Chippewa Customs

Chippewa Customs

. . .

Frances Densmore

With an introduction by
Nina Marchetti Archabal

MINNESOTA HISTORICAL SOCIETY PRESS

First published in 1929 by the Smithsonian Institution
Bureau of American Ethnology as Bulletin 86

www.mnhs.org/mhspress

The Minnesota Historical Society Press is a member of the
Association of American University Presses.

Manufactured in the United States of America

10 9

∞ The paper used in this publication meets the minimum requirements of the American National Standard for Information Sciences—Permanence for Printed Library Materials, ANSI Z39.48-1984.

International Standard Book Number 0-87351-142-5

Library of Congress Cataloging-in-Publication Data
Densmore, Frances, 1867–1957.
    Chippewa customs.
    (Publications of the Minnesota Historical Society)
    Reprint of the 1929 Ed. published by the U.S. Govt. Print. Off., Washington,
which was issued as Bulletin 86 of Smithsonian Institution's Bureau of American Ethnology
Bibliography: p.
    1. Chippewa Indians—Social life and customs.
    2. Indians of North America—Minnesota—Social life and customs.
    I. Title.
    II. Series: Minnesota Historical Society. Publications.
    III. Series: United States. Bureau of American Ethnology. Bulletin: 86.
E99.C6D38   1979   970'.004'97   79-15400

INTRODUCTION

There is no more significant figure in the study of American Indian music and culture than Frances Densmore. Her study of the customs of Minnesota's largest group of Indian people developed as a part of her research on music. Although she was a musician by training, her interest did not stop with music but went on to encompass the entire fabric of Indian life. So broad was the scope of her work that her full contribution is rarely appreciated. Her orientation was at once scholarly and popular, directed to the entire subject of North American Indian music and its cultural context, but sensitive to the most minute details that distinguished aspects of one group of Chippewa (Ojibway) from another.

From the Nootka and Quileute of the Pacific Northwest to the Seminole of Florida, Densmore conducted her research apparently oblivious to obstacles that would have discouraged a person of lesser determination. Beginning in the 1890s and continuing until her death in 1957, she worked determinedly to document and preserve the elements of disappearing Indian cultures. The urgency and commitment with which she approached her mission are best expressed in her own words. "I heard an Indian drum when I was very, very young," she recalled. "Others heard the same drum and the sound was soon forgotten, but I have followed it all these years. Unconsciously it has called me, and I have followed it across the continent . . . over the plains and the mountains, across the desert — always the Indian drum calling me."[1]

Densmore's interest in the culture of the American Indian spanned more than 60 years. A Minnesotan throughout her long life, she was born in Red Wing on May 21, 1867, to Benjamin and Sarah Adalaide (Greenland) Densmore, and grew up in a sympathetic and intellectually stimulating household. The family home looked out over the Mississippi River with a view of a nearby Dakota (Sioux) Indian camp at Prairie Island and within earshot of the drum that accompanied the Indian dances. "Those Indians," her mother explained, "are interesting people with customs different from ours." Curious to know more, Frances would fall asleep, she recalled, "with my mind full of fancies about the 'interesting people' across the Mississippi."[2]

After a traditional musical education with emphasis on piano, Densmore's interest in Indian culture was sparked by Alice Cunningham Fletcher's *A Study of Omaha Indian Music*, which she read shortly after its publication in

---

[1] Charles Hofmann, comp., ed., *Frances Densmore and American Indian Music*, 1 (Museum of the American Indian, Heye Foundation, *Contributions*, vol. 23 — New York, 1968).

[2] Nina Marchetti Archabal, "Frances Densmore: Pioneer in the Study of American Indian Music," in Barbara Stuhler and Gretchen Kreuter, eds., *Women of Minnesota: Selected Biographical Sketches*, 95 (St. Paul, 1977); Hofmann, ed., *Densmore*, 1.

1893. Fletcher's work included descriptions of Omaha customs as well as analyses and transcriptions of their music. Although Densmore gradually departed from Fletcher's notion that their music was based on the Indians' unconscious sense of harmony, she retained Fletcher's method of interpreting Indian music in relation to their customs. She adopted as her guiding principle Fletcher's idea that "Among the Indians, music envelopes like an atmosphere every religious, tribal and social ceremony as well as every personal experience. There is not a phase of life that does not find expression in song."[3]

Along with her study of Fletcher's writings, Densmore laid a solid foundation for her later work by undertaking an intensive study of every aspect of Indian life. "For the next ten years," she wrote, "I soaked my receptive mind in what army officers wrote about Indians, and what historians wrote about Indians [along] with some of the publications of the Bureau of American Ethnology. . . . All this was preparation for my life work."[4]

Densmore's first contact with the Chippewa people themselves occurred in 1901 when she and her sister Margaret made a trip to Port Arthur (now Thunder Bay), Ontario, an occasion she remembered as "a pleasure trip." Four years later Frances made what she regarded as her "first field trip." She again visited the Chippewa, this time at Grand Marais and Grand Portage on the north shore of Lake Superior in Minnesota. On this second visit she made notes on Chippewa customs and took photographs. "The most important event of the trip was a ceremony that Little Spruce and his sons gave for us in their house," she recalled. "It was part of a Grand Medicine ceremony."[5]

The following notes from her visit to Little Spruce's home reveal the broad scope of detail that caught her attention:

Hangers of twigs
Herbs tied up to dry
Guns on racks in two places
Four clocks, all of them wrong
Window held up by butcher knife
Hole in floor mended with red tin
Xmas *London Ill. News*
Deerskin folded ready to make into moccasins
Splint mats around wall
One family to each mat
Woman making moccasins
Lard pails (covered) held medicine
Tomato cans for cuspidors
All were smoking. He [Little Spruce] had dry green leaves in a beaded bag, took the leaves out, cut them on a wooden tray that had a long hollow place

[3] Harvard University, Peabody Museum of Archaeology and Ethnology, *Papers*, vol. 1, no. 5, p. 240 (Cambridge, Mass., 1893); Fletcher's work was reprinted in 1967 as a monograph.

[4] Hofmann, ed., *Densmore*, 2.

[5] Hofmann, ed., *Densmore*, 21, 22.

FRANCES DENSMORE AT MILLE LACS LAKE

in it. [sketch of bag and tray] cut with hunting knife and mixed with tobacco
— said to be some herb that he gathers in the mountains every year.[6]

Although she wrote down the song that Little Spruce sang for her, Densmore's interest was drawn as much to the surrounding Indian culture as to
the music. In 1907 she published an article in *American Anthropologist* setting
down the details of the Grand Medicine ceremony she had witnessed at the
house of Little Spruce. Already she had begun the meticulous practices she
would follow in her field work for the rest of her life: keeping detailed notes
and making photographs to document her observations of Indian customs.[7]

---

[6] Hofmann, ed., *Densmore*, 27.

[7] "An Ojibway Prayer Ceremony," in *American Anthropologist*, new series, 9:443 (April–
June, 1907).

The opportunity provided by field work to study the whole context of Indian life greatly expanded Densmore's horizons. Before she visited Indian people herself, she had given lectures on Indian music based on Fletcher's work. She gave the first of these lecture-recitals, in which she accompanied herself on the piano, before the Schubert Club of St. Paul on December 4, 1895, performing harmonized arrangements of songs from Fletcher's transcriptions of Omaha music. After 1903 Densmore's performances gained a measure of authenticity when she acquired a drum and four birch-bark medicine rattles used in Chippewa medicine rituals. Her work changed radically after her trip to the north shore in 1905. At that point, having heard it at firsthand, she begain to evolve a sense of Indian music on its own terms and to depart gradually from her dependence on what she had learned from the work of others. Through her own field experience she found what she considered a living culture. Of its music she wrote in 1910: "Chippewa songs are not petrified specimens; they are alive with the warm red blood of human nature."[8]

After two more field visits to the Minnesota Chippewa, during which, in October, 1907, she witnessed the rituals surrounding the death of Chief Flat Mouth at Onigum, Densmore wrote to the Bureau of American Ethnology in the Smithsonian Institution, "telling of the interesting material among the Chippewa that would soon be lost forever." William H. Holmes, chief of the bureau, responded with an initial grant of $150, followed in October by an additional $200 and a telegram which read, "proceed at your discretion." Frances did so, using the money to purchase an Edison Home Phonograph, "the best recording equipment available." With it she returned to Onigum where she began the systematic study of Chippewa music and customs.[9]

In February, 1908, Densmore traveled to Washington, D.C., to report to the bureau on her work. While there, she also delivered a lecture to the Anthropological Society. Her research, which focused on the cultural context as well as the structure of music, provided a logical meeting ground for students of music and of culture.[10]

The Bureau of American Ethnology in its 1907–08 annual report noted that its support of Densmore's research marked the first time the organization had taken up a serious study of native American music. The report remarked that Densmore's "investigation promises results of exceptional interest and scientific value." Frances pursued her work enthusiastically. During summer field trips she recorded the songs of Indian people with her phonograph and documented their customs in her notebook and in photographs. During the winter months she transcribed the songs and interpreted them in relation to tribal life. With the songs now directly available to her on recordings, Dens-

[8] Schubert Club (St. Paul), *Programs, 1899–1924*, December 4, 1895, in Minnesota Historical Society (MHS) Library; Archabal, in *Women of Minnesota*, 98; Densmore, *Chippewa Music*, 1 (Bureau of American Ethnology, *Bulletin 45* — Washington, D.C., 1910). The latter volume was reprinted by the Da Capo Press in 1972.

[9] Hofmann, ed., *Densmore*, xi, 24.

[10] Archabal, in *Women of Minnesota*, 102.

more began to have serious doubts about the appropriateness of harmonizing Indian music. Although she continued to look for western tonal implications in the music, after 1907 there were no more harmonizations.[11]

Her first book, *Chippewa Music*, published in 1910, was a considerable accomplishment. It included analyses and transcriptions of 200 songs collected during 1907, 1908, and 1909 from Minnesota Indians on the White Earth, Leech Lake, and Red Lake reservations. It also included a selection of 20 photographs and paintings, the latter probably executed by Frances herself (see plates 7 and 10), that documented aspects of Indian life she had observed. Although she presented a wealth of detailed information in *Chippewa Music*, she did not regard the Indian songs as lifeless data, but rather as products of a spiritual consciousness, of a "mental concept," as she phrased it. Herein lay their ultimate value. Her explicit recognition of this value in the introduction to *Chippewa Music* was to set the tone for all of her subsequent publications on Indian music.[12]

Three years later the Bureau of American Ethnology published Densmore's second work on Chippewa music. No less impressive than the first, *Chippewa Music — II* included analyses and transcriptions of 180 songs, along with 51 photographs of Indian artifacts and customs. Densmore explained her cultural approach in the book's foreword: "Chippewa music in its relation to tribal life constitutes one of the subjects dealt with in the present volume, as well as in the writer's first contribution to this study." In both works, the songs are arranged by function: the largest number in the first book are associated with religion, and the largest number in the second work are related to war. Both volumes include extensive information on tribal customs with detailed descriptions of specific rituals and practices. The Indian songs are cataloged and presented within the context of these descriptions.[13]

Even before *Chippewa Music — II* was published, Densmore had begun field research on the Dakota or Sioux Indians. In 1911 she went to the Sisseton Reservation in South Dakota to collect their music. The following summer she pursued her research at Fort Yates on the Standing Rock Reservation in North Dakota, where she interviewed and recorded the songs of men who had taken part in the Sun Dance. She visited a large gathering of Sioux at Bullhead, South Dakota, in 1913, and made two more trips to the Standing Rock Reservation in 1914.[14]

The Bureau of American Ethnology's annual report of that year again included an assessment of Densmore's research: "Excellent progress has been made. . . . The principal work in this direction has been the completion of

[11] Bureau of American Ethnology, *Twenty-ninth Annual Report, 1907–08*, 19 (Washington, D.C. 1916); Archabal, in *Women of Minnesota*, 108–110.

[12] Densmore, *Chippewa Music*, v.

[13] Densmore, *Chippewa Music — II*, v (Bureau of American Ethnology, *Bulletin 53* — Washington, D.C., 1913).

[14] Hofmann, ed., *Densmore*, 32–34; Densmore, *Teton Sioux Music*, 1–4 (Bureau of American Ethnology, *Bulletin 61* — Washington, D.C., 1918).

the manuscript on 'Teton Sioux Music,' consisting of 1,067 pages, in addition to transcriptions of 240 songs and about 100 illustrations.'' Densmore's massive study, entitled *Teton Sioux Music*, was published by the bureau in 1918. It offers tangible evidence of her indefatigable devotion to the mission she had set for herself.[15]

Although she continued to devote attention to Indian music, Densmore in June, 1917, visited the Chippewa White Earth Reservation in Minnesota to study the Indians' material culture. Reporting on the results, the bureau said: "Miss Densmore's main studies have been on ethnobotany of the Chippewa and include plants used in treatment of the sick and other subjects. The general economic life and the industries of the people were also studied and an extensive collection made, which she has photographed for use in her publications.''[16]

She presented these results in a short article entitled "Study of Chippewa Material Culture" published by the Smithsonian Institution in 1918. She continued her research on Chippewa material culture and the following year published a sequel to her first article on the subject. In July, 1919, she pursued this interest still further when she visited the Manitou Rapids Reserve in Canada to observe the customs of the Canadian Chippewa and compare them with those of the Chippewa she had studied in the United States.[17]

The Bureau of American Ethnology announced in its report for 1918–19 that it had purchased Densmore's papers on "Chippewa Remedies and General Customs" and on "Chippewa Art." The contents were impressive. "The latter article has 164 pages, with 42 pages of old Chippewa designs and numerous photographs pertaining to industries, medicinal plants, customs, and toys of children, games, processes of weaving, tanning, and other industries." These two papers were not immediately published. Not until 1928 did the Bureau of Ethnology issue Densmore's study of "Uses of Plants by the Chippewa Indians" in a collection of articles on various subjects written by different people.[18]

By that time Frances had over 20 years of direct experience in observing Chippewa culture, and the article included information she had been collecting since 1907. In that period she had also published eight major works whose primary focus was on Indian music. She explained that for the Chippewa there was a connection between plants and music. "Herbs were used in the treatment of the sick and in the working of the charms, and songs were sung to

[15] Bureau of American Ethnology, *Thirty-sixth Annual Report, 1914–15*, 27 (Washington, D.C., 1921).

[16] Bureau of American Ethnology, *Thirty-ninth Annual Report, 1917–18*, 23 (Washington, D.C., 1925).

[17] Densmore, "Study of Chippewa Material Culture," in *Explorations and Field-Work of the Smithsonian Institution in 1917*, 95–100 (Washington, D.C., 1918); Densmore, "Material Culture Among the Chippewa," in *Explorations and Field-Work of the Smithsonian Institution in 1918*, 114–118 (Washington, D.C., 1919); Hofmann, ed., *Densmore*, 44.

[18] Bureau of American Ethnology, *Fortieth Annual Report, 1918–19*, 14 (Washington, D.C., 1925); Densmore, "Uses of Plants by the Chippewa Indians," in Bureau of American Ethnology, *Forty-fourth Annual Report, 1926–27*, 275–397 (Washington, D.C., 1928).

make the treatments and the charms effective," she wrote. With its lengthy list of plants and descriptions of their uses as food, medicines, dyes, and in the decorative arts, the article showed the extraordinary depth of her interest in all aspects of Indian life. She interpreted the abundance of plants in the Chippewas' natural environment as an important influence in their culture, not only in material terms but as a source of inspiration: "The northern woodland," she wrote, "is a beautiful country, and knowing it in all its changing seasons, one can not wonder at the poetry that is so inherent a part of Chippewa thought." Here again was an expression of Densmore's respect for the spiritual essence of Indian culture, which she regarded as distinct from hers but having its own integrity.[19]

She followed her work on plants with an even broader portrayal of Chippewa life — the volume here reprinted — which was originally published in 1929 as *Bulletin 86* by the Bureau of American Ethnology. Although she would retain an interest in Indian ethnology throughout her life and would publish over 30 articles on the subject, never again would she attempt so comprehensive a synthesis. Like her other works, *Chippewa Customs* also contained voluminous, detailed information, but Densmore was still attentive to the human element of her story. The foreword speaks of her "friendliness with the people" and the "faithfulness of her Chippewa friends." On the facing page are portraits of two of those friends from White Earth, Mrs. Mary Warren English, her interpreter, and Niskigwun, one of her principal informants, whom she describes in the text as "a sincere man who has always led a quiet, respectable life, and has kept his native manner of thought." Other portraits throughout the work provide visual evidence that these were real human beings who had lived in the traditional ways she described. She prefaced the volume with a list of 63 informants; each one was identified by name in both the Chippewa language and in English, and by locale.[20]

Densmore viewed the Chippewa customs she described as part of a living tradition. She identified individuals who were the sources of specific information and lent the text a human quality by frequently embellishing her descriptions of particular customs with the reminiscences of her informants. Her discussion of puberty rites, for example, is enhanced by a little tale — not without a touch of humor and pathos — told to her by Henry Selkirk of White Earth. "A feast was held when a boy killed his first game. Henry Selkirk said that the first game he killed was a wild canary. He hung it up to wait until he had enough food to give a feast in honor of the event but it was so long before he had enough that the little bird had dried up."[21]

In other instances Densmore included lengthy narratives provided by her informants. Two examples are the stories of the first earth and Winabojo, a mythical hero, related by Odinigun of White Earth and the cycle of the work

[19] Densmore, in *Forty-fourth Annual Report*, 281, 285.
[20] Densmore, *Chippewa Customs*, 1, 84 (Bureau of American Ethnology, *Bulletin 86* — Washington, D.C., 1929).
[21] Densmore, *Chippewa Customs*, 72.

year narrated by Nodinens of Mille Lacs. By alternating between her own descriptive narrative and the reminiscences of her informants, Densmore transformed the Chippewa customs from the habits of some strange and faraway tribe to the daily ways of real people with interesting personalities.[22]

In this book Densmore drew together the information she had gathered throughout her field experience. She compared the data she had accumulated during the summers of 1907 and 1908 while recording Chippewa songs with that collected 10 years later while researching Chippewa material culture and customs. She generalized and made distinctions based on her observations of the Canadian and Wisconsin Chippewa. Her habits of careful notetaking and photographic documentation, established early in her career, served her well in compiling this comprehensive picture of Chippewa life. Only occasionally did her organization and presentation of masses of data deteriorate into a pedantic and repetitious patchwork. Considering the scope of the work, these occasional lapses, as in her discussions of "Payment of Annuity" and "Traders and Trading Posts," are understandable.[23]

For the most part, this book, as well as Densmore's work as a whole, reflects a remarkable objectivity. With the perspective offered by the passage of a half century, it is easy to fault her for never attempting to learn the Indian languages or for continuing to refer to their culture as "primitive." These faults were more a matter of common practice and usage in her day than of any implicit condescension on her part. On a more subtle level, there is no doubt that Densmore's analyses of Indian culture inevitably reflect her European-oriented background and training, but only occasionally do they seriously cloud her interpretations. Their very rarity makes it easy to cite an example: her reference to Ruskin in discussing the patterns of Chippewa beadwork adds little to the quality of her interpretation. That Densmore's scholarship would reflect some of the biases of a comfortable, well-educated, turn-of-the-century midwestern woman is to be expected.[24]

What is truly remarkable is that such a woman would dedicate herself in 1893, only three years after the Battle of Wounded Knee, to the preservation of knowledge of Indian culture. Writing in 1903 on the significance of that battle for the future of Indian traditions, she concluded sadly, "After the song — the silence." Densmore soon discovered, however, that the silence was not total — that there were "echoes . . . from the old days and life that is passing away." Although she was convinced that the traditions were vanishing, she hoped to preserve their echoes. To that mission she dedicated her life.[25]

After the publication of *Chippewa Customs* Densmore continued her study of Indian music and customs. She worked tirelessly among various tribes recording their music, noting customs, collecting objects, and making the results of her research available to a broad audience through lectures and

[22] Densmore, *Chippewa Customs*, 98, 119–123.

[23] Densmore, *Chippewa Customs*, 138–142.

[24] Densmore, *Chippewa Music*, 5; Densmore, *Chippewa Customs*, 186n.

[25] *Minneapolis Journal*, May 23, 1903, p. 11.

publications. She wrote 20 books and over 200 articles, ranging from columns in children's magazines to articles in scholarly journals. *Chippewa Customs* stands as a model of her dedicated scholarship and of the value and accessibility of her work 50 years later.[26]

At the time of her death in 1957, only three years after her last field trip among the Seminole in Florida, Frances Densmore had achieved what she set out to do. She had followed the Indian drum throughout her adult life. We have benefited from her mission and from her extraordinary dedication. She left a rich heritage of about 2,500 wax cylinder recordings and voluminous, detailed accounts of Indian life and customs — primary materials for the study of Indian cultures of the late 19th and early 20th centuries. Because of her work, the echoes of that rich cultural heritage can still be heard.[27]

NINA MARCHETTI ARCHABAL

St. Paul, Minnesota
April 15, 1979

Deputy Director
Minnesota Historical Society

---

[26] A bibliography of Densmore's publications is in Hofmann, ed., *Densmore*, 121–127. Her children's pieces were unique in their day, and their continuing value and interest for children is exemplified by the popularity of the Fall, 1978, issue of *Roots*, the Minnesota Historical Society's junior magazine, which was devoted to Densmore's photographs and accounts of the Chippewa and Dakota Indians.

[27] Hofmann, ed., *Densmore*, 65. For a list of these recordings, see "Catalogue of Phonograph Records of Indian Music in the Archives of the Bureau of American Ethnology," National Archives, Smithsonian Institution. The recordings total nearly 3,600, of which approximately 2,500 were made by Densmore. The wax cylinders have been re-recorded by the Archive of Folk Song, Library of Congress, in order to preserve their contents. Numerous notes, diaries (1907–33), scrapbooks, correspondence, various unpublished song transcriptions, and other manuscripts may also be found in the Densmore Papers, Archive of Folk Song, Library of Congress, and in the National Anthropological Archives of the Smithsonian. Others are preserved in the Frances T. Densmore Papers of the MHS, which also owns some of her personal photograph albums, and in the Frances T. Densmore Papers in the Goodhue County Historical Society, Red Wing, which also holds various artifacts collected by Densmore. Densmore also placed a collection of Indian artifacts with the Museum of the American Indian, Heye Foundation, in New York City.

SMITHSONIAN INSTITUTION
BUREAU OF AMERICAN ETHNOLOGY
BULLETIN 86

CHIPPEWA CUSTOMS

BY

FRANCES DENSMORE

UNITED STATES
GOVERNMENT PRINTING OFFICE
WASHINGTON
1929

LETTER OF TRANSMITTAL

SMITHSONIAN INSTITUTION,
BUREAU OF AMERICAN ETHNOLOGY,
Washington, D. C., March 1, 1927.

SIR: I have the honor to transmit the accompanying manuscript, entitled " Chippewa Customs," by Miss Frances Densmore, and to recommend its publication, subject to your approval, as a bulletin of this bureau.

Very respectfully,

J. WALTER FEWKES, *Chief.*

Dr. C. G. ABBOT,
Acting Secretary Smithsonian Institution.

CONTENTS

ILLUSTRATIONS

a, Cedar mat on frame

b, Woman weaving rush mat

a, Portrait of Mrs. Mary Warren English

b, Portrait of Niskigwun

CHIPPEWA CUSTOMS

By Frances Densmore

FOREWORD

The present work is related in many respects to material already collected among the Chippewa.[1] The study of tribal songs led to a friendliness with the people and a willingness on their part to give information concerning their customs.

A study of the Chippewa Indians was begun by the writer in 1905. The villages at Grand Portage and Grand Marais, on the north shore of Lake Superior, were visited, specimens and data were collected, and at the former place an interesting ceremony was witnessed.[2] The following year a trip was made to a primitive group of Chippewa living on Vermilion Lake, and to the Leech Lake and White Earth Reservations in Minnesota. The study of Chippewa music for the Bureau of American Ethnology was begun in 1907. The material herewith presented was collected on the White Earth, Red Lake, Cass Lake, Leech Lake, and Mille Lac Reservations in Minnesota, the Lac Court Oreilles Reservation in Wisconsin, and the Manitou Rapids Reserve in Ontario, Canada, the work continuing until 1925. (Fig. 1.)

The writer gratefully acknowledges the faithfulness of her Chippewa friends and especially the assistance of her principal interpreter, Mrs. Mary Warren English, which began in 1907 and continued during the work at White Earth. Assistance has also been received from members of the staff of the Bureau of American Ethnology and the United States National Museum, in their special fields of research.

The work on the Manitou Rapids Reserve in Ontario and with Canadian Chippewa summoned from Couchiching village was made possible by the courtesy of John P. Wright, Indian agent of the Canadian Government at Fort Frances, Ontario.

To all those who contributed to the result of the present undertaking the writer expresses her appreciative gratitude.

---

[1] Chippewa Music, Bull. 45, Bur. Amer. Ethn., 1910; Chippewa Music, II, Bull. 53, Bur. Amer. Ethn., 1913; "Uses of Plants by the Chippewa Indians," Forty-fourth Ann. Rept. Bur. Amer. Ethn., 1928.

[2] "An Ojibway Prayer Ceremony," Amer. Anthrop., n. s. Vol. IX, pp. 443–444, 1907.

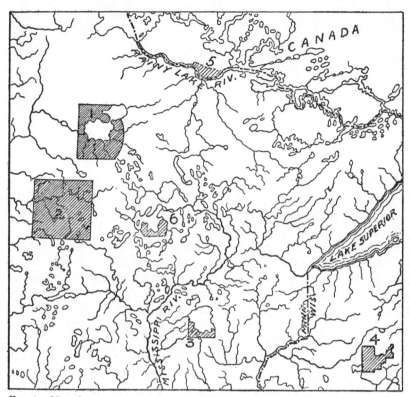

FIG. 1.—Map showing reservations on which material was chiefly collected. 1. Red Lake, Minn. 2. White Earth, Minn. 3. Mille Lac, Minn. 4. Lac Court Oreilles, Wis. 5. Manitou Rapids Reserve, Ontario, Canada. 6. Cass Lake and Leech Lake, Minn.

INFORMANTS[3]

WHITE EARTH, MINN.

Mrs. Mary Razer	Papa'gine' (Grasshopper).
Mrs. Louisa Martin	A'jawac' (Wafted across).
No'dinĕns'	Little wind.
Gage'wĭn [a]	Everlasting mist.
Mrs. Gage'wĭn	Nisĕd'nagan'ob (Nised, corruption of the French Lizett, or Elizabeth; Naganob, name of her father who was chief at Fond du Lac, Minn.).
Wa'wiĕkûm'Ig	Round earth.
Mrs. Wa'wiĕkûm'Ig [b]	Na'waji'bigo'kwe (Central rock woman).
Niski'gwûn [c]	Ruffled feathers.
Mrs. Niski'gwûn	Meja'kiya'bûndun (One who sees through to the bottom).
Star Bad Boy	Tci'anuŋg' (Big star).
Mrs. Star Bad Boy	Nenaka'wûbi'kwe (Woman who is sitting with every other one).

---

[a] Died Oct. 23, 1919.   [b] Died Sept. 16, 1923.   [c] Died Apr. 24, 1921.

[3] The purpose of this list is to identify the persons who chiefly contributed to the material herewith presented. The name given first is, therefore, the name by which the person is generally known.

Wase'ya [d] _____ Light.
Co'niä'kwe [e] _____ Money woman.
Mrs. Brunett [f] _____ Cai'yagose' (Shaken loose).
Mrs. Annie Davis_____ Ca'yabwûb' (Sitting through).
Mrs. George Walters_____ A'jawac' (Wafted across).
Mrs. Tom Swan_____ Bc'cakwûdo'kwe (Streaked cloud woman).
Mrs. Jackson_____ Ni'sûcwe'yaci'kwe (Woman blown about by the wind).
Mrs. Sharrett [g] _____ Ca'nodens' (Diminutive of Charlotte, by slightly changing word and adding *ens*).
Mrs. Sophia Agness_____ Memacka'wanamo'kwe (Woman with a powerful respiration).
Mrs. Margaret White_____
Mrs. Roy_____
Mrs. Nancy Macdonald_____
Mrs. Mary Warren English [h]
Mrs. Julia Warren Spears [i] ___ Co'nia'kwe.
Mrs. Sophia Warren_____
Mrs. Charles Mee_____
O'dïni'gûn_____ Shoulder.
Ĕn'dûsogi'jĭg [j] _____ Every day.
Albert Little Wolf [k] _____ Maĭŋ'gans.
George Big Bear_____
Tom Skinaway_____
Henry Selkirk_____
Joseph Sharrett [l] _____
William Potter_____ Bû'digons.
Rev. Clement H. Beaulieu [m] _ Ka'waëns (diminutive of his father's name Ka'wa), the Chippewa mispronunciation of "Clement."

PONSFORD, MINN. (WHITE EARTH RESERVATION)

Mrs. Fineday_____
Mr. Rock [n] _____ A'sĭnĭ'okûm'ĭg (Stony ground).
Weza'waŋge_____ Yellow wing.
Ne'yadji_____ Point of land.
Dĭ'kĕns_____ Diminutive of English "Dick."

RED LAKE, MINN.

Mrs. Defoe_____ Meya'wigobiwĭk' (Standing strongly).
Mrs. Ward_____ Ni'gida'wananĭk'.
Mrs. Joker_____ Bewa'becobenisĭk'.
Mrs. Roy_____ Zo'zĕd (corruption of Josette).
Mrs. Roy (daughter of above)_____ Ma'gidĭns (diminutive of Margaret).
Mrs. Lawrence_____
Mrs. John English_____
Mrs. Brunett_____
Mrs. Sha'wanokûm'igiskuŋ'_ Gi'wita'wisĕk' (Walking around).
Mrs. Gurneau_____

---

[d] Died Apr. 4, 1921.
[e] Died Dec. 29, 1921.
[f] Died Apr. 29, 1926.
[g] Died Apr. 14, 1925.
[h] Died Aug. 15, 1925.
[i] Died June 21, 1925.
[j] Died Oct. 24, 1926.
[k] Died Apr. 6, 1927.
[l] Died Feb. 15, 1920.
[m] Died July 7, 1926.
[n] Died Jan. 21, 1920.

MILLE LAC, MINN.

Tom Skinaway_____ Manido'bijiki (Spirit buffalo, or cattle).
Mrs. Tom Skinaway_____ Na'cine'kwe.
Migĭs'i°_____

CASS LAKE, MINN.

William M. Rogers_____ Bĭn'dĭgegi'jĭg (In the sky).
Mrs. Rogers_____ Bĭn'dige'ose'kwe (Walking woman).
William Dailey_____

LAC COURT OREILLES, WIS.

Mrs. John Quaderer_____ Ogima'bĭnĕsi'kwe (Chief bird woman).

MANITOU RAPIDS RESERVE, ONTARIO, CANADA

Mrs. Wilson_____
Mrs. Lewis_____
Mo'jagi'jĭg_____ (Always day).
Me'jaki'gonĕb_____
John Long_____

SKETCH OF THE LIFE OF MARY WARREN ENGLISH

Mrs. Mary Warren English (pl. 2, *a*), the writer's interpreter during a work which extended from 1907 to 1921, was born on Madeline Island in 1835. Her father was Lyman M. Warren, who was then in charge of the trading post of the American Fur Co. Her mother was the granddaughter of White Crane, a full-blood Chippewa, and the daughter of Michel Cadotte, a French trader. (See p. 140.) The employees of the fur company hired a woman named Miss Gates to come to the island and teach their children. Mrs. English attended this little school and later went to a school maintained there by the American Foreign Missionary Society of the Presbyterian Church. This school was in charge of a family named Wheeler, and in 1847, after the death of Mrs. English's mother, they took her into their family; papers being made out to the effect that she should live with them until she was 18 years old. The Wheelers moved to Odanah, Wis., and she was there trained to be a teacher, becoming so proficient that she acted as assistant in the mission school.

In 1854 the Indians asked the Government to give them schools and in 1856, when the reservations were set apart, the first school was established at Odanah. Mrs. English taught this school for two years and then went to the Twinsburg Institute, 5 miles from Cleveland, to improve her qualifications. After two years of study she returned to Odanah and resumed her teaching in the Government school. A year later she was transferred to the Government school at Red Cliff, where she taught for six years. She then obtained a

_____
° Died Mar. 17, 1927.

State certificate and taught in the district schools of the State, teaching two years at Madeline Island and two years at Eagle River. In the meantime the Wheeler family had moved to Beloit, Wis., and being still ambitious, she went to Beloit and remained there three years, studying music, which she believed would assist her in teaching. While there in 1873 she received a letter from her brother, Truman Warren, stating that a large school had been established by the Government at White Earth and suggesting that she join him at that place. She was the principal teacher at the White Earth school for two years, having several teachers under her direction. At that time a school had been started by the Government at Red Lake, Minn., and was in need of an experienced teacher. She accepted the position and taught there for 15 years. While there she married John English.

In recent years Mrs. English has lived at White Earth and on numerous occasions has done important interpreting for the Chippewa. Her death occurred in 1925.

Mrs. English was a sister of William W. Warren, the author of "History of the Ojibways," and of Mrs. Julia Spears, who contributed valuable data to the present work.

NAME OF TRIBE

The name " Chippewa " is comparatively modern and is the only name under which the tribe has been designated by the Government in treaties and other negotiations, but it has never been adopted by the older members of the tribe. They still refer to themselves as " Ojibway," or use the still older terms "A'nǐcǐna'be," meaning "original or first man " (*anic*, first, *nabe*, male). In the early mention of this tribe we find various spellings, as Achipoès (Prise de Possession (1671) in Perrot, Memoire, Tailhan, ed., p. 293, Paris, 1864), Ochipoy (York, 1700, in N. Y. Doc. Col. Hist., vol. IV, p. 749, Albany, 1854), Chepeways (Croghan, 1760, in Mass. Hist. Soc. Colls., 4th ser., vol. IX, p. 287, Boston, 1871), Tschipeway (Wrangell in Baer and Helmersen, Beiträge zur Kentniss des Russischen Reiches, p. 100, St. Petersburg, 1839), and Otchipwe (Baraga, Grammar and Dictionary of the Otchipwe Language, pt. 1, Montreal, 1878). Schoolcraft presents it as Odjibwa. (See Handbook of American Indians, Bull. 30, Bur. Amer. Ethn., pt. 1, pp. 280–281.) The spelling Odjibwe used in this and in Bulletins 45 and 53 is explained by the use of *j* to represent the sound of *zh*. The meaning of the word Ojibway has been the subject of much discussion. The derivation of the word from a root meaning " to pucker " has been conjectured. Many attribute this derivation to a type of moccasin formerly used by this tribe, which had a puckered seam extending up the front instead of having a tongue-shaped piece, as in present usage.

CHARACTERIZATION

While it is difficult to attribute one peculiarity to an entire tribe, it may safely be said that the Chippewa are a pleasant people. The older men and women are not lacking in dignity, but a ready smile and genial manner have, in the writer's experience, characterized this above other tribes. The Chippewa have a strong sense of humor and are fond of exchanging jokes among themselves. Their industrial life was marked by a cooperation of men and women, the man taking the heavier part of the women's work, and the women assisting in the lighter part of the men's work, as in the making of canoes. Even the children assisted in such parts of the industrial work as they were able to perform. In this, as in other tribes, the thrift of the women in their use of materials is worthy of special notice. Another interesting phase which the Chippewa share with other tribes is their high standard of excellence. Those who could not do a thing well either refrained from any attempt to do it or admitted that their work was not good. Those who excelled were given honor and, if their skill were particularly marked, they claimed that it was of supernatural origin.

HISTORY OF THE CHIPPEWA TRIBE

During the colonial period the Chippewa were remote from the frontier, but explorers and missionaries came into contact with them at an early date. History shows their prominence in transactions with the Hudson Bay Co. and the Northwest Fur Co. Although valiant in native warfare the Chippewa did not wage war against the white man, but seem to have been especially desirous of acquiring the customs of civilization.

The Chippewa are a part of a special group of central Algonquian, which group includes the Chippewa, Potawatomi, Ottawa, Algonquian proper, Illinois, and Miami.[4] Tradition states that the Chippewa, Ottawa, and Potawatomi separated at Mackinac. " They were first noticed in the Jesuit Relation of 1640 under the name Baouichtigouin (probably Bāwa'tigōwininiwŭg, 'people of the Sault'), as residing at the Sault, and it is possible that Nicollet met them in 1634. . . . In 1642 they were visited by Raymbaut and Jogues, who found them at the Sault and at war with a people to the west, doubtless the Sioux." [5]

---

[4] Twenty-eighth Ann. Rept. Bur. Amer. Ethn., p. 261 et seq.
[5] Handbook of American Indians, Bull. 30, Bur. Amer. Ethn., pt. 1, pp. 277, 278.

Our present interest is with that portion of the tribe which lived on the southern shores of Lake Superior and in adjacent territory, gradually extending toward the south and west. The War Department first placed an agency among these bands in 1822.[6] Ten years later a school at La Pointe, near the head of Lake Superior, contained 25 pupils.[7] In the following year the sum of $24,365 was expended by the Government for their education, for a blacksmith and his supplies, and for the 50 barrels of salt provided for in the treaty of 1829.[8] Their general development was probably similar to that of bands living near the foot of Lake Superior, concerning whom it was said: " The Chippewas cultivate corn and potatoes to a limited extent, but devote most of their time in quest of food, in the chase, or in fishing.[9]

The subagency at La Pointe, in 1839, controlled Chippewa to the number of 5,532, living at Grand Portage, Vermilion, Leech Lake, Red Lake, Gull Lake, Mille Lac, and other localities in Minnesota.[10] The subagent was D. P. Bushnell, and Henry R. Schoolcraft was " agent at Mackinac and acting superintendent of Michigan." The name of Schoolcraft appears first in 1838 and continues until 1840, his reports being included in those of the Office of Indian Affairs for those years. He married a woman of the tribe. It will be recalled that he wrote extensively on his travels and experiences among the Indians, his publications extending from 1820 to 1857. Longfellow's poem " Hiawatha " is based on the writings of Schoolcraft.

The Chippewa took part in the third treaty negotiated between the Government of the United States and the Indians, this being concluded at Fort McIntosh January 21, 1785,[11] a date two years prior to the formation of our present Constitution. Numerous treaties followed, among the most important being those at Prairie du Chien in 1829,[12] Detroit in 1837,[13] La Pointe in 1842,[14] and Fond du Lac in 1847,[15] by which the Indians ceded to the Government their possessions in Michigan and Wisconsin.

The scene of conflict between the Chippewa and Sioux was transferred from Wisconsin to Minnesota, and in 1850 the subagent at St. Peter, Minn., in his first report stated that "the deadly hostility

---

[6] Report, Dept. of War, Off. Ind. Affs., 1838, p. 455.
[7] Ibid., 1833, p. 188.
[8] Ibid., 1834, pp. 244, 245.
[9] Ibid., 1837, p. 531.
[10] Ibid., 1839, p. 488.
[11] Indian Affairs. Laws and Treaties, Chas. J. Kappler, ed., Vol. II, Washington, 1903, pp. 4, 5.
[12] Ibid., pp. 213–215.
[13] Ibid., pp. 358–360.
[14] Ibid., pp. 401–403.
[15] Ibid., p. 421.

for many years existing between the Sioux and Chippewas still exists, and their proximity is the cause of frequent outbreaks." [16]

The first Chippewa Indian agency in Minnesota was established in 1853, after which the problems of education and industrial development were paramount in the tribe.

In the mind of the Chippewa Indian, a history of the tribe is contained in the traditions of the Midewiwin (Grand Medicine Society) which are handed down from one generation to another. These traditions are marked by the poetry which characterizes all primitive religions. Warren, the native historian of the tribe,[17] relates the following which may be regarded as a cosmic tradition:

"While our forefathers were living on the great salt water toward the rising sun, the great Megis (sea shell) showed itself above the surface of the great water, and the rays of the sun for a long period were reflected from its glossy back. It gave warmth and light to the An-ish-in-aub-ag (red race). All at once it sank into the deep, and for a time our ancestors were not blessed with its light. It rose to the surface and appeared again on the great river which drains the waters of the Great Lakes, and again for a long time it gave life to our forefathers, and reflected back the rays of the sun. Again it disappeared from sight and it rose not till it appeared to the eyes of the An-ish-in-aub-ag on the shores of the first great lake. Again it sank from sight, and death daily visited the wigwams of our forefathers till it showed its back and reflected the rays of the sun once more at Bow-e-ting (Sault Ste. Marie). Here it remained for a long time, but once more, and for the last time, it disappeared, and the An-ish-in-aub-ag was left in darkness and misery till it floated and once more showed its bright back at Mo-ning-wun-a-kaun-ing (La Pointe Island), where it has ever since reflected back the rays of the sun, and blessed our ancestors with life, light, and wisdom. Its rays reach the remotest village of the widespread Ojibways."

As the old man delivered this talk he continued to display the shell, which he represented as the emblem of the great megis of which he was speaking.

A few days after, anxious to learn the true meaning of this allegory, . . . I requested him to explain to me the meaning of his Me-da-we harangue. After filling his pipe and smoking of the tobacco I had presented he proceeded to give me the desired information as follows:

"My grandson," said he, "the megis I spoke of, means the Me-da-we religion. Our forefathers, many strings of lives ago, lived on the shores of the Great Salt Water in the east. Here it was, that while congregated in a great town, and while they were suffering the ravages of sickness and death, the Great Spirit, at the intercession of Man-ab-o-sho, the great common uncle of the An-ish-in-aub-ag, granted them this rite wherewith life is restored and prolonged. Our forefathers moved from the shores of the great water, and proceeded westward. The Me-da-we lodge was pulled down and it was not again erected, till our forefathers again took a stand on the shores of the great river near where Me-ne-aung (Montreal) now stands.

"In the course of time this town was again deserted, and our forefathers still proceeding westward, lit not their fires till they reached the shores of Lake Huron, where again the rites of the Me-da-we were practiced.

[16] Rept. Comm. Ind. Affs. for 1850, p. 103.
[17] Warren, William W., Colls. Minn. Hist. Soc., vol. 5, St. Paul, Minn., 1885, pp. 78–80.

"Again these rites were forgotten, and the Me-da-we lodge was not built till the Ojibways found themselves congregated at Bow-e-ting (outlet of Lake Superior), where it remained for many winters. Still the Ojibways moved westward, and for the last time the Me-da-we lodge was erected on the Island of La Pointe, and here, long before the pale face appeared among them, it was practiced in its purest and most original form. Many of our fathers lived the full term of life granted to mankind by the Great Spirit, and the forms of many old people were mingled with each rising generation. This, my grandson, is the meaning of the words you did not understand; they have been repeated to us by our fathers for many generations."

The trading post at Fond du Lac, Minn., which was an important center of tribal activity for many years, is mentioned on page 140 in connection with the subject of traders.

The Chippewa were always a timber tribe and their principal native industry was the trapping of wild animals. With the coming of the white man they learned the commercial value of furs, which they had obtained only for their own use. The result was a slaughter of fur-bearing animals and the exchange of pelts for commodities offered by the trader. The Indians at first made yearly trips to Quebec and afterwards to Montreal, carrying their packs of furs and returning with firearms, blankets, trinkets, and fire water. They gradually curtailed the length of these journeys as the whites established trading posts at Detroit, Mackinaw, Sault Ste. Marie, and then, as stated, at La Pointe. It is said that the first trading post established by a white man in the present State of Minnesota was at Grand Portage,[17a] on the north shore of Lake Superior, where the distance across to the Pigeon River is only about 10 miles, this river flowing through extensive Chippewa territory in the present Province of Ontario, as well as forming part of the boundary between Minnesota and Canada.

TOTEMIC SYSTEM

The word *totem* is irregularly derived from the term *ototeman* of the Chippewa and cognate Algonquian dialects. The stem of this word is *ote*, signifying a consanguine kinship, and the suffix *m* indicates a possessive relationship. Groups of persons having a blood relationship were designated by the name of an animal which, in common usage, came to be called their "dodem animal." [18]

Warren states, "the Algics as a body are divided into several grand families or clans, each of which is known and perpetuated by a symbol of some bird, animal, fish, or reptile which they denominate the Totem or Do-daim (as the Ojibways pronounce it). . . .

[17a] Grand Portage was an important trading post when visited by Carver in 1767.— Minn. Hist. Soc. Colls., vol. XVII, p. 136.

[18] This subject is fully considered in the article "Totem," Handbook of American Indians, Bull. 30, pt. 2, Bur. Amer. Ethn., pp. 787–795.

The totem descends invariably in the male line, and intermarriages never take place between persons of the same symbol or family, even should they belong to different and distinct tribes, as they consider one another related by the closest ties of blood and call one another by the nearest terms of consanguinity." [19] The same authority states that "the Ojibways acknowledge in their secret beliefs, and teachings to each successive generation, five original Totems. The tradition in which this belief is embodied, is known only to their chief Medas or priests." He then summarizes the tradition, stating that six beings in human form came from the "great deep" and entered the wigwams of the Ojibwa. One was blindfolded; but his curiosity could not be restrained, and he lifted the veil. His eyes fell upon an Indian who immediately dropped dead. He was therefore sent back to the place whence these mysterious beings had emerged. The other five remained among the Indians and "became a blessing to them." From these visitants there arose the five original totems or clans—known as the Awaus-e, Bus-in-aus-e, Ah-ah-wauk, Noka, and Monsone or Waub-ish-ash-e. The entire list of 21 clans given by Warren are the crane, catfish, loon, bear, marten, reindeer, wolf, merman, pike, lynx, eagle, moose, rattlesnake, black duck or cormorant, goose, sucker, sturgeon, whitefish, beaver, gull, and hawk. He states further that "the crane, catfish, bear, marten, wolf, and loon are the principal families, not only in a civil point of view, but in numbers, as they comprise eight-tenths of the whole tribe." [20]

Personal informants stated that the bear and marten were the "most aristocratic" of the animal clans, and the crane and eagle among the bird clans. There were only a few of the sturgeon clan among the Mississippi Chippewa, but members of the catfish clan were very numerous.

PHONETICS

ALPHABET

The vowels and consonants employed in this work do not represent every sound that occurs in the Chippewa language. Thus an obscure sound resembling *h* in the English alphabet sometimes occurs in the middle of a word and is not indicated. No attempt has been made to indicate a slight nasal sound that frequently occurs at the end of a word. Prolonged vowels are also not indicated. The following letters are used:

Vowels.—a, pronounced as in *father; e*, as in *they; ĕ*, as in *met; i*, as in *marine; ĭ*, as in *mint; o*, as in *note; u*, as in *rule; û*, as in *but;*

---

[19] Warren, op. cit., pp. 34, 35.
[20] Ibid., pp. 43, 44, 45.

w, as in *wan;* *y*, as in *yet*. If two consecutive vowels are pronounced separately, two dots are placed above the second vowel.

Diphthong.—*ai* pronounced as in *aisle*.

Consonants.—*b*, *d*, *k*, *m*, *n*, *p*, *s*, *t*, have the ordinary English sounds. *s* is always pronounced as in *sense*, *g* as in *get*, and *z* as in *zinc*. *c* represents the sound of *sh*, *j* the sound of *zh*, *tc* the sound of *tch* in *watch*, and *dj* the sound of *j* in *judge*.

GLOSSARY

At the present time there is no strictly scientific grammar or dictionary of the Chippewa language in published form. The works of Baraga, Wilson, and Verwyst[21] were intended for a purely practical acquaintance with the language and accordingly are useful, although the phonetic system employed in most cases is very inadequate. Furthermore, the grammatical portions of these works are based essentially on Latin grammar, with the result that a number of important principles are entirely overlooked. A number of obscurities are present in Chippewa and are due to phonetic changes in the language. These obscurities do not occur in Sauk, Fox, and Kickapoo, which accordingly offer more important material for linguistic investigation. Much that has been written concerning these and other Algonquian languages applies also to Chippewa.

From the following glossary it will be seen that, as a general statement, there are few simple nouns, a majority of the nouns being formed by a composition of stems and affixes, more or less similarly to the formation of nouns in Fox.[22] Compound nouns also occur.

The Chippewa living in different localities differed in the pronunciation of the language, and these differences were recognized as permissible. Each man, however, was expected to be consistent with the locality in which he lived. It was said that the Chippewa were greatly amused by wrong pronunciation on the part of the people living in their own locality.

It will be noted that the sections of this glossary correspond to the sections in the text of the book.

---

[21] Baraga, Frederic. A grammar and dictionary of the Otchipwe language. Montreal, 1882.

Wilson, Edward F. The Ojebway language. Toronto, 1874.

Verwyst, F. Chrysostom. Chippewa exercises, being a practical introduction into the study of the Chippewa language. Harbor Springs, Mich., 1901.

See article, "Algonquian (Fox) language," by Truman Michelson, in Handbook of American Indian Languages, Bur. Amer. Ethn., Bull. 40, pt. 1, sec. 22, p. 809 ff., 1911.

See also "Ojibwa Texts," by William Jones (Truman Michelson, ed.), Publs. Amer. Ethn. Soc., vol. 7, Pt. II, New York, 1919.

[22] Cf. Michelson, Truman. The So-called Stems of Algonquian Verbal Complexes, Proceedings of Nineteenth International Congress of Americanists, 1915, pp. 541–544, Washington, 1917.

DWELLINGS [23]

wĭ′giwam_____ dwelling of any sort.

wa′ginogan′ (*wagi*, bent; *gan*, abode)__ lodge of bent poles covered with bark or mats.

gaka′gaŏgan′_____ bark dwelling, shaped like a house.

wanagĕk′ogûm′ĭg (*wanagĕk*, bark; *gûmig*, locative). dwelling made of any bark except birch bark.

cĭngob′igan (*cĭngob*, spruce; *gan*, abode)_ temporary abode made of evergreen boughs, spruce being commonly used.

nasa′ogan_____ tipi.

biwa′kobimĭj′_____ poles for frame of bark house.

wi′gwasapûk′we (*wigwas*, birch bark; *apûkwe*, mat). birch bark rolls for covering top of lodge.

apûk′we_____ bulrush mats for sides of lodge.

DRESS

wa′bowayan′_____ blanket.

mĭnĕs′aga′wûnj (*mĭnĕs*, sharp; *wûnj*, woody substance). thorn of the thorn apple tree, used as an awl.

a′sûbab′_____ thread (general term).

wa′nûsidĕns′iwigûn′ (*wanûsid*, heel; *ĕns*, diminutive; *iwi*, bone; *gûn*, article or thing). splint-bone of deer, used as an awl in sewing leather.

migos′_____ awl (general term).

bibu′giweyan′ (*wayan* suggests use as clothing. Thus, a Mide bag was considered so personal as to be part of a man's clothing and was called *wayan*, while a bag used as a container was called *mûckimûd*). cotton cloth; also shirt.

mĭske′gĭn (*mĭskwa*, red; *egin*, cloth)____ "list cloth," which was white woolen cloth with red selvedge.

manido′wegĭn (*manido*, spirit; *egin*, cloth). broadcloth.

zezega′manido′wegĭn (*zezega*, fine)_____ fine broadcloth.

ago′das (from *gode*, it hangs)_____ dress.

ma′djigo′de (*madji*, badly; *gode*, it hangs). woman's skirt.

mĭdas′_____ legging or stocking.

a′jigûn_____ sock.

ma′kizĭn_____ moccasin.

bĭne′odisi′makizĭn′ (*bĭne*, partridge or grouse; *odisi*, gizzard; *makizin*, moccasin). "partridge moccasin."

na′bĭkuwa′gûn_____ necklace or collar.

na′bice′bizun (*nabice*, piercing; *bizun*, through). earring.

gûc′kibida′gûn (*gûc* implies tucking in; *gûn* signifies an article). pipe bag carried in the belt.

---

[23] The assistance of Rev. C. H. Beaulieu and Mrs. Mary Warren English is especially acknowledged in connection with the compiling of this glossary.

FOOD AND ITS PREPARATION

nabob'_____ broth.

bimīte'igûn_____ pounded meat.

ta'goskawe'wīn_____ foot-trodden meat.

anib'ĭc or anibĭcabo (*anibĭc*, leaf; *abo*, tea.
liquid).

bûkwe'jigûn (literally, "sliced off," as bread.
the bread made by white women was
the first *loaf* seen by the Indians).

bĭŋgwa'bo (*bĭŋgwe*, sand or ashes; *abo*, lye (used in making bread).
liquid).

ona'gûn_____ dish.

bĭs'kitena'gûn (*bĭskite*, he or she bends dish made by bending birch bark.
it).

tci'gona'gûn (portion of *gĭtcĭ*, big; bowl.
onagûn, dish).

e'mĭkwan'_____ spoon.

mĭ'tĭgwe'mĭkwan (*mĭtĭg*, indicating wooden spoon.
wood).

cigwa'djiganak'_____ stick for extracting marrow from bones.

TREATMENT OF THE SICK

ako'siwĭn'_____ sickness.

nenan' dawi'iwĕd_____ one who treats the sick by administering
remedies.

dja'sakid_____ one who treats the sick by other than
material means, commonly called a
juggler.

mûcki'ki_____ herbs or other substances administered
to the sick.

LIFE CYCLE

a'dikina'gûn (*adikina*, cradle; *gûn*, ar- "cradle board."
ticle or object).

a'dikine'yab (this word contains the bands wound around cradle board.
ideas of length and flexibility).

a'dikina'gûna'tĭg (termination *tĭg* sig- hoop above end of cradle board.
nifies wood).

wewe'bizuwĭn (*wewe* is part of a word act of swinging cradle board.
meaning "to swing"; *wĭn* signifies
action).

a'sûbike'cĭn (*asûb*, net)_____ woven "charm" in the shape of a spider
web, placed on hoop of cradle.

wanda'wasud_____ person who names a child.

ni'awĕn_____ namesake.

ne'negeän_____ one who frightens children.

wewas'iŋgwe'igûn (*wewas*, shining; mask worn to frighten children.
iŋgwe, face; *gûn*, article).

odjib'aīgûn (*odjib*, ghost; *gûn*, article)__ term applied to a moccasin on a long
stick, thrust into the wigwam to
frighten children.

a'nĭcĭna'bĕns muzinak'giwi'djigûn (*anĭ-* doll (general term).
cĭnabe, first or original man, a term
applied by the Indians to themselves;
ens, diminutive; *muzinak*, picture;
giwidji, tied by hand; *gûn*, article.

mûcko'si   o'damĭnwa'gûn   (*mûckosi*, doll made of grass.
grass; *odamĭnwagûn*, play article).

bibu'giweyan' o'damĭnwa'gûn (*bibugi-* "rag doll."
weyan, cotton cloth or shirt; *odamĭn-*
wagûn, play article).

coco'man_____ snow snake.

ĭckwe'saĭgûn (*ĭckwe*, whirling or spin- spinning stone.
ning; *gûn*, article).

coco'kwadjiwe'wĭn (the e n d i n g *wĭn* coasting.
signifies action).

gagibiŋgwe'odamĭn'owĭn (*gagibiŋgwe*, blindfold game.
blind; *odamĭn*, play; *win*, action).

wĭn'digo'kazo odamĭn'owĭn (*wĭndigo*, "cannibal game."
cannibal; *kazo*, pretends; *odamĭn*,
play; *wĭn*, action).

o'mûkûki'mĭdas'un (*omûkûki*, frog; leaves of the "picher plant," used as
mĭdas, leggings; *ûn*, plural).   toys.

sisi'bûg beba'mûkwe'jiwed (*sisibûg*, ducks made of rushes, used as toys.
ducks; *beba*, around; *mûkwûc*, float-
ing).

nibawi'daban'   (*nibawi*,   standing; "coaster."
odaban, sled).

ni'bowĭn_____ death.

o'djitcag'_____ the soul or spirit of a person.

odjib'_____ ghost or shadow.

djibe'gûmĭg (*djibe*, spirit; *gûmig*, loca- house or shelter erected above a grave.
tive).

djibe'nak_____ wooden grave marker.

gidimag'iziwĭn' (*gidimag*, sorrowing, "spirit bundle."
also poverty; *iziwĭn,* token).

DREAMS

bawa'djigewĭn_____ dream (general term).

ninbawa'djige (literally, "I see a dream (term used in "medicine").
vision").

ina'bandûmo'wĭn_____ vision seen or thing dreamed (term used
in "medicine").

ina'puwe_____ important personal warning received in
a dream.

MIDEWIWIN

Mĭde'wiwĭn_____ a society commonly designated as the
Grand Medicine Society, though this
is not a translation of the native
term.

Mide'_____ a member of the Midewiwin. This also
forms part of compound nouns.

Mide'wigan_____ lodge in which meetings of the Midewiwin were held.

Mide'wayan_____ bag carried by a member of the Midewiwin. This is a general term. The
designation of these bags was connected with the degree of the lodge
held by the owner of the bag.
bijiü'wayan (*bijiü*, wild cat)_____ wild-cat bag.
caŋgwe'ciwayan' (*caŋgweci*, mink)_____ mink bag.
ciŋgu'siwayan' (*ciŋgusi*, weasel)_____ weasel bag.
koko'kaö'wayan' (*koko'ko*, owl)_____ owl bag.
cici'gwewayan' (*cicigwe*, rattlesnake) __ rattlesnake bag.
mĭtĭg'wakĭk_____ drum used in the Midewiwin.
ba'gaäk'okwan'_____ drumming stick used with this drum.
madodo'igan (*madodo*, sweat; *gan*, sweat lodge used by Mide.
abode).
madodo'wasĭnûn' (*madodo*, sweat; *asĭn*, stones used in the sweat lodge.
stone; *ûn*, plural).
sĭgaä'sĭnan (*sĭg* (*a*, *i*), stem of verb bunch of grass used in putting water on
meaning "to pour;" *asĭn*, stone).   stones in sweat lodge.
agwa'sĭnan_____ bent stick used in lifting the principal
stone in sweat lodge.

CHARMS [24]

bĭ'tûwi'wabos' (*wabos*, rabbit)_____ charm consisting chiefly of a rabbit.
mi'gĭsŏns'ibûg (*migĭs*, shell; *ŏns*, di- small seeds of a color resembling tiny
minutive; *bûg*, implies plant or leaf). shells.
cacabo'biïgi'nigûn (*cacabo*, gliding, also woven cord or round bead chain. Such
woven; *biïginigûn*, an article of a a chain, with lengthwise stripes, was
stringy nature). worn as a protection against snakes.
bebe'cabiïgi'nigûn (*bebeca*, striped)____ similar chain with crosswise stripes.
wawa'ckeci nonda'gotcigûn' (*wawackeci*, "deer call," a whistle used in hunting.
deer; *nondagotcigûn*, any article with
which a sound can be made).

GAMES

binige'wĭn_____ playing a game, used as the noun
"game."
oda'mĭno'wĭn_____ playing as a pastime.
ata'diwĭn_____ gambling.
gama'giwe'binigo'wĭn_____ snake game.
gine'bigog (plural)_____ "snakes," game implements.
bima'tĭgwanûg' (plural)_____ counters.
bipĭn'djigana'owĭn_____ dewclaw game.
bipĭn'djiganaün'_____ implement of dewclaw game.
wanasidĕns'iwigûn'_____ sharp bone or needle forming part of
this implement.
ozo' (tail)_____ oval piece of leather, forming part of
this implement.
mûckosi'bipĭn'djiganaün' (*mûckosi*, implement of grass game.
grass).
pĭnda'djiwe'bĭnige'wĭn_____ awl game.
migos'_____ awl (part of game implement).
wawië'atĭg (*wawië*, round; *atĭg*, wood)_ ring (part of game implement).

---

[24] The Chippewa have no general term corresponding to the English words "charm" and "fetish." It will be noted that the words indicate simply the characteristics of articles used in the working of "magic."

onĭndj'iwata'diwĭn (*onĭndj*, hand)_____ hand game.

jema'giwe'bĭnige'wĭn_____ stick game.

jema'giwe'bĭnigûnûn' (plural)_____ implements of stick game.

bû'gese'wĭn (from *bûgesan*, plum, also common term "plate game," literally, the pit of the plum; *wĭn*, indicating "plum-stone game." action).

bû'gese'wĭna'gûn (from *bûgesan*, plum; plate or shallow bowl used as implement *onagûn*, dish).   of game.

bu'gesa'nûg (plural)_____ flat disks, implements of game.

budû'kicigûn (this word contains an one of the carved figures used as game implication of thrusting).   implements.

makazĭn'ata'diwĭn (*makazĭn*, moccasin; moccasin game. *atadiwĭn*, game).

pupû'sikawe'wĭn_____ "woman's game."

pû'sikawa'nûg (plural)_____ two small billets of wood tied together (game implement).

pû'sikawe'atĭg_____ one of the "carrying sticks" used in woman's game.

i'nawa'wĭn_____ goal stake in woman's game.

INDUSTRIAL YEAR

a'nina'tĭg_____ maple tree.

zĭnzĭba'kwûd_____ sugar.

wĕndjidu'zĭnzĭba'kwûd_____ real sugar (maple).

    (1) zĭnzĭba'kwûdabo'   (s u g a r maple sap. liquid).

    (2) ciwa'gûmizĭgûn' (this term indicates the tendency of maple sap to become sour. *ciwa*, sour).

oji'gūigûn_____ tap in tree.

negwa'kwûn_____ spile.

bĭs'kitena'gûn (*bĭskite*, he or she bends birch-bark dish, a household article it; *onagûn*, dish).   placed beneath the spile to catch the sap.

nado'ban (*nadobe*, he or she goes and bucket in which sap is carried. gets; *an*, signifying an article).

ĭ'ckigamĭ'sĭge'wigûm'ĭg   (*ĭckigamĭsĭge*, lodge in which sap is boiled. it evaporates by boiling; *gûmig*, locative).

akĭk'_____ kettle.

djiba'kwana'tĭg (*djibakwe*, it cooks; pole from which kettles are hung. *kwan*, "this is its characteristic"; *atĭg*, wood).

ago'dakikwan' (*agode*, it hangs; *akĭk*, hook on which kettles are suspended. kettle).

ato'ban_____ trough in which sap is poured before boiling.

nase'ina'gûn_____ trough in which sap is granulated after boiling.

ga'ckagokwe'igûn_____ paddle with which sap is stirred while boiling.

mĭ'tĭgwe'mĭkwan (*mĭtĭg*, wood; *emĭkwan*, wooden spoon, for dipping sap. spoon).

ca'bobi'ginigûn'_____ strainer for sap.

ĭ'ckwaga'zĭnzĭba'kwûd_____ last run of sap.

sĭg'aĭgûn (*sĭg*(*a, i*), stem of verb meaning hard sugar, usually made by pouring "to pour"). into molds.

bi'giwi'sĭgûn (*bigiwi*, gum)_____ "gum sugar."

ma'kûk_____ birch-bark container used for grained maple sugar or any other commodity. Term commonly applied to any box.

asûn'jigo'wigûm'ĭg_____:_____ structure or "lodge" in which sugar-making utensils are stored.

kiti'ganĕns ("little farm")_____ garden.

mano'mĭn_____ rice.

mano'mĭnûck_____ rice stalk (straw).

gan'daki'iganak'_____ forked pole for pushing boat through rice field.

wi'gogwa'djigûn (literally, "a thing to hoop with which rice is drawn forward draw with"). for tying.

a'sigoban'_____ basswood fiber used for tying rice.

bikodjan'_____ ball of this fiber.

dako'bido' bûbin'sikuwa'gûn_____ special waist worn when tying rice.

dako'bidjĭgûn'_____ "tied rice."

o'bawi'gana'tĭgog (plural)_____ sticks with which rice is knocked from stalk.

nosa'tcina'gûn_____ winnowing tray.

a'neä'kokwûn'_____ paddle with which rice is stirred while parching.

gidû'sigûn_____ parched rice.

bota'gûn (*botaïge*, he or she pounds; mortar in which rice is pounded. *gûn*, signifying an article).

bota'ganak (*botaïge*, he or she pounds; wooden pestle used in pounding rice. *ak*, signifying that the article is made of wood).

mĭnigo'ckamo'wĭn_____ barrel or other container in which rice is trodden.

mani'mĭnĭwûc'_____ any native receptacle for storing rice.

oni'igûn_____ trap or snare (general term).

nagwa'djigûn (*nagwe*, he or she catches snare. by means of a trap or loop; *gûn*, article).

wabos'oni'igûn (*wabos*, rabbit)_____ rabbit trap.

wabos'inagwa'gûn_____ rabbit snare.

bĭne'nagwa'gûn (*bĭne*, partridge)_____ partridge snare.

wajûck'nagwa'gûn (*wajûck*, muskrat)__ muskrat trap.

TRANSPORTATION

o'daban'_____ sled.

METHODS OF MEASURING TIME, DISTANCE, AND QUANTITY

Divisions of the year

zi'gwûnoŋg (past), zi'gwûn (present), spring. api'zigwûn (future).

ni'bĭnong (past), ni'bĭn (present), api'- summer. nibiŋg (future).

de'gwagoŋg (past), dakwa'gĭg (present), autumn.
   api'dagwa'gig (future).
bi'nonoŋg (past), bibon' (present), api'- winter.
   biboŋg (future).

Months

gĭ'tĭcmanido'gizĭs (*gitci*, big; *manido*, January.
   spirit; *gizis*, month).
ona'bĭnigi'zĭs (snow-crusted month)___ February.
boba'kwudagime'gizĭs (broken snow- March.
   shoe month, so called because the
   crusted snow broke the netting on
   the snowshoes).
ĭ'ckigamĭ'sigegi'zĭs (maple-sugar-mak- April.
   ing   month.   Literally,   "boiling
   month").
wa'bigwûn'igi'zĭs (*wabigwûn*, flower)__ May.
ode'imĭn'igi'zĭs (*odeimĭn*, strawberry)__ June.
mĭn'igi'zĭs (*mĭn* commonly applied to July.
   blueberry.   ɪn combination it indicates any berry, fruitage, or seed).
mano'mĭnigi'zĭs (*manomĭn*, rice)_____ August.
wase'bûgogi'zĭs (*wase*, shining; *bûg*, leaf) September.
bĭnakwe'gizĭs (*bĭnakwe*. This word ap- October.
   pears also in *binakweĭgûn*, rake; and
   bĭnakwan, comb).
gûcku'dinogi'zĭs (*gûckudin*, it freezes)__ November.
manido'gizĭsons' (*manido*, spirit; *gizĭs*, December.
   month; *ons*, diminutive).

Divisions of the day

gi'jigûk_____ day.
di'bigûk_____ night.
mo'kaün, or mokaüŋ_____ sunrise.
buŋ'gecimo' (*buŋge*, it falls)_____ sunset.
gi'gijeb_____ morning.
na'wakweg_____ noon.
ĭckwa'nawakweg'_____ afternoon.
ona'gocĭg_____ evening.

Terms of measurement

diba'igûn (diminutive, *dibaïgans*)_____ "one measure," applied to time, dis-
                                        tance, or quantity.
non'godo'pwagûn_____᠆ "one pipe."
ningo'gabe'ciwĭn_____ "from camp to camp," usually a dis-
                                        tance of about 10 miles.
ningo'anwe'biwĭn_____ "from one resting place to the next."
                                        This was a term used by the traders
                                        and indicated the distance a man
                                        could carry a load of about 150 pounds
                                        in portaging. This was about one-half
                                        mile.
nijo'anwe'biwĭn_____ twice the above distance.

Linear measures

nin'godonĭnj'_____ width of the thumb, occasionally the width of a finger; also used in designating a handful.

ningodwa'kwaägŭn_____ span of the thumb and little finger.

nin'godo'nĭk_____ length or "spread" of one arm. Cloth was thus measured for a skirt length. Term used also to designate the spread of both arms.

nijo'nĭk_____ two such lengths.

Measures of quantity

nin'godonĕn'djigŭn_____ "one swallow," term used in connection with remedies.

nin'godo'bune'nindjigŭn_____ "hand hollow," term used in measuring powdered herbs, etc.

niji'godo'bune'nindjigŭn_____ two such amounts.

ni'jigodo'nikan_____ "double hand hollow," the amount held in the hollow of the two hands, placed together.

PAYMENT OF ANNUITY

de'baäma'gewĭn (debaámage, he or she term used to designate "annuity."
pays; wĭn, denoting action).

TRADERS AND TRADING POSTS

a'dawe'winĭ'nĭ, (adawe, he buys or sells; trader.
inĭnĭ, man).

FIRE MAKING AND USES OF FIRE

ĭ'ckode'_____ fire.

biwa'nŭg (bi implies smallness)_____ flint used in fire making.

ĭ'ckode'kan_____ steel used in fire making.

sa'gata'gŭn_____ decayed wood used in fire making.

gi'jĭk (cedar)_____ term used to designate the "hearth" of fire-making outfit.

a'gĭmak' (agĭm, snowshoe; ak, indicat- term used to designate the bow which
ing wood). formed part of fire-making outfit.

PIPES AND SMOKING

opwa'gŭn_____ pipe; also bowl when detached from stem.

okĭdj'_____ pipestem.

mĭtĭgo'pwagŭn (mĭtĭg, wood)_____ wooden pipe.

asĭn'ipwa'gŭn (asĭn, stone)_____ stone pipe.

ase'mawĭna'gŭn_____ tray in which tobacco was cut.

BOWS AND ARROWS

atcab'_____ bowstring; also bow.

mĭ'tĭgwab'_____ wooden portion of bow.

biwŭk'_____ arrow, commonly applied to the blunt wooden arrow for children's use.

a'sawan'_____ arrow with stone or metal point.

bĭn'dawŭn'_____ quiver,

SNOWSHOES

a'gĭm-------------------------------- snowshoe.
wag'ina'kweä'gĭm (*wag* implies a curve)   snowshoe with upturned toe.
m̩akwa'gĭm (*makwa*, bear; *agĭm*, snow-   "bear-paw snowshoe."
  shoe).
asûb'ika'gûn (*asûb*, net) ------------- netting on snowshoe.

PITCH

bigiü'---------------------------- pitch.
biwan'dago'biü--------------------- gum of a certain sort of spruce.
na'jikiwe'igûn--------------------- spatula used for spreading pitch.

TORCHES

waswa gûn (*was*, part of stem of words   torch (general term).
  referring to light; *gûn*, article).
was'ukonĕn'djigûn------------------- term used chiefly in designating candles.
i'kwewas'ukonĕn'djigûn (*ikwe*, woman)   long, slender torch used by the women
                                       when working around the camp.
                                       Commonly called "woman's candle."
bimûckwe'magi'nigûn   (*b i m u c k w e ,*   twisted birch-bark torch.
  twisted).
wawac'keciwaswa'gûn   (*wawackeci,*   torch used when hunting deer.
  deer).

CANOE MAKING

djiman'---------------------------- canoe.
wigwas'idjiman'-------------------- birch-bark canoe.
djiman'icĭg------------------------ extra thick bark for canoe making.
onade'skodjigan'------------------- frame on which canoe is made.
api'sidagûn'----------------------- one of the flat pieces of wood extending
                                       the length of the canoe.
waginak'--------------------------- rib of canoe.
gi'jĭk bi'midasan'----------------- crossbar of canoe.
bi'mikwan'------------------------- strip of wood around top.
wadûb'----------------------------- split spruce root for binding top.
migos'----------------------------- awl (general term).
bigiü'----------------------------- pitch (general term).
ci'jokiwaga'agûn------------------- spatula for spreading pitch in canoe
                                       making.
nimita'monaguŋg'------------------- front of canoe.
ada'kan--------------------------- stern.
abwi'------------------------------ ordinary paddle.
ikwe'abwi'------------------------- woman's paddle.

TWINE

wigo'bimĭc------------------------- basswood tree.
wigub'----------------------------- inner bark of this or similar trees.
bi'mute'igûn (*bimute,* twisted; *gûn,* ar-   twisted cord (general term).
  ticle or thing).
wigobi'mĭna'kwan------------------- cord made of basswood fiber.
ze'sûb----------------------------- cord made of nettle-stalk fiber.
atĭs'eyab' (*atĭs,* sinew)-------------- cord made of sinew.

FISH NETS

asûb'_____ net, commonly understood to mean the net used for catching fish.

asûb'ikeyab'_____ twine for making fish nets.

name'asûb (name, sturgeon)_____ large-meshed net.

sûgwa'sûb_____ small-meshed net.

MATS AND WEAVING

ana'kûn_____ rush mats for floor.

apûk'we (apûkwa, "to lap on to")____ bulrush mats for sides of dwelling.

namûŋg'_____ weaving needle.

aso'gabam_____ weaving cord.

mû'ckimûd_____ woven bag (container).

gijĭki'mûckimûd (gijĭk, cedar)_____ bag woven of bark.

okade'nigûn (okad, leg)_____ woven braid.

bi'nudabi'gûna'tĭg (binudabi, thread wooden frame on which braid was
woven in and out; gûn, article or   woven.
thing; atĭg, wood).

gi'jipizun' (gijip implies "circling the belt (general term).
waist").

BASKETRY

wa'dabi'makûk'_____ basket.

ozĭ'sĭgo'bimĭc_____ willow used in basket making.

wĭcko'bimûcko'si_____ sweet grass used in basket making.

DYES

adĭs'igûn (adĭsige, he or she dyes; gûn, dyestuff.
article or thing).

mĭskwa'_____ red.

miskwa'dûsigûn'_____ red dye.

oza'wa_____ yellow.

ozawa'dûsigûn'_____ yellow dye.

mûkûde'_____ black (also used to designate gunpowder).

mûkûde'wasigûn'_____ black dye.

oza'wûn_____ blue or green.

ozawûc'kûcigûn_____ blue or green dye.

TANNING

ase'kewĭn (aseke, he or she tans; wĭn, process of tanning.
denoting action).

ase'kwan, also bûckwe'igûn_____ tanned hide.

gica'kweĭgûn_____ scraper used in tanning.

apûkwa'igûn_____ log on which hide is scraped.

MUSICAL INSTRUMENTS

dewe'igûn (dewe, throb; gûn, article)___ drum.

mĭtĭg'wakĭk_____ Mide drum.

cicig'wan (cicig, rattlesnake)_____ rattle.

bĭbĭg'wûn (bĭbĭge, he plays)_____ flute.

BEADWORK

manido′mĭnĕs (manido, spirit; mĭn, seed bead.
  or berry; ĕs, diminutive).
manido′mĭnĕsikan′------------------ beadwork.
mûzina′bido′igûn (from mûzinûbe, he or woven beadwork.
  she pictures).
kwackwac′kûndjimĭnĕs′ikan   (kwac- "jumping pattern."
  kwackûn, jumping).
wawa′ckigwa′sûwĭn (wag is part of stem "zigzag pattern."
  of word applied to things bent,
  curved, or crooked).
ni′gigwa′sowûgwa′sûn (nigig, otter; sûn otter-tail pattern.
  implies sewing).
kuku′kigwa′sûn--------------------· pattern in squares.
wa′wië′gwasun (wawië, round)-------- round pattern.
ajage′cigwa′sûn-------------------- crawfish pattern.
anûŋg′egwa′sûn (anûŋg, star)--------- star pattern.
mûzini′jiganûn′ (from mûzinûbe, he or cut pattern.
  she pictures).

MISCELLANEOUS

gi′kĭno′igûn (gikĭno is modified stem of map, message, or record in picture
  verb meaning "to mark"; gûn, ar-   writing.
  ticle or thing).
gawe′ûg-------------------------- porcupine quill work.
na′gûmo′wĭn---------------------- song (applied only to human beings, a
                            different term being used for the song
                            of birds).
ni′miwĭn------------------------- dance.

DWELLINGS

The principal types of dwellings were the wigwam, the peaked lodge, the bark house and the tipi. To these may be added a conical lodge of evergreen boughs for temporary use.

(a) *The wigwam.*—This term is commonly applied to the dome-shaped Algonquian dwelling which in early times extended from Canada to North Carolina. The word wigwam appears in English as early as 1634 (Wood, Wm., New England's Prospect, 65, 1634). It seems to have been used originally by the Abnaki, an Algonquian confederacy centering in the present State of Maine. The proper term in Chippewa is *wigiwam*, from the root *wigiw*, " he dwells." [25] This term is applied by the Chippewa to any habitation. The type under present consideration is designated as a *waginogan*, from *wagin*, bent, *o* connective, and *gan*, dwelling. The materials entering into the structure of a wigwam were poles or saplings, birch bark, and bulrushes tied together with green basswood bark and basswood twine. The dwelling might be round or oval, and of any

---

[25] Cf. Article " Wigwam," Handbook of American Indians, Bull. 30, Bur. Amer. Ethn., pt. 2, p. 951, 1910.

size, but was characterized by a dome-shaped top. (Pl. 3, a and b.) The structure may be briefly described as consisting of poles planted in the ground, brought together in arches, and covered with mats. The framework was left on a camp site, and the coverings carried from place to place.

Dwellings of this type are still seen among the Chippewa, and the erection of such a one on the White Earth Reservation was described by its owner. This wigwam was 12 feet long and 10½ feet wide, with an entrance at one end. It was on slightly sloping ground, and a shallow ditch was dug across the back, terminating halfway down each side, to carry off the water in case of rain. The frame consisted of six slender poles (three on each side) set in the longer diameter, and eight poles (four on each side) set in the shorter diameter of the lodge. The poles on the longer diameter were about 38 inches apart, and on the shorter diameter about 14 inches apart. These poles were of ironwood, which is pliable when green and tough yet elastic when dry; thus it was possible to make a secure lodge of poles an inch or less in thickness. The poles were stuck firmly in the ground, those on the longer diameter being implanted first and the ends twisted together overhead, the length of the poles being such that the arch formed by them was about 5½ feet above the ground at its highest point. The poles at the ends of the lodge were then implanted and their ends similarly twisted, the overlapping portion being 1 to 1½ feet. The intersections of the two parts of the frame were then tied with freshly cut strips of the inner bark of the basswood tree. The lengthwise and crosswise supports having been placed in position, two similar ironwood poles were arranged around the sides of the lodge, the lower of these being about 4 feet from the ground, and the other about 3 feet higher. These encircling poles were fastened around the erect framework, each intersection being tied with basswood bark. At one end of the lodge an opening was left in the lower of these braces for the doorway. The framework having been completed, the sides, except the doorway, were covered with bulrush mats. The woven edge of the mats was placed at the top, and tied to the framework; the rushes at the other edge of the mat, not being fastened together, had enough "spring" to assist in holding the mat upright.

In the lodge herein described a second row of mats was fastened to the framework about 18 inches above the ground on the windy side, affording protection from a possible draft. For additional warmth in winter a second row of mats was frequently placed around the entire lodge overlapping the first row. The top of the lodge was covered with rolls of birch bark. These rolls were commonly about 10 or 12 feet long, and consisted of sheets of birch bark placed side by side, and sewed together with narrow strips of basswood bark.

The ends were finished with sticks, which prevented the tearing of the bark, and made it possible to roll the material. The rolls of bark were laid first across the shorter diameter of the lodge, a space about 2 feet wide being left in the middle for the smoke hole. Short braces were placed between the lengthwise poles to support the inner edges of the birch bark, adjacent to the smoke hole. The rolls of birch bark were then laid on the longer diameter, leaving an opening for the smoke hole. The corners of the rolls were firmly secured by means of strips of bark passed between the rushes of the side walls, and tied to the framework of the lodge. These rolls were further held in place by strips of basswood bark sufficiently long to extend entirely over the lodge from side to side. These strips were usually secured to stakes, or to a longitudinal pole on each side. In this lodge, however, the strips of bark were wrapped around heavy stones, which rested on the ground at either side of the lodge.

A blanket (or in older times a hide) was hung over the doorway, having a heavy stick or pole at the lower edge, which rested on the ground. A person entering the doorway usually lifted the stick at one end and rolled the lifted corner of the blanket inward and upward, thus holding the drapery as he entered. If the wind blew strongly into the doorway, it was customary to separate the rush mats at the opposite end of the lodge, and use the opening thus formed as a temporary entrance. If the wind were so severe as to blow through the rush matting, it was customary to tie a blanket on the outside of the lodge as a further protection. The fire space was in the middle of the lodge, being outlined by logs. A short pole was fastened

Fig. 2.—Wooden hook

across the smoke hole, and on this pole pieces of meat were hung to dry above the fire. Hooks to hold kettles were commonly made of crotched sticks of green wood and suspended from this pole by strips of green bark. (Fig. 2.) Similar hooks were suspended from the lower of the two encircling braces of the lodge. These hooks were commonly made of chokecherry wood. Rush mats were placed on the ground beside the fire, and personal belongings were stored in rolls or in woven bags of cedar bark, or of yarn, and placed along the walls of the wigwam. In the old days a dwelling of this or of the type next mentioned was occupied by two or three families, representing two or perhaps three generations.

In June, 1925, the writer watched the making of a wigwam at Mille Lac and photographed the process at various stages. A quantity of green tamarack poles, sharpened at one end, had been pre-

a, Frame of wigwam

b, Wigwam

a, Frame partially completed

b, Woman placing bark in position

c, Wigwam of black ash and birch bark

WIGWAM IN COURSE OF CONSTRUCTION

pared, together with large sheets of black ash bark for the lower part of the sides, and rolls of birch bark for the roof. An oblong space was first marked off by laying poles on the ground. This was measured and found to be 9 feet 8 inches long and 9 feet in width. A pole was set up at each corner. The next act was the placing of five poles in a slightly curved line outside the longer poles, these being the frame for the sides of the wigwam. The poles were thrust about 10 inches into the ground in a slanting position, with the upper ends slanting outward as shown in Plate 4, *a*. Six poles were similarly placed in a wider curve outside the poles which marked the back and front of the wigwam; a space was left for the doorway at the front, the poles at that point being farther apart than the others. Note the rolls of birch bark for roof at left of this picture.

Preparation was then made for tying the ends of the poles when they should be brought together to form the roof. The woman in charge of the work had a large pail of water in which she soaked wide strips of basswood about 1 yard in length. When these had softened she took them from the water and separated them into layers, then into strips or ribbons about half an inch wide. Her next act was to tie a basswood cord around her waist and put a number of the basswood ribbons in her waistband, so the loops stood up and the material could be easily drawn out for use.

A man then bent the ends of the poles downward and she tied them first in the middle, where they came together over her head, then she tied the ends of the poles in place. One of the poles was measured and found to be 16 feet from the ground to its tip. The poles erected at the corners of the framework, extending the length of the wigwam, were the last to be bent down and tied. To this framework four slender poles were tied in a horizontal position, extending along the sides and strengthening the frame, and several poles extending the length of the roof. A space was left between the latter in the middle of the roof for a smoke hole, this space being a neat square formed by the lengthwise and crosswise poles. For this purpose tamarack poles were used, with a few poplar poles. Each intersection was firmly secured by tying with the basswood fiber. The frame was then ready for covering. The sheets of black ash bark were notched at the upper end in order that they might more easily conform to the dome-shaped roof. Their height is shown in Plate 4, *b*. They were fastened in place by two women, one inside and one outside, who passed the basswood fiber through holes made with an awl. Each sheet of bark was fastened securely to each intersection of the framework below it. The bark on each side of the doorway was " sewed over and over " to the poles which formed the

" doorposts," and great care was taken to have the lines of the doorway perpendicular. The top of the structure was then covered with
rolls of birch bark. One corner of each roll was fastened in place
by a basswood cord which was passed between the sheets of ash bark
and tied to the framework inside the wigwam. The whole was
secured by basswood cord passed across the top and fastened to
stakes driven in the ground. (Pl. 4, c.) The poles which had
been used for measuring the size of the wigwam were taken up and
a few sheets of ash bark were laid on the ground to serve as mats.
The structure was neat, firm, and completed in a surprisingly short
time. All the work was done by women, except that of driving the
poles in the ground, bending them down, and holding them in
position while they were tied in place.

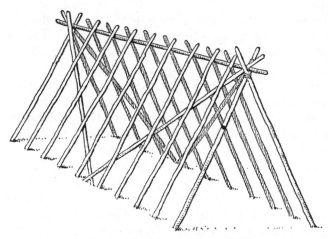

FIG. 3.—Sketch of frame of peaked lodge

(b) *Peaked lodge.*—This, like the wigwam, consisted of a frame
of poles covered with bark, but the structure instead of being dome
shaped had a long ridgepole and flat sides that sloped to the ground.
Sheets of elm or cedar bark like those used on the " bark houses "
were placed on the sides of this lodge. Birch-bark rolls were similarly used and a peaked lodge with such a covering was seen and
photographed in northern Minnesota by Bushnell in 1899.[26] A similar lodge was photographed by the writer at Grand Portage, Minn.,
in 1905. (Pl. 5, b.)

A Canadian Chippewa said that his people used this type of dwelling covered with birch bark or brush, and also made of logs. He
described the erection of such a lodge, Figure 3 being made from his
sketch. The crossed poles at the ends were first erected, then the

ridgepole and braces for the sides were put in place, after which the poles at the ends and along the sides were added. An entrance was provided at each end. These lodges were long, permitting three or even four fireplaces, but there were no smoke holes in the structure. It was said that the crossing of the poles left sufficient opening for the egress of the smoke. If the lodge were to be covered with birch bark it was necessary to put four horizontal bars on the sides, the birch bark being fastened to these bars. The birch bark covered only the upper part of the lodge, cedar mats being placed next the ground. The covering of brush was not explained, but was said to be used in winter. A dwelling suited to the rigors of a Canadian winter was made of split logs, 8 or 10 inches in diameter, laid on the frame above described with the smooth surface of the logs inside. The logs were chinked with moss on the outside and banked with earth. A log lodge was "made rather open at the top," but contained no smoke holes. The Canadian Chippewa used moose hide for the door of the lodge, also beaver hides sewed together or rabbit skins woven like a blanket.

(c) *Bark house.*—This type of dwelling consisted of a framework of poles resembling that of a broad, low house, having its walls and sides covered with sheets of bark. In some instances the roof was covered with rolls of birch bark, this being used chiefly in the sugar camps that were occupied for only a short time each year. The rolls of birch bark were carried by the women and it was often more convenient to use them than to take time for gathering the heavy sheets of elm or cedar bark. (Pl. 6, *a.*) The frame was usually of elm wood, the side walls being made of upright poles with the bark on them. No nails were used in either walls or roof in the old days. It is said that the poles forming the peaked roof were so securely tied together that the roof merely rested on the walls, not being held by the cords that seemed to fasten it. The side walls, and frequently the roof, were covered with elm or cedar or other suitable bark. (Pl. 6, *b.*) If such a lodge were occupied in winter it was made warm by banking the outside with cedar boughs and snow and by filling the crevices inside with dried moss. Cedar boughs were spread on the ground and mats laid over them. The lodge usually had a low platform extending along the sides, formed of branches supported by stakes. These platforms were used as seats. Dwellings of this type were used in the sugar camps as well as in other places where the people might wish to stay for a time, and similar structures were used as "weaving houses" for the making of rush mats.

(d) *Tipi.*—Among the Chippewa, as among the Plains tribes, this dwelling consisted of a conical framework of poles with a covering of birch bark or cloth. (Pls. 7, *a, b;* 8, *a, b.*) The Chippewa probably adopted the tipi from the Sioux, but all do not follow the Sioux custom of tying together the first three poles of the framework, putting them in place and leaning the other poles against their intersection. Instead, the older Chippewa leave a short crotch on two or three poles, which are thus locked together, the remainder of the poles being laid against them. Spruce wood was preferred for these poles in regions where it was available. If a high wind threatened the stability of the structure, its framework was reinforced by a thin pole of flexible wood tied horizontally to the framework about 5 feet above the ground and bent around the frame. At Mille Lac the writer witnessed the erection of the tipi shown in Plate 7, b. It will be noted that this tipi is not so pointed as those at White Earth (pl. 8, b), but the crotched pole makes what might be termed a very short ridge pole. The Chippewa at White Earth are in frequent contact with the Sioux, and the writer has seen a tipi on that reservation erected in the Sioux fashion, with the three poles together and put up in a tripod as its beginning. In the Mille Lac tipi a fire space was made in the old style, outlined with small logs, which were held in place by stakes. This space, extending from the door into the middle of the tipi, kept the fire and ashes within bounds. Over the fire a horizontal pole was fastened from one side of the tipi frame to the other and tied in place with basswood cord. To this, directly over the fire, a wooden hook was attached by basswood cord, and from this hook the cooking kettle was suspended.

Mention should be made of a form of temporary lodge, which consisted of a conical frame of poles covered with boughs of balsam or other evergreen. The boughs were fastened with the points downward. It is said this shelter would keep out the rain and was quite comfortable.

Logs were used for large structures at an early date, an old log dance house at Mille Lac, Minn., being shown in Plate 5, a.

MANNER OF LIFE IN THE WIGWAM

The winter habitation may be taken as representing the life in the wigwam, as at that time all the members of the family were usually at home. The family usually comprised two or three generations, living in a long wigwam with an entrance and a fire at each end, and a smoke hole over each fire. The one unfailing rule was that the youngest persons should live in the middle of the lodge, where they must pass their elders in entering or leaving. If the lodge was so long that there was more than one fire, the cooking was chiefly done at the fire presided over by the mother of the family, who prepared and served the food, sending portions to the branches of the family.

a, Old log dance house, Mille Lac, Minn.

b, Peaked lodge covered with birch bark, Grand Portage, Minn.

a, Lodge with mat sides and birch-bark roof

b, Elm-bark lodge

a, Frame of tipi

b, Tipi with covering of birch bark and cloth

a, Tipi covered with birch bark

b, Tipi covered with cloth

Thus a large piece of meat would be sent to the young men, each of whom would cut off what he wished to eat, using the knife which he always carried in his knife sheath. If any were absent at mealtime the mother put away a portion of food for them. There was not room to store much food in the lodge, and the supply of food was kept outside. A high rack or frame was put near the door of the lodge, and the food to be used during the day was kept there and covered with birch bark. The large supply of food was in a cache. There was usually a tipi or a storehouse of logs and bark near the lodge for storing implements of various sorts and for keeping extra clothing.

The arrangement of a family in a wigwam is shown in Figure 4. Informants differed as to whether the mother's place was at the left or right of the entrance, but the daughters were always next her. Each branch of the family had a possessive right to a certain part of the dwelling. The bedding consisted of blankets and deer or bear hide tanned with the hair on them. Some people had pillows and thin feather beds made of hide or cloth and filled with feathers, usually those of the wild duck. Cedar boughs were spread on the ground and covered with rush mats, the bedding being placed

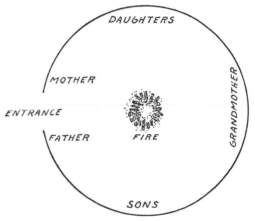

Fig. 4.—Sketch showing arrangement of family in a small wigwam

on these mats at night. During the day it was rolled up and used as seats or placed along the walls of the lodge. The winter evenings were social and pleasant. The fire burned brightly, but no work was done which placed a strain on the eyes. A favorite pastime was the making of birch-bark transparencies. The women made basswood cord or fish nets, and sometimes they made birch-bark makuks or dishes. The young men reclined in the wigwam and always had a drum conveniently near them. Sometimes they went to call on the neighbors or to hear the story tellers; it was, however, necessary for the men to do considerable woodwork during the winter, making and repairing their snowshoes as well as their traps. The winter was the time for story-telling, and many old women were experts in this art. One old woman used to act out her stories, running around the fire and acting while she talked.

Two photographs were secured showing the typical sitting posture of the man and the woman in the wigwam. The man sat "cross-legged." He said this position was the most convenient for a man's work. The woman "sat on her right foot" with the left foot extending out at one side. She said that in this position a woman could rise easily to "reach things," and the position of the left foot avoided a cramped feeling. If a woman were doing some handwork, her position would naturally conform to the implements used, but this was the ordinary position in the wigwam, as during the winter evenings.

In winter the family slept with their feet toward the fire, removing their moccasins and loosening their other clothing. If the weather was very cold, an old man or woman usually kept awake and smoked and watched the fire, keeping it burning and watching that the sparks did no damage.

In summer the Chippewa frequently slept in the open.

CLOTHING

(a) *Materials.*—The most primitive materials used as clothing by the Chippewas were tanned hides, the green leaves of plants, and a cloth woven of nettle-stalk fiber. The latter was woven in "tubular form" like the yarn bags (pl. 67) and used for underskirts by the women. The leaves were used as a protection to the head in hot weather, and the tanned hides were used for making garments.

The implements used in place of thread before the advent of the traders were nettle-fiber twine and sinew. A woman who wished to sew would often say to the children, "Go get me a stalk," and the desired twine would be quickly made. It is said that "there are lots of thread plants at deserted Indian villages." The nettle fiber could be twisted into fine or coarse thread, as occasion required. Every woman kept a piece of dried sinew (pl. 9, a (f)) ready for work upon leather. Moose sinew was rather coarse and was used for heavy work, but deer sinew could be split into exceedingly fine strands, and was used for fine sewing or with small beads. In place of needles the women used various pointed implements (pl. 9, a (e)), making a hole in the material with the implement and passing the sinew or twine through it. The thorns of the thorn-apple tree and the "splint bone" of a deer could be used without preparation. (Pl. 9, a (a, b).) Other materials were set in a handle or otherwise prepared for use. Wooden awls were the earliest form, followed by awls with a metal point set in a wooden handle. (Pl. 9, a (e).) The first yarn brought by the traders was too fine for weaving, and two strands were twisted together by the use of a distaff. (Pl. 9, a (d).) A woman kept her sewing materials in a bag. The type of workbag illustrated (pl. 9, b) was in much favor, as it could be placed upright on the ground beside the worker. It is made of the hide of four deer hoofs, and the flat piece at the base is about 6 inches in diameter. When obtained this bag contained a good supply of thorn-apple thorns and sinews in various forms which had been left by its former owner, dead these many years.

The tanning of hides (chiefly those of the deer) was the work of the women and was done in an expert manner, the hides being soft and colored a golden brown. An old woman said, " rabbit skin was a great help to the Indians." She said that the women hung the hides on bushes for several days and part of the soft fur was blown away by the wind, but the " firmer " hair remained. Hides prepared in this way were used inside a cradle board and inside children's moccasins; they were also used in the making of children's caps. Rabbit skins were sewed together in patches to make blankets. The Mississippi Chippewa did not make woven rabbit-skin blankets like those used by the northern divisions of the tribe.

(b) *Garments.*—In early times the clothing of a woman consisted of a single garment made of two deerskins, one forming the front and the other the back of the garment, the two parts being fastened together at the shoulders and held in place by a belt. When the traders brought broadcloth a woman might have a similar dress made of cloth, but she always had a dress of hides for use when she was at work. To this were added moccasins, leggings, and a blanket. A garment woven of nettle fiber has been mentioned in a preceding paragraph. One deerskin was enough for making the single garment worn by a child.

The usual costume worn by the men consisted of breechcloth, moccasins, leggings, and a blanket obtained from the trader. A man's leggings were rather tight and did not lap far at the sides. They extended from the ankle almost to the hip and were held in place by a thong tied to the belt. A band or thong was also tied below the knee. A woman's leggings were wider, with a wide piece that was folded over at the outer edge. They extended a few inches above the knee, but were fastened by a band or thong below the knee. The bands for men's leggings were made of woven beadwork with a long fringe of yarn which was used in tying them around the knee. (Cf. ornaments, p. 37.) Winter coats and pointed hoods were made from old blankets. The coats were belted, and the pointed hoods were often made to extend down to the waist in the back, with a belt fastening them in place. This winter costume was probably learned from the white man. A muskrat skin, tanned with the hair on it, was worn as a " chest protector " by men on hunting expeditions and was occasionally worn by women. This, as well as rabbit skin, was placed inside moccasins to make them warmer.

Four kinds of broadcloth were carried by the traders about 60 or 70 years ago and given to the Indians in exchange for furs.[27] The cheapest quality was dark blue coarse broadcloth with a white border. Enough of this for a woman's dress cost the equivalent of $5 in furs. The three other kinds cost about double that amount and were (1) a jet-black broadcloth which was very fine and shiny, (2) a dark-brownish broadcloth with a border of narrow stripes, and (3) a bright scarlet broadcloth. The last named was usually used as a decoration, embroidery of beads being placed upon it. Rev. C. H. Beaulieu, however, said that he once saw a dress made entirely of this material. To these cloths should be added gray list cloth with gray edge and the white list cloth with white edge which was coarser than the gray. Both were coarser than broadcloth and lacked the high finish of that material.

The amount purchased for a woman's dress was the length from her armpits to her ankles with about half a yard additional. The cloth was not wide enough to give the desired fullness, so the additional piece was put in the front of the dress as a " front breadth." The cloth was so wide that this breadth was too long, and the extra portion was turned over at the top of the garment, extending across the woman's chest and having the selvedge of the goods at its lower edge. This flap was called the " front piece " and was the first part of a woman's dress to be decorated in color. The traders brought worsted braids in various colors and several rows of these were put across the front piece of a dress and called a " rainbow." Later a more abundant use of colored braid arose. The braids in many hues were put around the lower edge of the dress. The decoration was no longer a " rainbow " against the dark, shining broadcloth, and the garish use of colored material had begun.

This garment was held in place by strips over the shoulders and confined at the waist by a belt or sash. Arm coverings were usually provided and could be worn or laid aside as desired. These consisted of two strips of cloth, each fastened at the wrist after the manner of a cuff, and the two attached at the back of the neck, forming a capelike protection to the shoulders. When calico was brought by the traders a loose calico sacque was frequently worn by the women over the above-described broadcloth dress without the arm coverings. The arm coverings are correctly shown in Plate 27.

The amount of broadcloth required for a breechcloth was measured by placing the two thumbs together with fists closed and thumbs extended. This width was then torn from the bolt. The ends

---

[27] The information concerning cloth was given by Nancy McDonald, whose mother was a Chippewa and her father a Scotch trader. She often went with her father on his trips when she was a child. At the time of giving this information she was almost 100 years old.

were bound with ribbon and decorated with beadwork. The quantity for a man's leggings was about a yard and was measured from the ear to the end of the thumb. These, like the women's leggings, were decorated with beads in line patterns and edged with beads. A black silk neckerchief was worn by the women about 60 or 70 years ago. (Pl. 42.) The typical dress of a Chippewa woman at the present time consists of a full, rather long skirt, and a fitted sacque buttoned neatly up the front.

Blankets were issued as part of the annuities, those for men being known as "three-point" and those for women as "two-and-a-half-point." Men wore the blanket over one shoulder and under the other arm, the lower part of the blanket being drawn closely around the waist. They took much pride in the arrangement of the blanket, practicing diligently to acquire a graceful folding across the arm. The blanket was usually worn over the left shoulder, leaving the right hand and arm free, but if a man were left-handed he wore the blanket over his right shoulder. The usual manner of wearing a blanket by a woman was as follows: The blanket was wrapped around the limbs like a tight skirt and fastened with a belt; the upper part of the blanket was then thrown loosely around the arms and shoulders, affording warmth and yet leaving the arms free for work. A woman could put her baby in the blanket between her shoulders, or, if desired, she could drop the upper part of the blanket entirely, drawing it around the waist.

The thrift of Chippewa women is shown in their use of old blankets. It was their custom to make coats for the little children from the discarded blankets of their elders, while small pieces were used for making pointed hoods and the socks that were worn inside moccasins. Old blankets were raveled to make yarn for weaving bags, and a thin, threadbare blanket was used to strain maple sap and remove twigs or bits of bark before the sap was boiled.

(c) *Head coverings.*—The leaves of the burdock were used as a protection to the head and were either sewed together or fastened upright on a wide strip of birch bark. The pointed hoods made of blanket were warm and comfortable in winter, especially to the hunters. A fillet of fur, decorated in various ways and with a strip of fur hanging from it, was worn in former years. A yarn sash was frequently worn around the head like a fillet, with the ends hanging at one side and with one or two feathers stuck in it. At the present time a handkerchief is worn around the head in a manner which is graceful as well as practical. It may be arranged tightly, affording warmth, and sometimes a fold of it is drawn forward as a shade for the eyes. A woman's shawl is often drawn loosely over the head in summer and is said to be an agreeable protection from the sun.

(d) *Moccasins.*—The hide of the deer and moose were used in making moccasins, according to the thickness desired. Four types of moccasins were in use among the Chippewa: (1) The simplest form of moccasin consisted of two pieces of leather with a plain seam extending the length of the sole and up the front and back of the foot. These moccasins were worn chiefly by infants and old women. Similar moccasins were made of blanket to wear under the puckered moccasins for additional warmth. It was customary for the women to make a supply of these and keep them on hand. (2) The moccasin with a puckered seam up the front and a plain seam up the back is probably the oldest type of Chippewa moccasin and is the article from which the tribal name is said to have been derived, *odjibwe,* meaning " puckered." (Bull. 53, pl. 36.) This moccasin was made of one piece of leather, and for winter use was made large enough so that the blanket moccasins above mentioned could be worn inside of it. Muskrat hide tanned with the hair on it was

FIG. 5.—Notched pattern for beadwork on cuff of moccasin

sometimes placed inside these moccasins. (3) A type of moccasins made for children was called the " partridge moccasin," because of derived, *odjibwe,* meaning "puckered." (Bull. 53, pl. 36.) This moccasins were made of one piece of leather, the sole being gathered in a straight seam across the top of the toe. (Pl. 10, *c, d.*) They were made large, and in winter a rabbit skin with the hair on it was placed inside them for warmth, or they were partly filled with moss or hay. (4) The present style of moccasin is said by some to have come from the Pembina Band of Chippewa and to have been introduced among the Mississippi Chippewa by mixed-bloods living along the Red River. This moccasin has a tongue-shaped piece of leather or black velvet in the front, to which the sole is gathered; also a " cuff " around the top, both the tongue and cuff being decorated. (Bull. 53, pl. 35.) For winter use a wide strip of cloth or buckskin is sewed around the top and tied around the ankle for warmth. Plate 10, *a, b,* shows these moccasins completed and partly completed.

Na'waji'bigo'kwe stated that among the Mille Lac Chippewa the earliest decorations for moccasin-cuffs were notched. Several pat-

terns cut by her are shown in Plate 11, *b*, *c*, *d*, *e*, and Figure 5.
These were laid on the buckskin and outlined with stitches, after
which the zigzag line was done in beads and the spots represented
by holes in the pattern were worked solid in beads. Informants
at Red Lake said this sort of moccasin decoration had never been
used among them. Two patterns for use on the front of moccasins
were cut by Nawajibigokwe. (Pl. 11, *a*.) These designs were outlined with a double row of beads. She said that "the young men
liked two strands of beads, white for the outer and blue for the
inner row." An old floral pattern for moccasin fronts, still used by
Mrs. Louisa Martin, is shown in Figure 6. Of a different and
modern type are the patterns for the fronts of moccasins used by
Mrs. Roy and her sister, of Red Lake. (Pl. 12.) These are the most
ornate of any Chippewa designs
seen by the writer and were part of
the regular equipment of these
workers. (Cf. p. 187.)

Around the curved front piece of
a moccasin there is usually a fine
cord, sometimes of silk but in the
better specimens made of horsehair.
This finish is used on the moccasins in addition to the bead work.
A pair of moccasins sewed with
sinew and decorated only with
horsehair was obtained. For this
decoration the hair of a white
horse is obtained and a part of it
dyed in several colors. In apply-
ing the decoration a strand of horse-

Fig. 6.—Old floral design for front of
moccasin

hair is laid along the line to be covered and held in place with the
thumb of the left hand while it is sewed in place with a colored hair,
threaded through a fine needle. The stitches are placed close together, giving the effect of a fine cord, and the strand of horsehair
gives a firmness to the edge of the curved front piece.

(*e*) *Necklaces.*—The material for necklaces which necessitated the
least preparation was a dentalium shell found among the rocks along
Lake Superior, which has a longitudinal hole, making it easy to
string. Necklaces made of bright scarlet berries were worn at an
early period. These berries were pierced with a sharp instrument
while green, the husks being removed by rubbing the berries between
the hands after they had dried. Four or five strings were worn
around the neck, no other substance being combined with them.

It was said by reliable informants that many kinds of large and small bones were strung and worn around the neck. Long, slender tubes were made of a bone in the hind leg of the rabbit (pl. 13 a) and used in this manner. Wooden beads were made before the bringing of glass beads by the traders. The beads worn by Nodinens (pl. 42) were said to be similar to the old beads, and she said that four was a suitable number of strings to wear. A later custom is shown by Mrs. Jackson (pl. 14), the beads being smaller and worn in larger quantity. These beads are like little sections of colored glass tubing and are greatly liked by Chippewa women of the present time. Another style of necklace consisted of about 20 strings of ordinary beads, the strings being of different lengths, so that the front of a woman's dress was ornamented by graduated rows of different colored beads, the whole decoration being 5 or 6 inches in depth. Strips of buckskin were used in tying the strings of beads at the back. A typical necklace of trade beads is shown in Plate 13, b. Woven bead chains were not worn by women in the old days. Braids of sweet grass were worn especially by the men. Two braids were fastened together at the ends and slipped over the head, one braid falling at either side of the face.

A plaited cord in two colors of yarn was worn around the neck as an ornament as well as a charm. Three sorts of plaited cord were noted, one being a charm to secure good health and the other two being said to resemble a striped and a spotted snake. The two latter might indicate that the wearer had dreamed of a snake, but more frequently they were worn as a protection against the bite of these reptiles. The manner of plaiting was similar to that of the bead chains worn for similar reasons. (See pls. 31 and 38, e.) The ends of these cords were finished in a manner suggesting a tassel, the cord being tied and the ends of yarn left free for about 2 inches.

(*f*) *Personal ornaments.*—Earrings were worn by old men more than by women and were seldom worn by young men. The lobe of the ear was pierced several times, the holes extending to the top of the ear. The most common sort of earring consisted of a bunch of small, elongated metal cones, suspended at the tip. It was not uncommon for so many of these to be worn that the ear was weighted down with them.

A ring in the nose was worn by the early Chippewa. This ring was so large that it hung below the lips. In winter a little bunch of fur was sometimes substituted for the ring. An informant said that she had often seen an old Indian with bunches of white fur in his nose and ears.

Armlets and bracelets of brass were obtained from the traders. If a man owned several, he did not hesitate to wear them all at once.

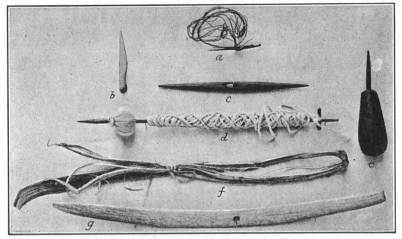

a, Implements and materials used in women's handicraft

(a) Sinew attached to thorn of thorn-apple tree, used as awl; (b) Splint-bone of deer, used as awl; (c) Needle for netting on snowshoes; (d) Distaff; (e) Metal awl set in wooden handle; (f) Dried sinew; (g) Weaving needle for cat-tail mats

b, Bag for sewing materials

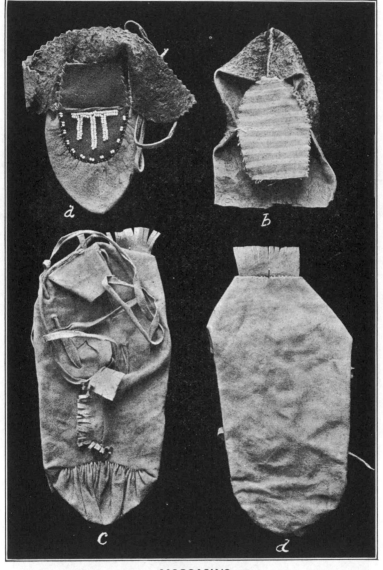

MOCCASINS

a, b, Present style of Chippewa moccasin, completed and partially completed; *c, d,* "Partridge moccasin," obverse and reverse

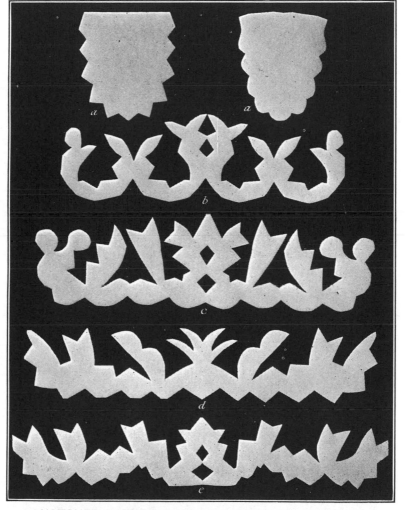

NOTCHED PATTERNS FOR MOCCASIN DECORATION

PATTERNS FOR DECORATION OF MOCCASIN FRONTS
(Native drawings)

a, Necklace of rabbit-leg bones   *b,* Necklace of trade beads

PORTRAIT OF MRS. JACKSON

a, Bead shoulder bag

b, Bead knee bands

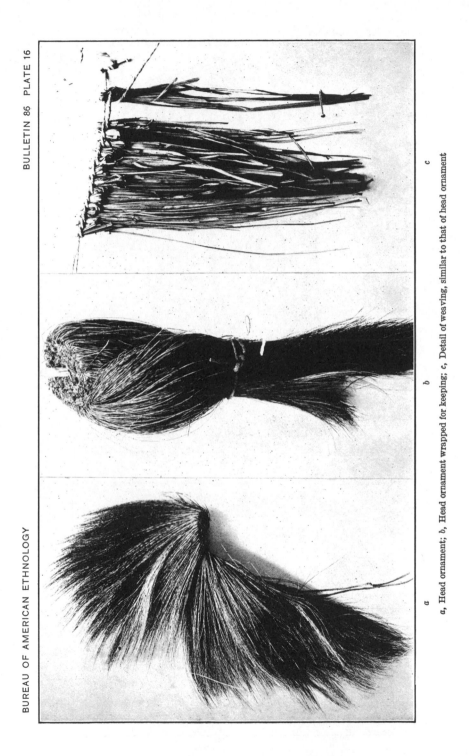

a

b

c

a, Head ornament; *b*, Head ornament wrapped for keeping; *c*, Detail of weaving, similar to that of head ornament

Bands of beadwork about seven-eighths inch wide were worn by the men as wrist bands and a strip 1¼ inches in width was worn close around the neck.

Young men sometimes wore narrow bands of fur around their wrists and ankles, the end hanging and decorated with beads.

The ornaments worn by dancers were of wide variety and showed much originality. In recent times they have been elaborated by the use of sleigh bells, small round mirrors, and bits of tin. Tassels of horsehair dyed red are frequently used on dance garments as well as on pipe bags, the tassel being partly covered by a top made of tin.

A man's beaded leggings were held in place below the knee by bands of beadwork 3 or 4 inches wide, with long strands of yarn at the ends. (Pl. 15, b.) This yarn was usually braided about half its length. In adjusting the ornament the beaded portion was placed in front and was the proper length to extend to the back of the leg. The braided portion of the yarn was crossed and brought to the front of the leg, where the loose ends of yarn were tied in a bow above the beaded band, so that all the beadwork would show.

A favorite ornament for dancers was a roach woven of stiff moose hair. This ornament consisted of a small circle with a long end, and was woven in one long strip of fringe, coiled and sewed in the desired shape. (Pl. 16, a.) In order to fasten it in place a lock of hair on top of the head was passed through a small hole in the circular portion of the ornament and tied, a short stick being inserted through the hair between the ornament and the knot. When not in use a stick several inches long was put in the same opening, the ornament was folded around it, tied, and wrapped in a cotton cloth. The ornament wrapped and a detail of the weaving are shown in Plate 16, b, c, the material in the latter being fine grass. (See p. 161.)

Beaded bags (bandoleers) were worn on festive occasions, the broad band passing over the shoulder. Sometimes two such bags were worn. (Pl. 15, a.)

(g) *Painting and other treatment of the face.*—Young girls reddened their cheeks with the juice of the bloodroot. Men greased their faces with deer tallow to keep them smooth. This was used before going out in the wind, as it kept them warm and also protected the skin. The faces of the men were usually painted in designs. This was done by two methods: (1) The pattern was applied with paint to the palm of the hand and transferred to the face by pressing the palm against it; or (2) the paint was applied solidly to the palm and a portion of the paint removed in a pattern, the palm then being pressed against the face. In the former method the pattern was in color, and in the latter the pattern was reversed.

The paint generally used was colored earth, powdered and mixed with grease. The face painting associated with the several degrees of the Grand Medicine is described and illustrated by Hoffman.[28] The bodies of the men were painted on occasions either in stripes and zigzag lines or in patterns as above described. When the men went to war they mixed "medicine" with the paint applied to their faces and bodies. The beard was removed by the use of tweezers.

(*h*) *Care and arrangement of the hair.*—The young men had handsome hair and took great pride in it, using ointments of various sorts. Sometimes they cared for their hair themselves, but more often this work was done by a sister. Their hair was kept smooth by greasing with bear's grease or deer tallow. It was usually cut in a fringe across the forehead and the remainder braided in two braids. Sometimes a fillet of beads was worn across the forehead to keep the hair in place. Older men often wore a short braid at each temple, the rest of the hair being in two braids, either hanging or tied on top of the head. They also wore the hair at the temples in small braids, each with an ornament at the end. Red and yellow paint was often put in stripes on the hair. Men wore feather headdresses of various styles, but feathers were never worn in the hair by women. In this connection it is interesting to note the manner in which the Chippewa regarded the long hair of the men. It is illustrated by the following incidents: Mrs. English said that she once went into a wigwam where a young woman was combing her brother's hair. The young man had long, handsome hair, and Mrs. English jestingly said, "Give me some of your hair." The young man replied, "No; I would lose all my strength if I cut my hair." His manner implied that he believed it. At a later time, when Mrs. English was connected with the Government school at Red Lake, a boy with long hair was brought to the school. Mrs. English asked whether she could cut the boy's hair and the mother objected. It was, however, a requirement of the school, and after the mother had gone home the boy's hair was cut, much against his wishes. When the mother returned some weeks later and saw the boy, she wept and refused to be comforted. Mrs. English said she could scarcely have showed more grief if the boy had been killed.

One informant said that her uncle once had a vision or dream of a woman, and he had long, beautiful hair, like a woman's. "It seemed as though his life was in his hair. When he went to war and was in the midst of a battle it seemed as though the Sioux could not see him because of the shining of his hair, but when the fighting cleared up his friends could see him."

[28] Hoffman, W. J. The Midē'wiwin or "Grand Medicine Society" of the Ojibwa; in Seventh Ann. Rept. Bur. Ethn., Washington, 1891, pp. 210–213.

Combs were obtained from English traders at an early date. A woman considered her comb as one of her most cherished possessions and kept it in a birch-bark case which she tucked between the frame of the wigwam and its outer covering. Little girls wore their hair in two braids. Young women arranged their hair in three different ways: (1) The most common and convenient mode of hairdressing was in a queue, the hair being wound with cloth in a stiff mass. Beadwork was wound over the cloth if ornamentation was desired. This method kept the hair from tangling and obviated the necessity of arranging it often. (2) The hair was sometimes braided in two braids and a long roll of otter fur was attached to each braid, almost concealing the hair. This was worn only on festive occasions. (3) Before playing a game in which opponents might try to catch a woman by her hair it was customary to weave the hair tightly across the neck with a cord, which was brought around the head and tied. This weaving kept the hair firmly in place at the neck, though it hung loose down the back below the "weaving." (See pl. 27, b, showing doll with this style of hairdressing.) The manner of wearing the hair by women in mourning is described in the section on mourning customs. (See p. 77.)

FOOD

(a) *Vegetable foodstuffs.*—The country of the Chippewa abounded in vegetable products, which the women prepared in a variety of ways and stored for winter use by drying.[29]

The principal vegetable foods were wild rice, corn, and maple sugar. Rice was the staple article of food and was boiled in water or in broth, as well as parched. Corn was roasted in the husks or parched in a hot kettle, or dried and boiled. Pumpkins and squash were cultivated in gardens and either eaten fresh or dried for winter use. Maple sugar was prepared in the form of granulated sugar, "hard sugar," and "gum sugar." The grained sugar was used as a seasoning, and all forms of the sugar were extensively eaten as a delicacy. Wild ginger, bearberry, and mountain mint were used as seasonings, and corn silk and dried pumpkin blossoms were used to thicken broth as well as to give it an agreeable flavor. The Chippewa did not habitually drink the water that they encountered when traveling but boiled it and added leaves or twigs. This decoction was drunk either hot or cold. Among the materials used in this manner were the leaves of the wintergreen, raspberry, spruce, and snowberry, and the twigs of the wild cherry.

Wild potatoes were used, and the Chippewa obtained white potatoes at an early date. Acorns were gathered and cooked in several

---

[29] Cf. section on the industrial year, pp. 123–128; also Uses of Plants by the Chippewa Indians, Forty-fourth Ann. Rept. Bur. Amer. Ethn.

ways. The flowers of the milkweed, the root of bulrushes, the sap of the basswood and aspen, a sweetish substance beneath the outer bark of the woodbine, and the moss from white pine were among the somewhat unusual vegetable foods of the Chippewa. Berries and fruits were extensively used. Dried berries were boiled when used and either seasoned with maple sugar or combined with other foods. A Canadian Chippewa said that his people combined dried berries with moose fat or deer tallow. Salt was unknown in the old days.

The Chippewa claim to have had both pumpkin and squash before the coming of the white man.

(b) *Storing of food.*—It was the custom to store food obtained during the summer in caches or pits dug near the village. The food kept perfectly, the pits were never disturbed, and this method of storage was safe and practical. The women of two or three families usually combined in the work of storing food, and often put rice, sugar, and vegetables in separate pits. Seed potatoes and seed corn were stored in a similar manner.

A food cache was usually about 6 feet deep and was lined with birch bark. The rice and sugar were in makuks, and after they were in place the spaces between them were filled with hay. When the pit was nearly filled a covering of birch bark or hay was added. Beams of wood were laid across and the whole was covered with a mound of earth.

Dried meat was stored in bags and dried fish were packed together and tied in bundles.

(c) *Meals and cooking utensils.*—It was said by some informants that only one meal a day was prepared, this being a substantial meal at a time equivalent to about 10 a. m. Other informants stated that two meals were prepared, one early in the day, and a second one in the late afternoon, the latter being a light lunch. It was also said that they sometimes began to cook a heavy meal about sundown and continued eating until late at night. Aside from the morning meal it seems probable that the preparation and eating of food depended upon circumstances and the convenience of the family. A man sometimes went out and killed game, and if the people were camped near the fishing ground the nets were lifted and fish cooked for the morning meal. A typical complete meal comprised meat or fish, broth, rice with maple sugar, and dried berries prepared in some way. The meal was cooked and served by the mother, who sat next the door of the lodge. Beside her there was usually a small set of shelves on which she kept her utensils or small portions of food. Pointed sticks were used to remove the meat from the kettle if it were too hot to use the fingers. Buckets and shallow trays made of birch bark (pl. 17, a) were used as food containers, and

a, Bucket and trays made of birch bark

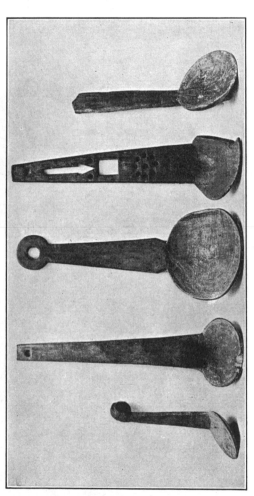

b, Wooden spoons

a, Portrait of Mojagijig

b, Portrait of Mejakigoneb

a, Kettle hung from tripod

b, Kettle hung on slanting stick

a, a′, Fish caught in seine; *b,* Fish drying over fire

for these trays it was customary to use unsplit bark, sometimes comprising six layers, making them strong and not likely to leak. Broth was drunk from wooden bowls made from the knots of hardwood trees. Occasionally cups or small bowls made of birch bark were used for broth or beverages, but they were not very satisfactory. Knives were made of the ribs or other bones of animals, and were sharp enough to cut meat. (See pl. 53, *d.*)

Large wooden spoons were used in dipping broth, and smaller ones were used by individuals for eating rice or similar food. (Pl. 17, *b.*) Birch-bark spoons were used, and clamshells were also used as spoons. An indispensable utensil in eating was a narrow willow stick used to scoop the marrow out of bones. A man had this beside him and used it like a spoon. Inquiry among Chippewa of several bands is always met with the statement that the old people say that their grandparents said that the old-time Chippewa had vessels of clay for boiling water. One informant stated that she had been told that the substance used in making these vessels was "mud and sharp sand and glue, made by boiling the hoofs of animals." It is also said that cooking was done without metal kettles by making dishes of freshly cut birch bark with the inside of the bark as the outside of the dish. So great is the moisture that the cooking was accomplished before the bark dried sufficiently to take fire. Mo'jagi'jig (Always Day) (pl. 18, *a*), a Canadian Chippewa, said that he had heard of heating water by putting hot stones in one of these birch-bark receptacles containing water. He and his brother Mo'jaki' goněb (commonly known as Kawa' kato, Thin Man) (pl. 18, *b*) were together when giving their information and were the only Canadian Chippewa questioned on this class of material.

Kettles were suspended over the fire from a tripod, a wooden hook and heavy basswood fiber cord being used for that purpose in the old days. This was the method used in a permanent camp. If the camp were temporary, the kettle was hung on the end of a pole thrust in a slanting direction into the ground. (Pl. 19, *a, b.*)

At a Winnebago camp the writer saw a double hook, two crotched sticks being wired together, making a hook at each end, one hook placed over the pole across the fire and the other holding the kettle. Green bark may have been used before wire was available. The Chippewa probably used the same device.

(*d*) *Bread.*—A form of bread called "Legolet bread" was made from flour and salt, mixed with water, and kneaded very hard into round, flat loaves. If the woman had a frying pan, she baked the bread in this pan, placed upright in front of the fire. If she had no pan she fastened the bread on sticks, which she stuck in the ground before the fire.

Soda was used when it became available, and, lacking this, the women put a little lye in the bread.

(*e*) *Fish.*—Fish was caught in a seine (pl. 20, *a*, *b*) and was eaten fresh, or stored by either drying or freezing. Fresh fish was prepared as follows:

(1) The fish was cleaned and placed between the sections of a split stick, which was thrust into the ground before the fire. By this means the fish could be turned so that all sides would be equally cooked. Such a stick, with a fish in it, may be seen projecting over the fire in Plate 20, *c*.

(2) The fish, without being opened, was impaled head upward on a stick, which was placed upright in the ground before the fire. As the fish cooked the stick was turned so as to expose all sides to the fire. When thoroughly cooked the fish was split open and seasoned with maple sugar.

(3) The heads of fresh fish, especially suckers, were boiled and greatly liked.

(4) Fresh fish were boiled and the broth used.

(5) A large fish was selected which was rich in oil. The intestines were cleaned and turned, and with the roe were fried in grease and seasoned with maple sugar.

(6) Another manner of preparing fish was as follows: When the fish was partly dry the skin and bones were removed, the fish was then spread on clean birch bark and again allowed to dry slightly, after which it was rubbed with the hands until very soft and fine. It was then mixed with new sugar and packed in makuks. Fish prepared in this way would keep a long time. It was eaten with a spoon and considered a great delicacy.

(7) Fish eggs were boiled or fried with the fish.

Fish were dried by laying them on a rack over a slow fire (pl. 20, *c*) or by stringing them on wigub and hanging them in the sun. The fish were dried until hard and then packed in layers without salt. When needed for food they were boiled. Small fish, such as perch, were dried without cleaning. Sunfish were split lengthwise and laid on the horizontal poles of the rack, while large fish, such as pickerel or bullpouts, were cleaned and cut along each side of the backbone, leaving the head attached to the body of the fish and also to the backbone. The fish was then hung over one of the top rails of the frame, the body being on one side and the backbone and tail on the other. When the fish was partly dried the flesh was split lengthwise, making a thinner strip, the inside of which was exposed to the fire.

For winter use the fish were frozen without cleaning. It was said to be better not to clean them if they were to be kept in this manner.

If sunfish were to be packed they were split down the back and laid flat. The usual way of packing them was to lay three fish in the bottom of a barrel as the lowest layer, piling the others on top of these. A Canadian Chippewa said that in the fall his people strung the fish in bunches of 10 and froze them for winter use. He said they "peeled off the skin when they cooked the fish."

(*f*) *Ducks, pigeons, and other wild birds.*—(1) Boiled with wild rice; also with potatoes and meat. (See p. 123.)

(2) Cooked in hot ashes without cleaning or removing the feathers.

(3) The feathers were removed and the birds cooked by impaling them on sticks, which were placed before the fire.

(*g*) *Meat.*—(1) Deer: The fresh meat of the deer was prepared as follows:

(a) Boiled.

(b) Cut in pieces and roasted on sticks before the fire.

(c) Cut in thin slices, roasted, and then pounded on a flat stone, the pounding being done with a smaller stone. After being pounded finely it was stored in makuks.

The method of drying deer meat depended on the time of year. If the deer were killed during the winter season, it was customary to dry the meat only enough so that it would keep until spring, when the drying process was completed in the sun. A good supply of meat was usually obtained during the winter and was thus partially dried on a large frame over the camp fire. (See p. 120.) If the deer were killed in the autumn, a portion of the meat was cut in strips, dried on a rack over a slow fire, and wrapped in large packets, an entire deerskin tanned with the hair on it being sometimes used for this purpose. The meat, having been dried, was prepared as follows:

(a) Boiled.

(b) Chopped, mixed with bear's grease, and stored in birch-bark makuks.

(c) The meat of an entire deer was spread in layers on a tanned deer hide and pounded with a board until it was in shreds. It was then thoroughly mixed with hot deer tallow and put in a deer-hide bag. When desired for use it was cut in slices.

(d) The dried meat was cut in pieces, spread on birch bark, and covered with birch bark. A man then trod on it until it was crushed. This was called by a term meaning "foot-trodden meat."

The bladder and large intestine were used as containers for the tallow, which was rendered and poured into them while hot, birch-bark funnels being used for this purpose.

(2) Moose: The use of moose meat was similar to the uses of venison. The moose is abundant in the northern regions, and a Canadian Chippewa said that his people kept moose fat in strong

birch-bark makuks, with tops sewed in place with spruce root. He said that moose fat freezes readily. Its use with dried blueberries has already been mentioned.

(3) Bear: The flesh of the bear was cut in strips about 6 inches wide and hung on a frame to dry. If intended for winter use, it frequently was put on high racks to freeze. When used it was cut up a little and boiled. Bear meat was liked because it was so fat. All parts of the bear were eaten or utilized. The head was considered a luxury. They singed it, removed the inside, and boiled it whole. The paws were singed, scraped, and boiled. The liver was good to eat and the intestines were so fat that the Chippewa cleaned them and fried them crisp. The stomach was filled with tallow, known as "bear's grease," which was used for seasoning. In filling a container of this sort a funnel of birch bark was used. The gall was dried, mixed with cedar charcoal, and "pricked into the skin" as a remedy for rheumatism and other ailments.

(4) Rabbit: The Chippewa used rabbits as food, catching them near their winter camp. Detailed information was given by a Canadian Chippewa, who said that his people caught rabbits with snares of nettle twine and prepared them as follows:

(a) The meat was removed from the bones, roasted, and pounded. The bones were then pounded with what meat remained on them. The pounded bones were boiled in a small kettle and the grease skimmed off and eaten with the pounded meat.

(b) The meat was cut in pieces and dried, the bones being dried also. The bones were pounded to a powder and mixed with the dry meat and any available grease. This was eaten dry, and not boiled at the time of using.

(5) Trapped animals: The Chippewa cooked and ate all trapped animals except the marten. Otter and muskrat were eaten, and beaver tails were considered a great luxury, as they were so fat.

TREATMENT OF THE SICK [29a]

Among the Chippewa, as among other tribes, the sick were treated by two different methods, one of which was entirely mental in its method, while the other employed material remedies.[30] He who treated the sick without material remedies was called a djasakid (juggler) and might be a member of the Midewiwin (Grand Medicine Society), though this was rarely the case. He who administered herb and other remedies was almost without exception a member of the Midewiwin, as the knowledge of herbs constituted

---

[29a] This subject is more extensively considered in "Uses of Plants by the Chippewa Indians," Forty-fourth Ann. Rpt. Bur. Amer. Ethn.

[30] Cf. Bull. 45, Bur. Amer. Ethn., pp. 92–96 and 119–125; Bull. 61, pp. 244–283; Bull. 75, pp. 127–144; also Seventh Ann. Rept. Bur. Ethn., pp. 197–201, 226.

one of the secrets of that organization. Songs were used by both the djasakid and Mide, and considered an essential part of their treatment. Having recorded these songs, the Chippewa were willing to impart information concerning the herbs and their uses. An important informant was O'dini'gûn. (Pl. 21.)

It was the chief purpose of the djasakid to work upon the mind of the sick person, and by that means to produce a recovery. To that end he startled, amazed, terrified, and stimulated the sick person, and it is not impossible that in some cases the excited nervous condition produced an apparent or even a real improvement in his condition. The members of the Mide, in their treatment of the sick, used a mental influence in addition to their material remedies, but used it intelligently. This mental influence was exerted chiefly through the words of the songs that they sang when administering their medicines. It was also the belief that initiation into the Midewiwin would cure a man of bodily illness, this belief being so strong that persons too ill to be carried to the Mide lodge were initiated by proxy, a relative or friend representing them in the initiation ceremony. Before beginning a treatment the member of the Midewiwin prayed or " talked to the manido," saying that the sick person wished to have his life prolonged by means of the Mide, and also smoked tobacco provided by the relatives of the sick person. It has been noted that a djasakid, before beginning a treatment, narrated his personal dream as a guaranty of his success. A Mide, on the other hand, placed the emphasis on the power of the Midewiwin transmitted through many generations of faithful adherents.

The following song affirms the recovery of the sick person and states that it will be accomplished through the power of the white shell, which is the emblem of the Midewiwin. It was addressed to a person whose infirmity was such that he could not walk. This song occurs as No. 47 in Bulletin 45. " You will recover; you will walk again. It is I who say it; my power is great. Through our white shell I will enable you to walk again."

The following song is one of a group that was sung after a man had been initiated into the Midewiwin. (Bull. 45, No. 51.) " Come, let us sing. Come, we are now standing before you, bending down. My Mide brethren, we ask long life for you, that is what I myself am seeking for you."

A djasakid frequently gave the following demonstration of his magic power. He caused a tall, slender tipi to be built and then required that he be bound hand and foot with the strongest thongs. His power was so great that, as he lay bound in the tipi, he could cause it to sway and shake, though the outside air were quiet. He could " call the animals " so that their voices were heard in the tipi, and he also had power to " call the spirits of the air," among which was a " spirit turtle." He sent this turtle to search for lost persons or articles, and its return was made known to the persons in the darkened tipi by a heavy sound as of a large body striking the ground. After various demonstrations of a mesmeric or hypnotic character he would call for a light, and it would be found that he was free from his bonds, the thongs frequently being entangled in the highest poles. The djasakid were accustomed to swallow and regurgitate short sections of tubular bones as part of their treatment of the sick.

In September, 1917, at Pine Point, on the White Earth Reservation in Minnesota, the writer talked with a woman who had been treated for quinzy sore throat by one of these men, the treatment being of recent occurrence. She said the " doctor " first related the story of his dream, as his authority for the treatment he was about to administer. He then requested that the room be darkened in order that he might " see what was the matter with her." After singing for a time and shaking his " medicine rattle " he said that the cause and cure of the illness had become apparent to him. Small sections of tube-like bones were swallowed and regurgitated according to the custom of the djasakid. He then placed one of these bones against her congested throat and blew through it repeatedly and with such violence that the congestion " broke internally," the poisonous matter issuing freely from her mouth. This relieved her distress and she recovered rapidly.

In this connection it is interesting to note that a djasakid commands that there be absolute silence during his swallowing and regurgitating of the bones, even insisting that children and dogs be kept away from the place where he is performing. Mr. Henry Selkirk, of White Earth, stated that he once saw a djasakid in a violent fit of choking which was caused by an unexpected noise when he was regurgitating the bones. He fell forward with his face on the ground and was revived with considerable difficulty. A man who treats the sick by this method frequently wears one of the bones attached to his hat, with the feather of an eagle or hawk in it. This is worn as an evidence or badge of his profession. Odinigun (pl. 21) is wearing a long string of these bones, indicating that he is a djasakid of unusual proficiency.

HEALTH MEASURES

The following data collected from many individuals should be understood as representing the best ideals of the tribe rather than the practice of each individual or family:

Cedar boughs were frequently burned in a lodge to purify the air,

Sage was burned in a lodge during a contagious illness. It was also used to fumigate the head and hands of those who had cleansed the dead.

Bedding was aired daily in summer and spread on the snow in winter.

Woven bags, when soiled, were brushed, pounded, and turned the other side out.

Damp clothing was dried over the fire. It was said that the smoke had a healthful effect and prevented vermin.

Bathing in a lake or river was frequent, and the hair was thoroughly washed.

A small sweat lodge was often built in a corner of the living lodge for use during the winter.

Stiff brushes were used in washing the hands and in scouring kettles. These brushes were identified as *Equisetum hyemale* L.

Travelers did not drink water if uncertain of its purity. The usual custom was to boil the water and put in twigs or leaves of plants or trees known to be healthful. The decoction was drunk hot or allowed to cool.

The space of hard ground between the fire and the mats in a lodge was swept clean, the sweepings being put in the fire. The Canadian Chippewa made brooms of ash, the entire broom being made of one piece with narrow strips of wood turned back and tied to form the brush.

Refuse that could not be eaten by the dogs was burned.

Lye for household use was made from hardwood ashes. The directions were: " Boil the ashes, let them stand, strain them out, and use the water." A specimen of this was obtained and found to soften water in an acceptable manner.

For washing dishes they "took the lye down to the beach, put it in the dishes, and scoured them with sand."

Washing of clothes was done as follows: The soiled clothes were soaked in warm, weak lye, after which they were "shaken and pounded " and rinsed in the lake. Lye used in washing clothes was of such strength that they could dip their hands in it without discomfort.

Washing of blankets was as follows: They were washed in "not too strong " lye. If a flat rock were available, the blankets were spread on the rock and pounded with a flat board, after which they were rinsed in plenty of clear water and dried.

In winter the face and hands were washed with snow.

It was said that the Chippewa never immersed their bodies in icy cold water.

LIFE CYCLE

(*a*) *Care of infants.*—In the old days the Chippewa did not have large families, several informants stating that the average was two or three children. A mother had her infant constantly with her, and the daily relation between mother and child was closer than in the white race.

If a baby was born during the night it was customary to notify the people by firing guns. Immediately the men of the father's gens and those of one other gens went to the wigwam and attempted to gain possession of the child, the father and the men of his gens defending the child against the other party. The child's relatives threw water, and sometimes a mixture of flour and water, on the attacking party, and the men fought and wrestled.[31] It is said that "everybody was wringing wet" when the struggle was finished. The men who secured the baby took it to the leader of the gens who carried it four times around the fire while the people sang a song with words meaning "We have caught the little bird." The parents gave presents to the men to secure possession of the baby. It was said, "This was done to make the child brave from hearing so much noise as soon as it was born."

It was the desire of the Chippewa that their children should be straight and vigorous, and to that end the mother began a child's training in early infancy.[32] Two means were employed for this training as well as for convenience in taking care of the child. These were (1) the cradle board and (2) a custom which arose after the Chippewa obtained cotton cloth and which may be designated as "pinning up the baby." With these forms of restraint they alternated periods of freedom when the child was "let out for exercise." It was frequently bathed but clear water was seldom used, a warm decoction of some strengthening herb being preferred for this purpose.

The cradle board, in which a baby spent most of its time for the first year of its life, consisted of a board about 24 inches long with a curved piece of wood at one end to confine the child's feet and a hoop at right angles above the other end. (Pl. 22, *a.*) A light rod was fastened loosely to one side of the cradle board and to this were attached the two binding bands, about 6 inches wide, which were pinned or tied over the child. In the old days the upper end of the board was cut in points and painted red or blue, and the entire structure was held together by thongs. Inside the curved wood at the foot

---

[31] Mrs. English said she remembered that Coniäkwe had a baby when the people were at the rice fields and the men dipped each other in the lake during their struggle for possession of the child.

[32] A Chippewa said with pride, "An Indian never stooped except for age."

of the cradle board was birch bark of the same shape filled with soft moss. The hoop above the child's head served as a support for a blanket in winter or for a thin cloth in summer, thus protecting the child's head from the weather. On this hoop were hung small articles intended as charms or for the child's amusement. The leather strap fastened near the hoop enabled the mother to carry it on her back. (Pl. 22, *b*.) If she were carrying only a cradle the strap was across her chest, but if she were carrying a pack, she put the pack strap across her chest and the strap of the cradle board across her forehead. The binding bands were formerly of list cloth and decorated only on the portion above the cradle board, but as beads and worsted braid became more common the decoration was extended over the entire length. The women took great pride in the decoration of these bands. Strips of hide were used in early days to hold the bands in place; these were followed by flat woven braid about an inch wide, made of yarn, one such braid being tied over each band.

In old times a baby wore little or no clothing, being surrounded by moss, which, with the birch-bark tray, was removed when necessary. Wood moss was occasionally used, but the moss in most common use was that found in the cranberry marshes. It was dried over the fire to destroy insects, then rubbed and pulled apart until it was soft and light. In cold weather a baby's feet were wrapped in rabbit skin with the hair inside, or the soft down of cat-tails was placed around them. Care was taken that the arms as well as the legs and back should be straight, and the arms of a very young infant were fastened straight against its sides practically the entire time. When it was able to move its arms freely they were released above the binding bands for a little while at a time. The cradle board afforded warmth and protection, and it is said that children cried to be put back in the cradle board after being out of it for a time. A mother often released a child and let it play until it was tired, then she put it in the cradle board to sleep. When the mother was at work or was walking the cradle board usually was hung from her head, but if the baby were asleep or if the family were traveling it might be placed horizontally in her shawl and swung across her waist at the back. A mother might put a child to sleep by holding the cradle board in front of her and rocking it by moving her feet from side to side. The cradle board rested on her toes as she sat on the ground. (Bull. 53, pl. 39.) Sometimes the cradle board was put in an upright position near the mother when she was at work and the baby was entertained by watching her. When the child was old enough the cradle board was put near the family at meals and the child given bits of food, or it was given a duck bone to keep it quiet. In recent times a rind of bacon was used for this purpose.

The second phase of an infant's physical care consisted in pinning it tightly in cloth.[33] (Pl. 23, *a*.) Its arms and legs were as closely confined as in the cradle board, but sometimes the hands and fingers were uncovered. This was cooler than the cradle board in hot weather and was the manner of preparing a child for sleep at night or for carrying in a shawl or blanket on its mother's back. In this wrapping, or even with the cradle board, it could be put inside the pack which its mother carried when the camp was moving. The outside of this pack was the roll of bulrush mats, and the blankets were rolled inside the mat. In case of a snowstorm the mother threw a shawl over the child's head. (See section on industrial year, p. 120.)

For convenience during the day a little hammock was made of a piece of blanket by passing a rope through each of two lengthwise

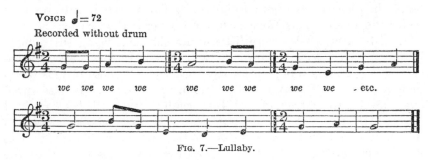

FIG. 7.—Lullaby.

folds and tying the ends to low tree branches or to objects in the lodge. Occasionally a cradle board was placed in such a hammock, but the baby was usually " pinned up " before it was put in the hammock. (Pl. 23, *b*.) The writer has seen this hammock in use in a house, in a tent, and under the trees. The mother sits beside the hammock and swings it to and fro as she sings this lullaby. (Fig. 7.) The syllables " *we, we* " are part of a word which means " swinging."

At an early age a child's head was encased in a close-fitting hood, soft deer hide being used for this purpose before cloth was available. The deer-hide hoods were made with a wide front which could be turned forward to serve as a shade for the child's eyes, the hide having sufficient texture to hold it in place. Two reasons were given for this custom. Gagewin said it was to accustom the child to a head covering so that when such a protection became necessary it would not pull it off. Other informants said it was to affect the shape of the baby's head, and for this reason the hood was carefully

---

[33] It is the belief of many Indians that a child will die if its picture is taken (see p. 79). The mother of this child said that she " was not superstitious," but the child died in a few months. The mother said later that she attached no blame to the taking of the picture.

PORTRAIT OF ODINIGUN

b, Cradle board carried by mother. Lac Court Oreilles, Wis.

a, Chippewa infant in cradle board. White Earth, Minn.

b, Chippewa infant in hammock

a, Chippewa infant in wrappings

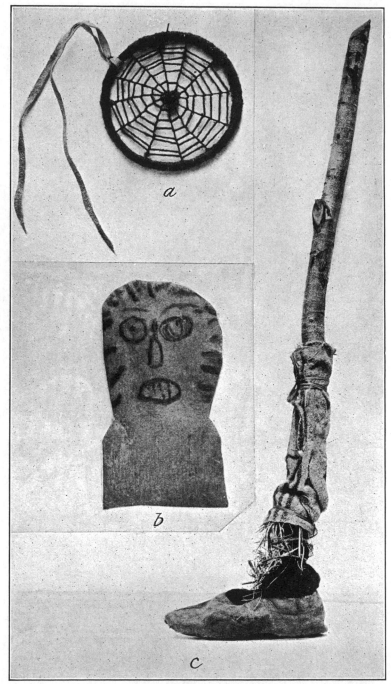

a, "Spider web" charm, hung on infant's cradle; *b*, Mask used in game; *c*, "Ghost leg," to frighten children

cut. The desired shape did not differ from the symmetrical and normal.

If a child were " ailing " it was held in the warmth of the fire and its body rubbed with grease, goose oil being approved for this purpose. If it were too fat and chafed, a healing powder was made from rotten oak, rubbed to extreme fineness and freely applied. A baby was weaned by giving it fish broth or wild rice boiled very soft. Indian mothers, however, nursed their children until they were about 2 years old and instances are known in which a mother nursed two children at the same time, the older being 3 or 4 years old.

As soon as a child "knew anything" it was held up and "danced" while some one made a drumming sound like that of an Indian drum. This was done before a child could stand alone, and perhaps it is for this reason that very young children react immediately to the drumming of the fingers on a table or any similar sound. Chippewa women never allowed a baby to cry if this could be avoided by any mode of pacification, and for this reason the small children were somewhat "spoiled." The devotion of a mother to her children was intense, and if necessary to defend them she fought with ferocity.

Three sorts of articles were hung on the hoop of a child's cradle board: (1) Articles intended as "charms," (2) the article given to the child by the person who named it, and which was supposed to convey a definite benefit, and (3) articles intended solely for the child's amusement. First among the " charms " should be noted the decorated case in which the umbilical cord of the child was preserved. Gagewin stated that the chief reason for this was the securing of wisdom for the child. Another said that if it were not done the child " would become foolish," and other informants said that if the cord were not kept the child " would always be searching for something." One said it would poke among the ashes around the fire, and older persons would say, " He is looking for the cord." It was desired that a child should play with this as it lay in its cradle and should keep it during its whole life, and for that reason the case in old times was sewed with sinew and hung from the hoop by nettle-stalk twine, both of which were very strong. This little case was treasured by a mother in the event of the death of a child. The writer knew a woman who had kept such a case for 25 years after the death of her infant son. A butterfly was sometimes embroidered or worked with beads on such a case, the butterfly being regarded as " the spirit of childish play." A similar case of plainer design was obtained from a woman who had kept it many years.

Two articles representing spider webs were usually hung on the hoop of a child's cradle board, and it was said that "they catch everything evil as a spider's web catches and holds everything that comes in contact with it." These articles (pl. 24, *a*) consist of wooden hoops about 3½ inches in diameter filled with an imitation of a spider's web. In old times the web was made of nettle-stalk twine and colored dark red with the juice of bloodroot and the inner bark of the wild plum. In a similar Pawnee charm the netting symbolized the Spider Woman, a deity who controlled the buffalo. In later times the web is made of dark-red yarn. Various playthings were given the child and suspended from the hoop, in easy reach of the little hands. Small white shells were favorite toys, also bunches of tiny cones made of birch bark. Sometimes one of these little cones filled with hard maple sugar was hung in such a manner that the child-could put it to its mouth and get a little of the sweetness.

(*b*) *Naming a child.*—The names of Chippewa under the old conditions of life may be divided into six general classes: (1) Dream' name given ceremonially by a "namer," (2) dream name acquired by an individual, (3) "namesake name" given a child by its parents, (4) common name or nickname, (5) name of gens, and (6) euphonious name without any significance. In recent years there are also translations of Chippewa names into English, the adaptation of English names into Chippewa, and the mispronunciation, in English, of Chippewa names. These classes may be described as follows:

(1) This name was given ceremonially to either an infant or adult by some one who had received "spirit power" in a dream. The child or person receiving the name was supposed to receive a definite benefit from it, but he could not transmit this acquired power to anyone else; thus a person who received a ceremonial dream name in his infancy could not on attaining maturity give this name with its accompanying power or protection to another child or person.

(2) The dream name acquired by an individual was usually received in the fast and isolation attendant upon the period of puberty and was associated with the tutelary spirit he acquired at that time. (See pp. 71 and 81.) This name was seldom mentioned. The experience of this dream gave its possessor a spirit power or protection which he could transmit to others, bestowing at the same time either his own dream name or some name which he composed from the incidents of his dream. Thus Odinigun said he had named several children, giving them names which were different but were in some manner connected with the events of his dream.

(3) The "namesake name" given by parents was frequently a dream name, but it was not bestowed in a ceremonial manner and carried no power with it. Thus a man might bear the name

Carried-across-the-sky, which he received either from a namer or in a personal dream, and which gave him a certain spirit power or protection. A friend might name his child Carried-across-the-sky because he had a high respect for the owner of the name, but the child would receive no benefit from it. In many instances the "namesake name" was not in any way associated with a dream but belonged to the class next following.

(4) The common name or nickname was that by which a Chippewa was known throughout his life. It was short and frequently contained an element of humor. A child might be given a name derived from some circumstance at the time of its birth, or it might be named from the first person or animal that entered the lodge after its birth. Children were sometimes named from a fancied resemblance to something. Mrs. Julia Spears was called Co'niäns' (Little Money) because her face was so round when she was born that it reminded the people of a small piece of silver money. Her brother, Truman Warren, was known as Makons' (Little Bear) for some similar reason. Adults sometimes bear the names that were given them because of some childish trait. Thus a certain woman was known all her life as Ga'sigĕns' (Little Cat) because as a child she scratched savagely. A certain man carried the name Stands Alone because he was reserved in manner and kept aloof from other children. The element of humor is shown in the fact that a child who was a long time in teething received the name Without Teeth, and a child who was short in stature was named Stump, both names being carried by men who lived to an advanced age.

(5) In old times a chief was sometimes known by the name of his gens or ododem (kinship group).

English names have been adopted into the Chippewa language and in some instances they have been so mispronounced that the original form is lost. Thus the French Josephette or Josephine has become Zozed, and Margaret has become Magid, or, as noted later in this work, Magidins, meaning literally "Little Margaret." Sophia becomes Sope, and Minnie becomes Minin. In recent years the Chippewa have, in many instances, been known by the translation of their native names, as Hole-in-the-day.

Soon after the birth of a child its parents selected a person to name the child. This person was called a namer and usually gave to the child a name connected with his or her dream. The bestowing of a name was not, however, the principal function of a namer. Indeed, the giving of a name was sometimes omitted. The principal function was the transmission to the child of the benefit which he or she derived from their dream. Odinigun, who had named several children, said that he always took the child in his arms and pressed it close to his body. He said that every namer did not do this, but he believed that more power was transmitted to the child by this action. A child was given power by its namer, but it rested somewhat with the child whether this power was developed. Throughout the Indian's belief in spirit power we note the necessity of cooperation on the part of the individual in order that he might have the full benefit of that power. Odinigun related an incident of a woman whom he had known since they both were children. This woman's name was Me′dweä′ckwe (noise of wind in the trees). She was named in infancy by a man who told her parents that as soon as the child was able to walk the mother must take one of the child's dresses and hang it on a certain sort of tree. This must be done once a year. As soon as the child was old enough the mother instructed her to do this for herself. She continued this during her entire life and lived to be 95 years old. Odinigun said he had often seen the dress hanging on the tree, but knew nothing more than that the placing of it was a requirement of the woman's dream name.

The following account of the ceremonial naming of infants was given by Gagewin, a member of the Grand Medicine Society, who had named several children. He said that when the parents had decided on the namer they asked this person and a few others to a feast. The name of the child was not made known at this time, only that of the person who was to give the name. The namer put tobacco in the child's hand, saying that he (or she) would later give a feast and announce the name of the child. He asked all who were present to attend this feast and made a speech in which he expressed his appreciation of the honor conferred upon him. The time of this feast was indicated as several months in the future. Thus if the namer were chosen in the spring he usually gave the feast and named the child in the following autumn. As the season drew near he went to the parents of the child and told them the exact time of the feast at his house. He had already procured part of the necessary food and went at once to hunt for ducks and game. His wife got the wigwam ready, put fresh boughs on the ground, and had everything clean. She also provided dried berries, dried meat, and other adjuncts of the feast. Only five or six highly respected persons were invited. When the people were assembled the namer told his dream and for the first time made known the name of the child. As already stated, this name expressed in some manner the substance or the story of his dream.

Let us suppose the namer had seen a clear sky in his dream and that he intended to name the child Gage′ana′kwad, meaning "clear sky." He would have a right to say before the feast, " I invoke the spirit of the sky to make clear, fair skies for this child." If he had dreamed of an animal, he made a speech at the feast in which he dwelt at some length upon the power of that animal to guide and protect the child. If his dream were pertaining to some material object, as a bow and arrow, he told of the mysterious power that his dream had imparted to these articles. If he had dreamed of an event or of a mythical being, he explained its significance and told of the influence it would have on the life of the child. After the namer had talked and given a name, the other invited guests, as witnesses, signified their approval and acceptance by "taking a few puffs" from a pipe. In this manner the namer conferred on a child what he believed to be its best equipment for a successful and upright life. Then followed the smoking of the pipe and the feast.

The gift of a small article representing the dream subject could be made at the feast but was usually postponed until a later day, and the occasion for the presentation of the article might be an illness of the child. Its parents, anxious concerning its recovery, might summon the namer who would make an article suggesting his dream and bring it with him. He would first "talk over the child," then tell of his dreams, give medicine to the child, "bless it," and assure the parents that it would recover.

FIG. 8.—"Token" worn by child

Gage'wĭn said that very sick children often recovered after this had been done.

Two instances of these dream articles were mentioned. No'dĭnĕns said that her father dreamed of a knife of a peculiar pattern (see p. 80) and that he always gave a miniature of this knife to the boys that he named. Another man always gave a little bow and arrow to his namesakes. A dream article given to an adult by a namer is noted in a subsequent paragraph. A small object or "token" was sometimes given to a child by the medicine man who named it "in order that the child might care for him." This consisted of something that might attract the fancy of the child and was usually worn around its neck by a cord. Such an article is shown in Figure 8 and is of cloth decorated with beads in a pattern that has no significance. At Mille Lac several little boys were seen with round pieces of cloth sewed on their coats. The pieces of cloth were neatly bound with braid and each bore a design like those which are known to be symbolic. The trader, Mr. H. D. Ayer, said that one of these designs had been worn by children in the better families of Mille Lac for several years. No explanation was asked, but it is probable that the design was a symbol representing a " dream name."

Some parents neglected the naming of their children until illness overtook them. A namer was then summoned in haste, the belief being that his power could save the life of the child. Odinigun said that he had been summoned several times to name children that seemed near to death, and that the children in every instance recovered and lived to old age. He regretted that he had never been asked to name a child in health, as he felt that the power he could transmit to such a child would be of great benefit. His power and authority to name children were derived from one of his dreams.[34] He related the story of his dream, which was interpreted as follows:

" In my dream I saw a wigwam with the door toward the north. Three men were there, one from the sky, one from the north, and one whose body was half under the ground. The man whose body was half under the ground was beside the door, outside the wigwam. He had a messenger and had sent this messenger for me. I stood in front of him wondering why he had sent for me. At last he spoke and told me to enter the wigwam, and to sit next the door on the same side as he was sitting. I went in. There was no one else in the wigwam. I sat down and after a while a woman came in with a baby in her arms. She came toward me and handed me the baby. After I took the child she asked me to name it. Then the man whose body was half under the ground spoke, and I could hear voices in the air, as of many people, answering him. After I had returned the child to its mother another woman came with a child which she asked me to name. The first mother kept her place next me, and as others came they stood in order one after another. Others brought children who were a little older, and then a little older. They came until the wigwam was full, and I named them all. Then they went away. The three men remained. The man whose body was half under the ground spoke to me and told me to stay, as perhaps the children would come back. I waited quite a long time. The man whose body was half under the ground spoke again and said, ' Your namesakes are coming soon.' So they came. First the smallest ones who were just able to run, then those who were a little older. They came in four groups, each a little older than the one before it. So I believe that the children I name will grow up. All my dreams have come true and I believe that I will name many more children."

<hr>

[34] Cf. section on dreams, pp. 78–86.

This dream gives him the right to "make up names" in some way connected with the dream. For instance, he was once summoned to a house where a child about 3 years old was very sick. He did not know why he was sent for until he arrived; then they asked him to name the child. He took the child in his arms and gave it the name "Ne'soga'bo" (three standing) because of the three men seen in his dream. The child recovered and is still living. It was not unusual for a man when naming a child to give some evidence of his spirit power. Thus Gagewin related the following incident concerning Odinigun, which the latter corroborated: A woman had a little girl who was sick unto death. She took the child and went to the house of Odinigun, begging him to name the child and cure it if possible. Odinigun gave a feast and talked of his dreams. He took the child in his arms and walked around the fire, telling of his dreams. In his hand he held four small stones. After a time he returned the child to her mother, saying, "Her name is Stone-sky-woman (A'sini'wagi'jigo'kwe), and these stones are her 'charm.'[35] If you see streaks in the sky this evening, the child will recover; otherwise she will die." Odinigun had studied the appearance of the sky and knew what was favorable to him and what was not. He knew that a streaked sky indicated success for him.

Odinigun related the naming of a boy by a certain old man. When the child was about 10 years old he became so ill that, the parents were afraid that he would die. So they sent tobacco to the old man and asked him to name the child. The old man came, looked at the child, and said he would name it the next day. He told the child's parents not to be afraid that the child would die before the next day. Most of the people assembled there did not believe that the child would live until night, but the man "talked and prayed" so the child would live until the next day. He gave tobacco to each of those present and told them to return the next day. He told the people that when he named the child they would hear a sharp sound of thunder. The child was alive when the old man came next day, and he named the child Ce'nawickûŋ'. ("He who produces a rattling sound with the movement of his being"). As soon as he had named the child they heard the sound as of sharp thunder, though there were no clouds in the sky and no sign of a storm. Many people talk of this event until this day. The child recovered and lived to old age. The writer was present when an adult was ceremonially given a dream name. Both the namer and the person to be named were women. The namer shook hands with the person to be named and kissed her on the left cheek. (In old times the action would probably have been a stroking of the arm or body.)

---

[35] Cf. mention of a "stone charm," p. 113.

The namer then related her dream, announced the name, and presented an article made to resemble the subject of the dream.[36]
Tobacco was provided by the person receiving the name. A pipe
filled with this tobacco was lifted and smoked by the namer, and was
puffed by a witness who was present. The person receiving the
name was instructed to carry the "dream representation" when
going on an important journey and to keep it always. She was told
that if it were accidentally destroyed she should make another,
which would have the same power. This was similar to the custom
in naming children.

(c) *Government of children.*—Throughout the information given
by the older Chippewa we note the elements of gentleness and tact,
combined with an emphasis on such things as were essential to the
well-being of the child. Fear was often used to induce obedience, but
not to an extent which injured the child. For example, it was said
to be a frequent custom to put a scarecrow where it was unsafe for
the children to go. Mrs. English said that she remembered a very
steep hill where she and other children liked to play. One day they
found a frightful scarecrow at the foot of the hill and they were so
scared that they never went there again.

The Chippewa gave much attention to the training of their children. Odinigun said, "In summer the children could play out
of doors, but in winter they had to be amused indoors." It was hard
to keep the little children quiet in the evening so they would not dis-
turb the older people. The mother often said, "Keep still or the owl
will get you." If they did not keep still she went to the door of the
wigwam, held back the blanket, and said, "Come in owl; come and
get these children, who won't keep still." Then the children put
their heads under the bedding and were soon asleep. In the daytime
they constantly wanted to run outdoors. Some had no moccasins
and were barefoot. The only way to keep them in was to frighten
them. So the older people made a birch-bark "mask" of an owl
and put it on a stick where the children would see it if they went
outdoors. This frightened them and they were glad to stay in.
When they were old enough to mind what they were told and to
understand things they were taught that they must not go peeking
in the wigwams after dark and that they must not laugh at anything
unusual nor show disrespect to older people. They were also taught
that they must not go to the neighbors when they were eating and
look wistfully at the food. Little children were taught not to go
between older people and the fire. (Cf. fasting incident, pp. 129–
130.)

Further information concerning the government of little children
was given by Gagewin and his wife, who said that in old times the

---

[36] This is described in the section on dreams, p. 80; see also pp. 84–86.

mothers sometimes frightened their children by saying that a bear's paw would come and get them. There is a tradition that a woman once told this to her children and that a bear reached into the wigwam, took a child and carried it away. Then the Indians forbade the frightening of children with this story and substituted the owl because it could not go into the wigwam and carry children away. The owl is thus feared by all Chippewa children. A song concerning this was composed by a little boy when he was left alone in the tipi. It was at the time of sugar making when the people were camped close together and his little song was heard in a neighboring tent. The melody was so interesting that the men took it up and used it in the moccasin game. (See Bull. 45, Song No. 121.)

An article which may be said to have represented the bear paw was called a " ghost leg." (Pl. 24, *c.*) It consisted of an old moccasin stuffed with straw and fastened at the end of a stick. It was sometimes called a " bear paw." If a child were persistently naughty the mother would call aloud for the bear paw. The blanket hung over the wigwam door would be drawn aside and the old moccasin at the end of the stick would be slowly thrust into the wigwam by an older person on the outside. This was said to be an effectual form of discipline. When the children were old enough to listen attentively it was still desired to keep them quiet in the evening. For this purpose the older people devised a game called the " Game of silence." (See Bull. 53, pp. 302–304. Song No. 179.) In this game a song was sung by an older person in which the most novel and interesting events were related. The song suddenly ceased at the most exciting point, and the children tried to avoid making a sound at this surprise. The song was repeated over and over with new words and new pauses, a prize being given to the child who showed the most self-control. It is said that the children were usually asleep when the game ended.

If the children were reluctant to leave their play in the summer evenings a man wearing a mask went among them. He was called the frightener, and the purpose of his visit was to make the children go home and to bed. He wore ragged clothes and walked with a cane. Sometimes his mask was of birch bark that shone with a pale light in the dusk. (Pl. 24, *b.*) At other times he wore a horrible mask with a projecting stick for a nose. It was expected that the children would keep still when the frightener came, not bursting into shouts as when they were pursued in the cannibal game (see p. 70). The ability of a child to keep still when surprised or frightened was more important to the Indian than to the white race. For example, the scream of a child might cost the lives of many people if an enemy were approaching the village. When the children went to bed the

father or mother told them to lie still and try to think of something
nice so they would have good dreams. They were encouraged to
remember and relate these childish dreams. There appears to have
been a belief that the mind of the child was thus rendered more
receptive to the important dream, or vision, that was sought a few
years later.

When everyone had retired and the camp was quiet an old man
walked around the camp circle, passing in front of the dark tents.
This man was a crier and he made the announcements for the next
day, telling whether the people would go hunting or what would be
done in the camp. He also gave good advice to the young people
who were taught to respect him and obey his words. Only a man
who was known to embody in his own life the excellent principles he
uttered was allowed to act as crier. He usually announced that it
was time for the young men who were calling upon the young maidens to go home. He spoke impersonally of the conduct of the young
people, describing incidents in such a manner that those concerned in
them would know to what he referred. He taught sterling principles
of character and gave such advice as he thought necessary. Odinigun said that the old man emphasized the teaching that the young
people must not steal, also that they must keep away from fire water,
use very little tobacco, and never say anything disrespectful concerning women.[37] He told the women that they must "keep from quar-
reling, live peaceably, and not say bad things about each other."
The advice to young men and women was "Obey your parents, take
their advice, and respect them. If you live in that way while you
are among your own people you will be respected when you go to a
strange village."

Mention has been made of the fact that one or more grandparents
were usually in every household. A man usually lived with his wife's
family, hence the old people were her parents. The grandmother
talked to the mother and told her how to bring up the girls, and
the grandfather advised the father how to instruct and bring up the
boys. One advice which was strong and often repeated was "if
your children go among the neighbors and make a quarrel, don't you
take their part. You must bring them home and make them behave
themselves. Do not get into a quarrel with your neighbors because
of the quarrels of the children." Another precept was "teach the
children what it is right to do, and they will live that way and get
on well in the world."

Nodinens said, "I had four brothers and two sisters. My father
gave counsel to the boys and taught them the best way to live, and

<hr/>

[37] Song No. 49, Bull. 45, Bur. Amer. Ethn., contains the words "Do not speak ill of a
woman, my Mide brethren."

my mother told the girls how to conduct themselves. The first thing
I can remember was my mother's saying 'always be industrious.
Get up early and do your work. Do you hear me? Do you hear
me? Do you understand?' She took hold of my ear and pulled
it hard as she said this, and she kept on until I said that I understood. She told me that I must live a quiet life and be kind to all,
especially the old, and listen to the advice of the old. She said that
people would respect me if I did this and would be kind to me. She
said, 'Do not run after a boy. If a young man wants to marry
you, let him come here to see you and come here to live with you.
This is the reason I am always telling you to be industrious and how
to live, so when you have a home of your own you will be industrious
and do right to the people around you.' She taught me to make
mats and bags, to make belts and moccasins, leggings, and coats for
my brothers, so they would never lack for these things."

Nodinens added, " I have tried to do as my mother taught me.
Now, at my age I look back and am so grateful to her for giving me
this advice, and I think it is the reason I have been so blessed and
prospered all my life." Nodinens said the advice which her father
gave to her brothers was similar to that quoted above. He told them
not to be idle and "run around" but to hunt and to work so they
would be prosperous. She also said that her father told the boys not
to destroy birds' nests as "the birds were put here for the good of
the earth." [38] Children received their first lessons in the value of
plants by being encouraged to gather every flower they saw in the
fields. These blossoms were dried, pulverized, and used in the making of a beverage, but at the same time the child learned that some
plants had a medicinal value, while all were placed on the earth for
the good of mankind.

The companionship of a Chippewa girl and her mother was very
close and the child learned many household tasks by watching and
helping her mother. Thus a little girl was early taught to chop
wood and carry it on her back, and as she grew older she carried
larger and larger bundles of wood until she could carry enough into
the wigwam for the night's use. A girl was taught to make
little birch-bark rolls like those which covered the wigwam, her
mother saying "you must not grow up to live outdoors and be made
fun of because you do not know how to make a good wigwam." She

[38] Radin, writing concerning the Ojibwa of eastern and southeastern Ontario, mentions
" the system of instruction to which it was customary to subject all children from the age
of 5 or 6 to the age of puberty, and which consisted almost exclusively in directions concerning the actions necessary to take in order to insure a happy and successful life. One
of the most insistent prayers in this instruction is that without a guardian-spirit (manito)
no individual could possibly surmount the crises in his life." Radin, Paul, Some Aspects
of Puberty Fasting among the Ojibwa. Geol. Surv. Can., Dept. Mines, Ottawa, 1914, Mus.
Bull. No. 2, Anthrop. Ser. 2, p. 76.

was also taught to make maple sugar, gather wild rice, and do all a woman's tasks. Odinigun said that "a man had no bother thinking he must go home and do this or that, for he knew that his wife would attend to it." He said that if a girl was well brought up and was capable she usually got a good husband. Her reputation often went to other villages, and a young man would seek her out because he had heard that she was quiet and industrious. Such a couple usually had a fine family, the children were well governed and did not quarrel. In concluding this subject Odinigun said that in his old age he noticed that those who had kept the advice of the old people had lived long and led a quiet life, but those who did not regard their advice had had much trouble and died.[39]

A little girl was trained in what might be termed the accomplishments of feminine life, as well as in its household tasks. Her first lessons in applied beadwork were the decoration of her doll's clothing, straight lines, either continuous or interrupted, being the easiest patterns, from which she progressed to diagonal patterns and the familiar "otter-tail pattern." In woven beadwork she frequently began by making a narrow chain with horizontal rows of beads of different colors, two or three rows of each color. This gave pleasure to the eye and involved no counting of the beads except in the multiple of the number of threads on the little loom, less the "end thread." A simple pattern for a child consisted in a stripe of contrasting color down the middle of the chain, after which she might attempt a diagonal or zigzag pattern in two colors. In such easy, yet intelligent, lessons a Chippewa girl was trained by her mother.

(d) *Pastimes for little children.*—The following pastimes show the simple means devised for entertaining little children. A multitude of other pastimes have been forgotten in the advance of the race toward a new mode of life.

1. The summer child: A child born in summer was called a summer child. The first winter in which such a child could talk was usually when it was about a year and a half old. If the weather were very cold, the child was taught to take a handful of ashes, go to the door of the wigwam and throw the ashes around, saying, "South wind, your child is getting cold." It is said that the weather would then turn warmer. Sometimes, when a shaft of sunlight came through a hole in the wigwam cover, the summer child was told to try to take hold of it, as though it could climb upward on it, and to say, "Summer, summer." It was said that sometimes this action would make the child quite warm.

---

[39] It is the custom of the old men to reiterate again and again that which they consider of importance, repeating it with a slight change of words. The same manner of speech is used in telling ancient stories, such as those on pp. 98–106. This peculiarity makes the material difficult to translate.

2. The winter child: A child born in winter was called a winter child. When he was able to walk around the wigwam he sometimes held up his hands to warm them at the fire. This was said to be an unfailing sign of very cold weather.

3. Stopping a snowstorm: During a heavy snowstorm it is a frequent custom to tell a boy to go out and shoot the snow. The child's father put a piece of birch bark on the end of the child's arrow, fitted it to his bow, and set fire to it, saying, "Shoot; hit the snow right in the eye." The boy shot the arrow with its flaming tip into the thickly falling snow; then he went into the wigwam and went to bed. It was said that the snow always ceased before he woke in the morning.

4. The new tooth: When one of a child's "first teeth" came out he was told to take the tooth in one hand and a piece of charcoal in the other hand. Then he was told to throw the tooth toward the east and the charcoal toward the west, saying, "I want a new tooth as soon as possible."

5. Calling the butterflies: By members of the Mississippi and Mille Lac bands of Indians living at White Earth the butterfly was regarded as "the spirit of childish play," and a butterfly was often used as a decoration on children's articles, as well as a figure in birch-bark transparencies. Inquiry among the Red Lake Chippewa did not disclose a similar belief among them. The White Earth Chippewa stated that children were never allowed to destroy butterflies. They were taught to call the butterflies to join in their games, especially in the game of hide and seek. A child would hold its nose between its thumb and forefinger and run about calling "Me-e-mĕmgwe" (Butterfly—butterfly). Mrs. Martin said she had often seen the butterflies come when the children called them in this manner. The term for butterfly is memĭŋgwa', but was pronounced as indicated when used in this pastime.

6. The spirit of the woods: When children went into the woods they were taught to watch and heed the "Spirit of the Woods." This was said to be like the "Spirit of the Water" which is mentioned in connection with dreams, and which has power to quiet the waves if so requested by a person who has dreamed of the water. Children were told that if they were going into danger the spirit of the woods would break a little branch and throw it in front of them as a warning. It is interesting to note the friendly guardianship of the wood spirit; also that waves did not indicate anger on the part of the water spirit. (See p. 81.)

(e) *Stories told to children—a typical example.*—The Wren Family, related by Mrs. Mary English.

The little wren grandmother sat by the fire in the little wigwam. Some one came in and said, " You have a grandchild."

" A boy or a girl? " asked the little wren grandmother.

" A girl," said the visitor.

" Throw her out; throw her out," said the little wren grandmother.

Another day, as the little wren grandmother sat by herself in the little wigwam, another visitor came to tell her that she had another grandchild.

" A boy or a girl? " asked the little wren grandmother.

"A boy," said the visitor.

"Bring him in; bring him in," said the little wren grandmother, " He will kill deer and I shall have plenty of marrow bones. He will bring water for me and I shall never lack for anything as long as I live."

And the old lady danced round and round the fire in her little wigwam.

One of the stories most widely told is that of the raccoon and the crawfish. It is said that the crawfish determined to make war on the raccoon, who continually disturbed their village. The raccoon pretended to be asleep and allowed the crawfish to pinch him with their claws as they sang a song with the words " The raccoon is dead." Suddenly he jumped up and ate all the crawfish.[40]

(*f*) *Playthings and toys for children.*—Among the first playthings given a child was the skin of some small animal filled with maple sugar and imperfectly sewed, so that the child in handling the article and putting it to its mouth would obtain a little of the sugar. Squirrels and other animals were stuffed as playthings for children, wild rice being sometimes used for the purpose.

A Menominee informant said that birds as well as animals were stuffed and used as toys, and that it was customary in old times to tie some small object to a baby's wrist, the object being something that the child could put in its mouth. A peculiar toy described by the Menominee consisted of the leg of a freshly killed deer, a muscle being left so that an older person could pull it, thus causing the toes to move for the amusement of the child. The Menominee also drew pictures on the ground for the entertainment of the children.

The leaves of the pitcher plant (*Sarracenia purpurea* L.) formed a favorite plaything for Chippewa children. The native name of the plant means " frog leggings." If the older people were gathering berries the children filled the pitcher-shaped leaves with berries or sand and used them in various forms of childish play.

The gathering and stringing of certain red berries formed an interesting pastime. The fresh berries were pierced with a sharp

[40] Bull. 53, Bur. Amer. Ethn., p. 305, and Song No. 180.

instrument and strung on nettle-fiber twine. After they were dry the husks were removed by rubbing with the hands. No other berries and no beads were combined with them and four or five strands were usually worn around the neck. These berries were said to grow on a little bush about 18 inches high which grew on dry ground.

" Little snowshoes " were made of the needles of the Norway pine. In making a little snowshoe the point of the pine needle is bent over and inserted in the socket of the needle at its base, forming a loop which somewhat resembles the frame of a snowshoe. Many of these are interlaced and worn as a necklace.

Large flat lichens were cut from trees and etched in patterns resembling those on woven-yarn bags. These were used by little girls in their play, being placed along the walls in imitation of the yarn bags in the wigwams.

In more recent times bright-colored autumn leaves were used by the children to represent letters, and the children "played post office," receiving these "letters" and pretending to read them. Leaves were selected with distinct markings, which they read as words.

The little girls made miniature mats from rushes and were encouraged to take the bark from small birch-bark trees and make rolls similar to those used for wigwam covers; they also made little birch-bark utensils similar to those made by their mothers.

It is said that animals were often modeled of clay by the Chippewa. One such specimen was obtained, and the boy who made it said that it was his "kwin'gwaäge," though it looked like a dog. The kwin'gwaäge is the wolverine, which lives in thick woods north and east of Lake Superior. Children going into the woods in the old days were told to beware of it.

Ducks were made of bulrush roots, similar to the dolls described in a subsequent paragraph, and were floated on little pools of water.

As soon as a boy was able to hold anything in his hands he was given something resembling a bow and arrow, and taught to go through the motions of shooting. A bow and arrows were first given a boy when he was 5 or 6 years of age, and with this he took his first lessons in the craft that was most necessary to a hunter or warrior in the old days. In the specimen illustrated (pl. 25, a) the bow is about 11 inches long. The bowstring is of basswood twine, and the arrows are blunt. The boy was taught to hold the bow horizontally, the arrow resting on the bow and passing under the bowstring. He held the bow in such a manner that his thumb was inside the bow while the arrow passed between two fingers. The projection at the end of the arrow was held between the thumb and finger of the right hand, making it an easy matter to " draw the bow." It was said that boys were encouraged to use this bow and arrows and that they " could be trusted not to do any damage with it."

(g) *Dolls.*—These will be considered in the order of their elaboration. The simplest form of representing a human being was by means of a large tuft of the needles of the Norway pine. This tuft was cut squarely across the end and about halfway up a part of the needles were cut across, suggesting the length of the arms, or perhaps a shawl hanging from the shoulders. A bit of the wood was left at the top of the tuft suggesting the head. These little figurines

Fig. 9.—Dolls cut from slippery-elm bark

were placed upright on a piece of zinc or in a large tin pan which was gently agitated. This motion caused the figurines to tremble in a manner suggesting an Indian dance and even to move back and forth, according to the skill of the person manipulating the tin on which they were placed. Dolls were also made of green basswood leaves and of bright autumn leaves, fastened with little splinters of wood.

Figures of men and women were made from a portion of the root of bulrushes that is below the water. This was partially dried and made into figures by tying it with basswood fiber, after which the figures were thoroughly dried and could be handled without breaking.

A step higher in development were the figures of men and women cut from the inner bark of the slippery elm. This is the same material from which is made the " wigup cord " so extensively used in Chippewa industries. The two figures illustrated (fig. 9) were cut by a woman at Red Lake from bark she took from the tree. The figure of the woman shows the old manner of dressing the hair and both figures are so cut that they can be easily held by little hands. The same is true of the grass doll (pl. 26, *b*) whose body is admirably shaped for a child's grasp. The grass is wound with narrow strips of basswood fiber, and a bit of color is introduced by the red breechcloth. A similarly elongated figure is seen in a doll made of willow, by a woman living at Grand Marais, on the north shore of Lake Superior. (Pl. 26, *a*.)

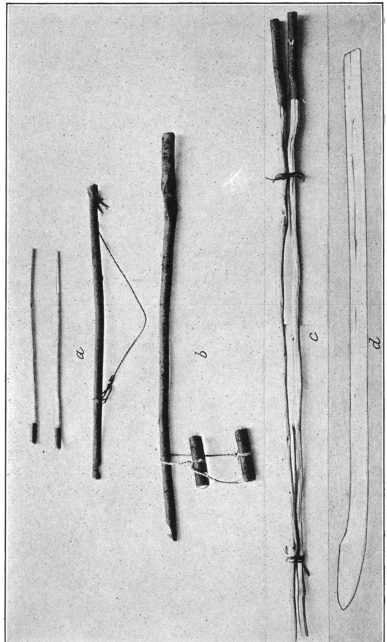

a, Bow and arrow for child's use; *b*, Game implements for little girl; *c*, "Deer sticks"; *d*, Snow snake

a, Doll made of willow withes; *b*, Doll made of grass

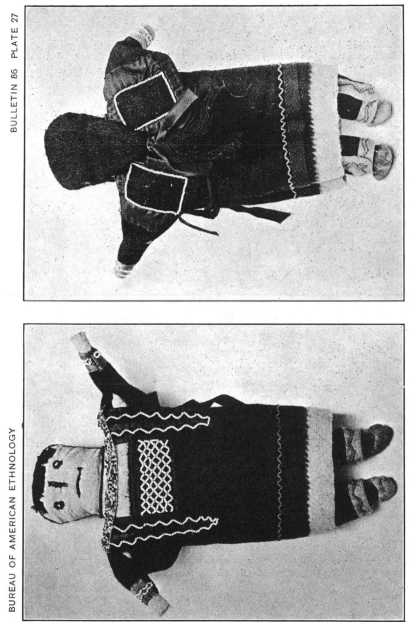

ʃ. .L IN WOMAN'S COSTUME

PORTRAIT OF THOMAS SKINAWAY

Attention is directed to the fact that in the four types of dolls above mentioned there is no attempt to outline the features of the face. It appears that in this stage of primitive art it was not necessary to show the details of an object; in brief, the articles represented nature without being a close imitation of nature. A similar stage of development was noted in the patterns used in beadwork (p. 186).

Dolls made of cloth and stuffed with soft moss were made when cloth became available, the little girls receiving their first lessons in beadwork by sewing the beads on a doll's dress. The cloth doll (pl. 27, *a*, *b*) shows the complete costume worn by a Chippewa woman in (approximately) the years 1850–1860. The sleeves are separate from the dress and fastened together jacketwise across the back, while the decoration of the " front piece " shows beads and the colors already mentioned (p. 32), which suggest the rainbow. The hair is woven across the back of the neck, a mode used by those engaged in work or other activity that would tend to loosen the braids. (See p. 39.) In explanation of the shape of this doll's face the woman who made it said that " the faces of the Indians were wider in the old days than now."

A doll in man's winter costume shows a combination of Indian apparel with that obtained from the trader. and may be said to represent the transitional period of Indian development. The coat and shirt are in imitation of manufactured articles, while the fringed leggings bound around the knee with bead bands, the breechcloth, woven sash, and moccasins are of the native style. The hood made of cloth is of a type widely used among the Chippewa and said to be very practical in winter. The face of this doll is of brown cloth and there is an attempt at modeling the features, all of which mark the passing of the imaginative and the dawn of the imitative period in native art.

(*h*) *Sports and games for children.*—In all outdoor sports the girls were as proficient as the boys. All were expert swimmers. An old woman said, " The children were like ducks, in-and-out of the water all day. They never stopped to take off the little clothing they had on, and their clothes dried on them when they came out of the water."

(1) Coasting erect: In winter a boy strapped to one of his feet a strip of wood or of slippery elm bark about 3 feet long, 4 inches wide, and curved upward at the forward end. This resembled the "toboggan" or "traineau" drawn by dogs and described in the section on transportation, but was, of course, much smaller. To the curved end was attached a cord or thong which the boy held in his hand, both for guiding his course and as an aid to balancing himself.

Standing erect on this one support the Chippewa boy coasted down the hills. It was permissible to hold a long stick for balancing in addition to the cord attached to the "coaster," but this was not looked upon with favor. The steepest hills were chosen for this sport, and by it the boys acquired bravery and self-control.

(2) Snow snake: This article is common to many tribes of Indians,[41] and was made in different sizes by the Chippewa, according to the age of the boys who were to use it. Plate 25, *d*, shows one which is about 20 inches long and would be suitable for quite a small boy. The throwing of the snow snakes required sufficient skill to make it interesting for young men, and the sticks used by them were about 3 feet long. In the specimen illustrated the handle is decorated by burning or searing the wood, giving it a shaded brown color. Personal marks often were put on the sticks in this manner or with paint, so the owners could claim their sticks when many fell near together.

There were two designs for the tip of a snow snake. In one the tip was upturned and finished smoothly as in the illustration. These were thrown through soft snow or across hard crusted snow. The other type had its tip carved to represent the head of a snake and was thrown under and through the snow, the object being to have the stick travel a long distance and then reappear above the surface. The lower surface of either type could be flat or slightly convex. In throwing across the snow it was customary for several boys to stand in a row and throw their sticks, after which they would run forward, identify their sticks, and determine who had thrown farthest. It is said they threw the sticks several hundred feet if the conditions were favorable. Eastern Chippewa drew a log through the snow and allowed the sides of this trench to freeze, often sprinkling it with water. In this smooth, icy trench the snow snakes were thrown long distances.

(3) Marbles: Stones similar to marbles were used by the boys. These stones were of two sorts, spherical and slightly flattened. In playing with these a number of holes about the size of the marbles were made in the ground, the round stones being "thrown sideways" toward the hole, the object being to place as many stones as possible in the holes.

(4) Deer sticks: A favorite pastime of little boys was to take two sticks and use them in the manner of "arm stilts." By means of these sticks they produced an effect of being four-legged and imitated the motions of a deer, cavorting about and kicking those who happened to be behind them. The sticks illustrated (pl. 25, *c*) are 2 feet

[41] Culin, Stewart, Games of the North American Indians, Twenty-fourth Ann. Rept. Bur. Amer. Ethn., Washington, 1907, pp. 399–420.

11 inches long, and the bark is removed except for 5 inches at one end. This form of stilts is not mentioned by Culin.

(5) Spinning stone: This form of top was a favorite plaything of boys and was also used by men. The game implements consisted of a smooth stone of a shape which would spin well and a wooden whip with a leathern thong. The game was usually played on the ice, the stone being set in motion with the fingers and kept in motion by striking it with the whip. (Pl. 41, *b*.) The " whip top " is widely used among Indian tribes of the United States and Alaska. (See Culin, op. cit., pp. 733–735.)

(6) Woman's game: There is a game among the Chippewa which is known as the woman's game (see pp. 118, 119) and little girls were early provided with simplified implements of this game, as the boys were provided with simplified bows and arrows. The implements of the woman's game consisted of two long sticks carried by each player and two billets about 3 inches long fastened together by a thong and tossed from one player to another. In the set intended for a little girl there is a notch in one of the sticks, making it easier to catch and hold the thong between the short sticks. In the specimen illustrated the sticks are 2 feet 4 inches long. (Pl. 25, *b*.)

(7) Bunch of grass game: A certain game played by the little girls was a miniature of a woman's game. As played by the little girls the bunch of grass and stick were very small. The manner of play was the same as in the adult game, the grass being tossed upward and caught on the pointed stick.

(8) Playing camp: Boys and girls joined in this sport. They made a little wigwam and " fixed it up," making a fire in the center. The boys caught fish, or killed rabbits or birds, and " threw them into the wigwam for the girls to cook." The little girls roasted them or cooked them in the ashes, and sometimes were given potatoes to cook in the ashes.

(9) Hide and seek, or the butterfly game: This game was preceded by the drawing of lots. Four sticks were prepared, one of which was longer than the others. A set of these sticks was obtained. The longer was 3 inches in length and the others 2⅜ inches, the four being tied together with basswood fiber. These sticks were held by one of the children, the others being told to draw a stick in turn. The one who drew the longer stick was the one to cover his eyes while the others hid. When all were ready he began his search, singing " Me-e-mĕm-gwe, me-e-mĕm-gwe (butterfly) show me where to go." He held his nose between thumb and fingers as he sang this, giving it a peculiar nasal sound, and he prolonged the first syllable, the rhythm of the call being 1–2–3–4, with the " 3–4 " corresponding to the two last syllables.

(10) Blindfold game: This was played as follows: One child was blindfolded and before the chase began he held out his hand and each of the other children "tapped his hand" and asked a question which he was required to answer. The following were said to be the usual questions and answers:

"What do you want?" "I want a fire."
"Who is with you?" "My horse."
"How high is your horse?" "As high as a pine tree."
"How far can your horse go?" "As far as you can see."
"Try to catch your horse."

Then came the chase as the blindfolded child tried to catch the other children.

(11) The windigo game or cannibal game: The most exciting game of the Chippewa children was the windigo game, and in order to understand its interest we must enter somewhat into the native idea of a windigo. This name implies all that is fear compelling, as the windigo were said to be terrible beings who were cannibals. If a stranger came to a lonely wigwam he was closely watched as he "might be a windigo," and if he stayed all night some one sat up and watched him constantly. The children absorbed the idea and made it into a game. One child was chosen by lot to play the part of the windigo. Four sticks were prepared, one longer than the others. These were held in the hand with the tops even and offered for choice among the older boys, the one who drew the longest stick acting the part of the windigo. He did not wear a mask but put leaves on his head to give him a grotesque appearance. He hid in a clump of bushes. The other children then formed in a long line, each holding the belt of the child in front of him. A large boy was chosen to lead the others and he carried a club. When they came near the windigo's hiding place he rushed out with fearful yells. The leader fought with him, and the younger children clung screaming to each other. Sometimes the windigo seized a child and pretended to eat it. This game was a favorite among the children.

(i) *Puberty customs.*—At the time of her maturity a young girl was required to isolate herself for four days and nights. Her mother made a little wigwam for her at some distance from the lodge, and it is said that in old days she was allowed absolutely no food during this period. A feast was given after her maturing, and she continued her fast until that time. In later days an older sister or other relative brought a little food to the girl. During her isolation she was not allowed to scratch her hair or body with her hands, a stick being provided for that purpose.

The writer's informant said that during the first summer of her womanhood she was not allowed to taste any fruit, berries, or vegetables until the proper ceremony had been enacted. The first fruit was the strawberry, which she gathered. Her parents invited the Mide and others to the feast. Each had a dish of berries, and she had one for herself. The old Mide drummed and sang, then he held a spoonful of the berries to her lips, but as she was about to take it he withdrew it. This was repeated four times, and the fifth time he gave her the berries. Then she took her dish of berries and ate with the others. This was a great trial to the child who hungered for the fresh fruit, but in it we see the teaching of patience and the discipline which underlies so many Indian customs. The same procedure was repeated with the first of every product of nature, even to the wild rice of the autumn.

At about the same age a boy was required to undergo a fast in which he hoped and expected to obtain a dream or vision. The father taught the boy to prepare for this and insisted that he persevere until he secured the dream. The boy blackened his face with charcoal and usually went away from home for his fast. Sometimes the father took the boy a considerable distance and made a nest for him in a tree. He left the boy there several days, going occasionally to "see if he was all right." It was not unusual for a boy to make several attempts before he secured a dream, but complete failures were very rare. (See narratives, pp. 78, 79, 84.) Odinigun said that he prepared himself by fasting. In his first attempt to secure a dream he scarcely tasted food or water for eight days, but he saw no vision. The next time he fasted for 10 days. He said that "by that time his mind was clear" and he knew that he would have power to heal the sick. It was not stated that he received a name in this dream, though he may have done so. A song that he used in healing the sick is recorded as No. 79 in Bulletin 45. The words are "In a dream I was instructed to do this." The melody is one of unusual vigor and force.

The following is an instance of a dream in which a man received a name. Mr. Tom Skinaway (pl. 28) said that he was born at Mille Lac, Minn., and received his early teaching from his mother. When he was about eight years old his father talked to him and told him that ever since the oldest times the Indian boys had blackened their faces and fasted and waited for their dream. His father told him to blacken his face with charcoal, saying, "When you sleep to-night perhaps something will appear to you. If you get a good dream, it will be a good thing for you. Perhaps you will see a big town. That would be good luck and would mean that if a white man sees you he will like you." But the boy did not see anything in his sleep that night. He had to try ten times. After each attempt his father would say, "Didn't you see anything?" and he would answer, "No." After a while he got his vision. In his dream a man came to him

and told him that his name would be " Bi'jiki." This is the word by
which the old Chippewa designated the buffalo; in later years its
meaning has been extended to domestic cattle, but in its use as a
dream name it always indicates great strength and endurance. In
relating this Mr. Skinaway called attention to his splendid physique
and said he was well named. In the dream he received certain
instructions which he had faithfully fulfilled.

A feast was held when a boy killed his first game. Henry Selkirk said that the first game he killed was a wild canary. He hung
it up to wait until he had enough food to give a feast in honor of
the event but it was so long before he had enough that the little
bird dried up. In older times, when the tribal customs were strictly
observed, he would have provided a simple repast, perhaps rice and
dried blueberries, or corn, fish, or potatoes, and would have asked
five or six old men to the feast. They would have "talked to the
manido and made petitions concerning the boy and his family."

(j) *Courtship and marriage.*—The young maidens of the Chippewa were closely guarded and were modest in their behavior toward
the young men of the tribe. If a young man wished to call upon a
young woman he talked first with the older people who lived next
to the door of the lodge. He might then proceed to the middle of
the lodge, where the young people lived, and talk with the girl in a
low tone, but she was not allowed to leave the lodge with him. If
a young man came to call rather late in the evening when the fire
had burned low, the mother or grandmother would rise and stir up
the fire so that it burned brightly, then fill her pipe and sit up and
smoke. The young man could continue his call, but was conscious
of being watched. The young men played the "courting flute" in
the evenings, but it was never permitted that a young girl leave the
lodge in response to the flute.

If a young man's intentions were serious, he killed a deer or some
other animal and brought it to the girl's parents. This was to indicate his ability and intention to provide well for his family. If
the parents approved of the young man, they asked him to stay and
share the feast. This was understood as an acceptance of his wish
to marry their daughter, and he was allowed to come and go with
more freedom than formerly.

Jealousy among the young girls was a marked feature of
Chippewa life and frequently resulted in spirited fighting. The hair
seems to have been the special point of attack, being ferociously
pulled and frequently the braid being cut off with a knife. The
clothing was torn, but "slapping" with the hand was not a method
of this conflict. It was said that a girl who "flirted with several
young men" was punished by them, an instance of this sort hap-

pening at White Earth in recent years. One of the young men took the girl into the country, leaving her to find her way home alone. She was waylaid by others of the group, her clothing was torn, and she was thrown into a mudhole.

The young couple might go away quietly for a few days, or they might go at once to live in a lodge of their own. The first-named custom was usually followed if the couple intended to live with the woman's parents. It was the usual custom for a girl to remain at home for a while after her marriage, after which time the couple might, if they desired, build a lodge of their own or, occasionally, they might live with the husband's parents. Mrs. Julia Spears, who was 88 years old when giving the information, said she remembered an instance which occurred in 1848 among the Bad River band of Chippewa, near the present site of Odanah, Wis. The chief had a daughter of whom he was very fond. His wife built a wigwam for the young couple near their own, making it as pretty as possible and furnishing it with new floor mats and other articles. When the young people were ready to begin life together they quietly took up their abode in the wigwam which had been provided for them.

In early days, if a couple living in a lodge of their own could not get along together, the wife went back to her own people and the man could do as he liked. It was said that "if she got over her pouting spell she might go back to him." A man might have two or three wives and all lived in the same lodge, each having her appointed part of the lodge. The writer witnessed a ceremony in the house of a Chippewa at Grand Portage who had two wives. (Shown at left in pl. 5, b.) Two of his sons lived with them and the family seemed to be living harmoniously. A Canadian Chippewa said that many Indians had two wives, adding that "the man sat between them." He said that in old times some men had five wives, and that one was the "head wife" and the only one who had children.

On being questioned concerning the courting customs among the Canadian Chippewa he said that he never heard of a courting song except that sung at a dance where all could hear it. He said that for such an occasion a man might "make up a song on account of some girl." This statement was translated back into Chippewa for him in order that there might be no misunderstanding of his meaning. He said that his people had a "long whistle" which the young men played so that the girls might hear.

(k) *Customs pertaining to death, burial, and mourning.*—As soon as a person died he was washed, his hair braided, and his best clothing put on him, also a great quantity of every sort of bead work. If he were a member of the Grand Medicine Society his Mide bag was placed under his arm. Frequently his face, moccasins, and blanket were painted with brown fungus [42] and vermilion. A round spot of brown was placed on each cheek and over it was painted a horizontal line of vermilion. (Fig. 10.) His moccasins were painted brown, and there were brown streaks on his blanket.

This custom has its origin in the following tradition: It is said that a woman went into a trance for half a day and, on recovering, said that she had been to the ghost land where the northern lights are shining, and that the ghosts held this fungus in their hands and painted their faces in stripes with it. She said that northern lights are ghosts rising and falling in the steps of a dance, that the women are dressed in gay clothing, and that the warriors have their war clubs. Thus the dead were arrayed to join the dance of the ghosts where the northern lights are shining. With the dead were placed any trinkets or articles particularly valued in life. A pipe and tobacco pouch, with flint, steel, and punk were buried with a man and,

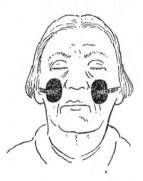

FIG. 10.—Painting on face of dead

if he were a good hunter, his gun might be placed beside him. A woman's favorite ax or pack strap might be buried with her. The only articles of utility placed with the dead (unless because of some personal attachment) were those articles needed on a short journey, such as a little kettle, a dish, and a spoon. It was the Chippewa belief that everything necessary for life and its occupations awaited the person in the " Hereafter." His friends therefore made provision only for his comfort on the four days' journey to that distant place. Mr. William Dailey, son of Ĕn′dûso-gi′jĭg, said, " My father was buried with his jackknife and pipe, the Grand Medicine man who buried him requesting this and saying that his soul might crave those articles and not leave at once for the Hereafter." Endusogijig was an expert maker of bows and arrows. (See pp. 131, 136.)

After the proper preparations had been made the relatives sent for the Mide, who conducted a form of funeral ceremony. The writer was outside the lodge in which the Mide were holding such a ceremony beside the body of Flat Mouth, a Chippewa chief. (Bull. 45, p. 54.) They rehearsed the beliefs of the Mide and assured the family of Flat Mouth of their reality. Then they addressed the spirit of the dead chief as it is believed that the spirit lingers near the body for some time. One after another they sat beside him telling him to be careful to avoid certain turns in the road to the spirit land, or to trust certain spirits who would meet

[42] Identified as Bovista pila B. and C.

and assist him. They spoke with extreme rapidity, punctuating the words with occasional sharp beats on the drum. Rev. J. A. Gilfillan, who witnessed many native burials at White Earth while a missionary among the Indians, quotes an address by an old Indian to the dead body of his daughter, beginning with the words, " Your feet are now on the road of souls, my daughter." [42a]

Before the Chippewa obtained lumber, the body, with the several articles beside it, was wrapped in very heavy birch bark and tied with basswood cord. It was placed in a shallow grave, after which the mother or other relative danced around the open grave. This lasted some time, and then the grave was filled. Winter burial was accomplished by building a fire to thaw the ground. Food was placed beside a grave, and for four nights a fire was kept burning to aid the spirit, the purpose of the fire being for warmth and for cooking. Food was placed on the graves at any time, and poor persons, or members of the same clan, or friends of the deceased person were welcome to take it.

Burial was with the feet toward the west, as tradition states that to be the direction of the spirit's journey. Opinion seems to differ, however, as Bû'digons' (known as William Potter) states that in his youth he was told that the old belief of the Mide is that the land of departed spirits is not of necessity toward the west but "somewhere—as though in *space*." He said there was day and night in that place, but that during the day there was absolute silence. When night came the drums were beaten at some particular spot, and the spirits assembled from all directions and danced during the entire night, dispersing at daylight. Over a grave in old days there were spread sheets of birch bark or rush mats with stones at the side to hold them down. A survival of this custom is seen in the placing of coverings of white cotton cloth over the Chippewa graves, with stones along the sides. The usual custom, however, was to erect low houses over the graves. Birch bark was used for this purpose before lumber was obtained. In the grave houses there is a small opening resembling a window, and usually a ledge outside the window. The relatives of the dead person placed food there, the first maple sugar and the first berries being cooked in a special dish and placed on the graves. Sometimes the relatives would go to a friend and say, "Go to a certain grave and take what you find there." These gifts of food were arranged in an attractive manner, usually in birch-bark wrappings. Markers placed at graves bore the " totem " of the deceased, the symbol being inverted, to indicate death. (Pl. 29, *a.*) Thus a man passing a grave in a strange part of the country would pause to ascertain to what gens the person had belonged, and if it were his

---

[42a] Gilfillan, Joseph A., The Ojibway, p. 50. New York and Washington, 1904.

own gens he would, if possible, leave an offering of food on the grave. The birch-bark grave house shown in Plate 30, *a*, was seen in an isolated place, but groups of grave houses (pl. 30, *b*), as well as single burials, are common throughout the Chippewa country.

If a death occurred while the family were traveling they moved as soon as possible to a new location, and certain marks placed on the grave marker indicated the number of days which elapsed between the death and the removal of the family to their new camping place.

Informants differ concerning tree sepulture among the Chippewa. Some say that if a death occurred when the people were away from their customary camping ground the body was wrapped in birch bark and placed in a tree, on a scaffold made by tying poles together, this being a temporary arrangement until the people returned home. It seems probable that the custom varied with circumstances and with individuals.

A permanent village had its burial ground. Thus at Leech Lake and at Odanah the burial ground was in the middle of the camp circle. An informant said that the camp circle at Leech Lake had its opening toward the lake, and she remembered passing alongside the graves as she went to the lake for water.

A Canadian Chippewa said that when a death occurred they often buried the body inside the wigwam and then took down the wigwam. He said that if the burial were to be outside a tipi they took down the poles and threw them aside. These poles were never used again.

Carved birds were seen on posts above the graves of Canadian Chippewa. Two of these were over one grave and a third was over another. (Pl. 29, *b*.) Reference to the interpretation of the Mide roll (p. 92) will show that posts surmounted by carved birds were used in the Midewiwin, a carved hawk in the second, and a carved owl in the third degree. These posts were provided by the candidate for initiation. It seems possible that these posts were over the graves of members of the Midewiwin who had taken these degrees.

Among the Chippewa, as among all races of people, there were certain established customs of mourning and others that varied with the individual. The grief of some persons was so extreme that they cut gashes in their bodies when the death occurred. Wailing usually began immediately after a death, but this was not required by custom; indeed it is said that some persons who were " of strong mind " did not wail at all. Relatives usually went to a grave at evening and wailed for a long time in a plaintive manner. A death was announced to strangers by wailing. Thus if the Sioux were coming on a friendly visit, and the Chippewa had not seen them in some time, it was customary (or permissible) for a Chippewa in mourning to

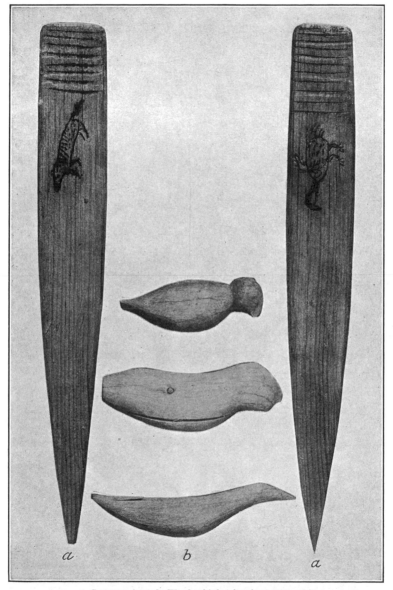

a, Grave markers; *b*, Wooden birds taken from grave posts

a, Birch-bark covering above grave

b, Wooden structures above graves

go toward them wailing. This would acquaint the Sioux with the fact that a death had recently occurred in that person's family, and they would be prepared to express their sympathy.

Two customs of mourning were observed, (1) the wearing of outward signs of mourning for about a year, this period of mourning being terminated by a ceremony, and (2) the keeping of a "spirit bundle." A man in deep mourning painted his entire face black; in less extreme mourning he painted a black circle covering each eye. Informants differ on the custom among women, some saying that a woman in mourning covered her face entirely with black paint, others that she painted her face with black streaks, and others stating that she used no black paint. Probably the observance was decided by the individual. The custom of cutting the hair or wearing it unbraided, and of wearing old clothing was universally observed. Some women cut their hair off at their shoulders, others greased it and cut it straight across the forehead after the manner of "bangs." They tied back the rest of their hair with a thong and let it hang without braiding. Narrow strips of buckskin were braided and worn around their necks and waists during the period of mourning. A woman with loosened hair because of mourning is shown in Plate 75.

In every case it was required that a widow present an outward evidence of mourning for her husband at least a year. During that time she did not go to any public place, she wore ragged clothing, clipped her hair across the ends, combed her hair very seldom, and wore it unbraided. If she disregarded these customs or wore any bright adornment, the relatives of her husband, even so distant a relative as a cousin, had a right to tear off the ornaments. If she presumed to marry within the year, her wigwam might be torn down and all her belongings scattered and torn. During that period her husband's relatives had a claim upon her time, and she frequently lived with and worked for them.

Among the Wisconsin Chippewa a ceremony of "restoring the mourners" was held once a year. Those who had lost relatives were escorted to the ceremony. They were publicly "comforted" and presented with bright shawls, bead chains, and other ornaments, after which they were expected to lay aside their grief and mingle with their friends. Such a ceremony was attended by the writer in 1910. (Bull. 53, pp. 153–161.)

If a relative of the dead intended to keep a "spirit bundle," he or she cut a lock of hair from the back of the dead person's head soon after death occurred. The lock of hair was wrapped in birch bark and formed the nucleus of the "spirit bundle." The relatives built a fire on the night of the burial, took this "spirit bundle" to the fire and "sat and talked"; then they took the "spirit bundle" home with them. This was repeated for four consecutive nights. The requirements of those who kept a "spirit bundle" were similar to the custom of the Sioux. (Bull. 61, pp. 77–84.) The "spirit bundle" of a child was made by its mother. She carried it on her back if she went around the camp, or placed it upright in the wigwam, laying food before it as though it were a living thing. Sometimes instead of carrying a "spirit bundle" a mother placed the child's clothing in its cradle board and carried that for a year. If a woman were keeping the "spirit bundle" of her husband, she treated it as if it were the habitation of his spirit, laying food before it and placing it beside her at night. At first the bundle was small, but it grew larger as she wrapped around it whatever she obtained that was new and of value, as cloth, blankets, or beadwork. She also made all kinds of beadwork, such as moccasins and belts, and wrapped them with the bundle. At the end of a year she took this on her back and went to the lodge of her husband's relatives asking for her freedom. If she had been frivolous or indiscreet, they could require her to carry the pack still longer. If, however, they were willing to release her they gave a great feast, at which the "spirit bundle" was unrolled, and the articles therein were given to the husband's relatives, who painted her face and in turn gave her presents of fresh clothing and other articles. She was then declared free and could marry again if she so desired.

A husband carried a "spirit bundle" for his wife, but it was much smaller. If a man had two wives he was not required to do this, but the woman's mother carried the bundle and mourned for her daughter, the husband supplying all the goods for the bundle.

After the feast which followed the keeping of a "spirit bundle" the lock of hair which formed the nucleus of the bundle was buried beside the grave of the person whose spirit had been kept. The lock of hair was still wrapped in the birch-bark wrapping, as when in the "spirit bundle."

DREAMS

(a) *Significance of dreams.*—In order to understand the character of the Chippewa we must take into consideration the influence of the dream on the life of the Indian. An aged Chippewa said: "In the old days our people had no education. They could not learn from books nor from teachers. All their wisdom and knowledge came to them in dreams. They tested their dreams, and in that way learned their own strength." The ability to dream was cultivated from earliest childhood. "Try to dream and to remember what you dream," was a frequent admonition to children when they were put to bed. Thus the imagination was stimulated, and there arose a keen desire to see something extraordinary in sleep. No significance was attached to these childish dreams, but they prepared the way for the really important dream that the child sought on attaining its maturity. Parents instructed both girls and boys concerning the importance of this dream and the means of securing it. Purity of life and thought was one essential to the revelation of one's guardian spirit or tutelary. Fasting, isolation, and mediation were the principal conditions under which such a dream might be secured. (See p. 70.)

The dream thus secured was of greatest importance in the life of the individual, though he or she might have other dreams. We note the confident expectation in the mind of the child, the stimulating of the brain by lack of food, and the unfamiliar waking impressions that may have combined with the child's own character to determine the subject of its dream. This is a matter of physiology and of psychology. The Chippewa say that in their dreams they often returned to a previous state of existence; also that they saw things which no Indian had seen at that time, but which they themselves saw and recognized in later years, such as sailing vessels and frame houses. It was said the power of the dream was so great that a man had been known to assume the form which had been his in a previous existence, and which had formed the subject of his dream. Thus it was said that a warrior who had dreamed of a certain animal would call on it in time of danger, and if he were wounded, his comrades would hear the cry of that animal and see it run away. On searching they would be unable to find the body of the warrior, and believed he had returned to his previous existence and escaped in the form of an animal.[43]

It was a belief of the Chippewa that by possessing some representation of a dream subject one could at any time secure its protection, guidance, and assistance. There seems to be inherent in the mind of the Indian a belief that the essence of an individual or of a "spirit" dwells in its picture or other representation. To this belief was due the reluctance of the old-time Indian to being photographed, his reason being that harm would come to him if harm befell his portrait. A further instance is as follows: A picture of President Wilson was given to Tokala Luta (Red Fox) (see Bull. 61, pl. 56), who placed it on his wall. A year later he wished to send a message to the President saying that he felt the President had been his guest during the year, and that he appreciated the honor thus conferred upon him. Perhaps there lies beneath this belief a tribute to art and its mystery of achievement, but there is also the element

---

[43] Cf. an incident among the Sioux in which a man who had dreamed of an elk left the footprints of an elk behind him when enacting the events of his dream. Bull. 61, Bur. Amer. Ethn., p. 178.

of imagination on the part of the observer, without which art would fail in its purpose.

The representation of a dream subject took the form of an object or of an outline, and might be either an exact representation or an article or outline more or less remotely suggesting a peculiarity of the dream. The representation published the subject of a man's dream, but seldom indicated the nature of the dream. Thus the writer once asked the significance of a turtle as seen in a dream, and the reply was "It might mean many things; no one would know except the man who dreamed the dream. Perhaps it would be a sign of danger, and perhaps it would mean that the turtle would protect him." It was considered desirable that the representation should be put in as enduring a form as possible.

An aged man said to the writer, "A picture can be destroyed, but stone endures, so it is good that a man have the subject of his dream carved in a stone pipe that can be buried with him. Many of his possessions are left to his friends, but the sign of his dream should not be taken from him." A stone pipe carved to represent a bird was unearthed in Canada and had probably been buried with its owner. Similar carved pipes were made of wood by the Minnesota Chippewa. Nodinens said that her father dreamed of a knife of peculiar pattern, and that he made one of metal and wore it whenever he went to fight the Sioux. He explained its advantages, saying the pointed blade made it easy to drive into the body of the enemy, and the notch above the blade afforded a hold by which the knife could be pulled out. He said further that the length of the blade was such that it was sure to kill a man who was stabbed with it. Nodinens said it was her father's custom to give such a knife to the boys whom he was asked to name. If the child were a baby, he made the knife very small, so that it could be hung on the hoop of the cradle board as a plaything.[44] Nodinens made a knife of wood, making it about 9 inches in length, the proportions and outline being that of her father's dream knife. (Pl. 31, d.)

The representation was sometimes an article which interpreted rather than imitated the subject of the dream. Thus Mrs. Louisa Martin, a Mille Lac Chippewa, living at White Earth, carried a woven yarn cord with white as one of its colors, representing a dream of a safe voyage on a wide lake. She said that if she were to make such a cord for another person she would use the white yarn, and yarn of whatever color the person wore most frequently. When a young girl she was given the name A'jawac, meaning "wafted safely across." This name was given her by a woman who dreamed of

---

[44] The gift of a dream representation to a namesake with the sharing of its "spirit power" is described on p. 58.

crossing a great lake in a sailing boat. The woman had never seen a sailing boat, but at a later time she saw one and recognized it as similar to that seen in her dream. She dreamed that she got into the boat and crossed the great lake. When she arrived safely the person who escorted her said, "Your name shall be *A'jawac*, and you will always cross water in safety." With this name Mrs. Martin received a cord woven or braided of two colors of yarn. She can travel in security on stormy water with this cord tied around her waist next her body, and it is a protection in travel by land if placed with her personal belongings. By virtue of this transmitted dream power she can make effective requests of the "Spirit of the Water."

Niski'gwûn (pl. 2, *b*) said that when he was a young man he dreamed of smooth, quiet water. He did not have occasion to test the power of this dream for many years. At length the opportunity came under the following circumstances: Niskigwun was returning with a party of Indians from La Pointe where they had received their annuities. When they reached the place where the Fond du Lac River empties into Lake Superior they found the lake very rough with the wind blowing directly toward them. A mixed blood who was with the party said, "We are likely to be delayed here several days. Does anyone know how to treat with the Spirit of the Water?" Niskigwun replied that he had seen smooth, quiet water in a dream but had never tested its power. He said that he would "try and see what he could do." There was a little whisky in the canoe and he took that as being something very valuable and sprinkled it on the water; he also strewed tobacco on the water and said that he desired the water to become like that which he saw in his youthful dream. In half an hour the wind veered and they were able to proceed on their way. (Cf. placing tobacco in the fire, p. 145.)

Several informants said that the following custom was familiar to them. This is of interest as the offering was alive, and the person making the offering was a child who was too young to have had a dream: It was customary to make a little birch-bark dish and to put in it a head louse and a little tobacco. A child was told to put this in the water and watch it float away. The child watched it, and if the waves upset it the people were sure the storm was almost over and that they could soon resume their journey. This, however, may be interpreted as a "sign," rather than an instance of an offering to the Water Spirit.

In reply to a question as to whether the presence of waves indicated anger on the part of the Water Spirit it was said that "Waves do not mean that the Water Spirit is angry with those who wish to cross. It is natural that there should be waves and rough weather as well as smooth water, but if the Water Spirit is asked by the right person, he can quiet the waves at that time so the people can proceed in safety." It was said that those who dreamed of water were usually the most successful in treating the sick. In this connection it is interesting to note that dreams concerning water are most frequently observed in persons of highly sensitive and nervous temperament.

A picture of a dream subject could be painted, outlined with beads, or woven in beadwork. Such representations of the turtle and bear are shown in Plate 31, a and b. While the chief purpose was the benefit of the dreamer, it was possible for him to extend this benefit to others. Thus a certain well-known member of the Mille Lac band of Chippewa saw a bear in his youthful vision. He believed that he derived from the bear a rugged strength that is his characteristic. As a representation of this dream he had in his possession an outline of a bear drawn on white cloth. When his wife was dangerously ill he spread this cloth over her so that the strength which came to him from the bear might be hers also. In a short time she began to recover, and he fastened the cloth on the wall above her head, where it remained until she was entirely well. She related this incident to the writer many years after it occurred. The article is shown in Plate 32, a. The streaks on it were said to have been made by the " medicine " that had been placed upon it.

Dream symbols often were painted on a man's blanket or on the covering that hung before his wigwam door, the man who dreamed of a wolf or a bear displaying a picture of that animal. A more elaborate and individual pattern is shown in Plate 32, b. This is the pattern painted on a blanket and worn by a man who is still remembered among the White Earth Chippewa. The blanket was covered by the dream picture. All who saw it were aware that the man had dreamed of a rainbow, the thunder bird, the lightning, and the earth (the latter indicated by the circle) ; yet the relation of these to one another and to the dreamer remained a secret known only to himself and those to whom he revealed it. His blanket was worn in such a manner as to show the pattern to best advantage, being spread its full size around him and fastened across his chest with a sharp bone or a wooden skewer, thus falling free behind him. It was said that a dream of a rainbow was one in which a woman appeared, the colors of the rainbow representing the bright and varied colors of worsted braid on the " front piece " of a woman's dress. The most common manner of wearing a dream representation was in woven beadwork, either on the headband or on a woven band that was worn tightly around the neck. Plate 80, b, shows three patterns used in this manner, the rainbow, the moon, and a star. The custom of wearing a dream pattern has not entirely disappeared among the Chippewa.

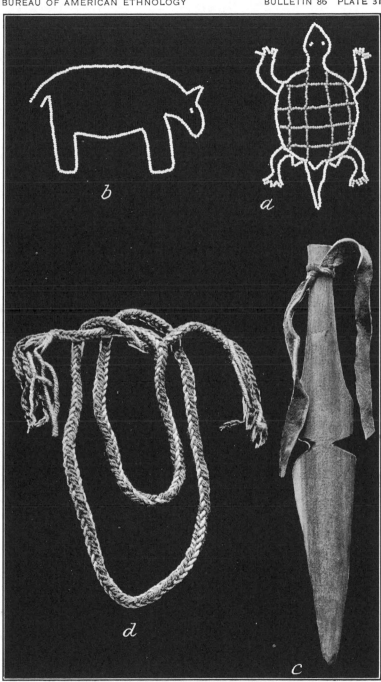

a, Dream symbol, turtle; *b*, Dream symbol, bear; *c*, Knife, representative of dream; *d*, Cord, worn as charm

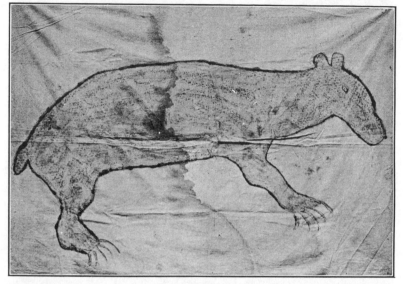

a, Bear, dream representation

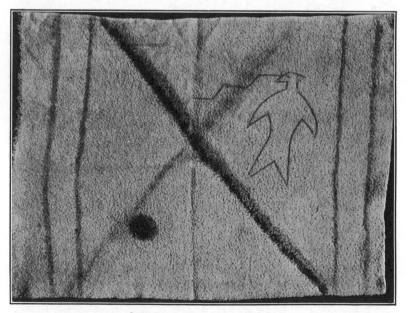

b, Dream symbols used on blanket

A certain Indian who is particularly active and industrious in following the white man's ways always requests his wife to put a star in the pattern of the beadwork she makes for him. Even she does not know its significance to him nor the story of his probable dream of a star.

From the foregoing instances it is evident that the subject of a man's dream was clear to all intelligent observers, but its significance was a secret that he might hide forever if he so desired.

Three personal dreams were related to the writer, two by Niskigwun, an aged man, and one by Ajawac, a woman (pp. 80, 86). The man expressed the belief that in his first dream he returned to a previous state of existence and also saw things that were in his human life subsequent to the dream, and the woman said that in her dream she also saw things she had never seen in actuality, but which she saw and recognized at a later time.

(*b*) *Dream narratives by Niskigwun.*—It is interesting to note that Niskigwun (pl. 2, *b*) recorded the song concerning this dream in 1908, 10 years before relating the present narrative. The song appears as No. 6 in Bulletin 53, but the dream was not related.

The subject under discussion at that time was war, and the principal informant was his friend Odjib'we, whose position as a warrior was higher than his own. The circumstances were not favorable to relating his dream, nor did he feel called upon to do so. He contributed three of his war songs and assisted Odjibwe in recalling the old customs and incidents of wars against the Sioux. But in 1918 the circumstances had changed. Odjibwe had passed from earth and Niskigwun had become so frail that he could scarcely stand. The writer returned and asked him directly about his dreams. The time was propitious for relating them, and he said that the song above mentioned was connected with his first dream, this being indicated by the words "my bird plumage will be flying." He wore eagle feathers in the wars against the Sioux. When it was possible for him to secure fresh feathers of the proper sort he might substitute a new for an old set of the feathers, but some of them of this sort had been in his possession continuously since he had his dream of the eagle. The Chippewa recognize two varieties of the eagle. The bald eagle (wabĭcûc'kwe) is considered a war bird because of its high and rapid flight and the beauty of its feathers which are black and white, firm, and lustrous. This species of eagle is very rare in the Chippewa country, and when seen is hard to capture. It was this variety of eagle that Niskigwun saw in his dream. It is difficult for a member of the white race to accept Niskigwun's statement that the banner seen in his dream was afterwards identified by him as the United States flag. In this, as in similar instances, one must take into account the character and reputation of the man who makes the statement. Niskigwun is known as a sincere man who has always led a quiet, respectable life, and has kept his native manner of thought; his statement is therefore recorded as worthy of consideration.

Niskigwun said that his parents instructed him as to what he ought to do in seeking his first dream, and that one morning when he was about 12 years of age he blackened his face with charcoal. He remained quietly in the wigwam all day and ate nothing until after sunset when his mother gave him a very little food to refresh him. That night he lay down in the wigwam and slept but he dreamed of nothing except the blackening of his face. This was said to mean that his "real dream" when it came would be a "true dream," and that he must have faith in it. He fasted 10 days, not all at once but at such periods as he could endure. At last his "real dream" came to him, the wonderful dream which he said had given him mysterious powers throughout his long, eventful life. In this dream he imagined himself to be flying through the air.[45] A large eagle was with him, and in one account of the dream he said that the eagle carried him. They alighted on top of a tall pole. There was a strange piece of cloth hanging on the pole and a small frame house with open doors stood near by. The eagle gave him to understand that the piece of cloth would in some way be a protection to him, and that he would live in such a house during many years of his life. The eagle scattered his tail feathers. The eagle told him to keep these feathers as a remembrance, and said that he would be with him in spirit all through his life. Then the eagle flew away.

Niskigwun gathered up the feathers, promising to keep them and to live as high and pure a life as he could. Then he looked around him and saw the frame house. He saw a woman's footprints and followed them into the house. There stood a woman. She went out the other door and he followed her. After a while she turned and looked at him, then she disappeared. Niskigwun said that the piece of cloth on the pole was afterwards identified by him as the United States flag, and that the woman who led him through the house when he returned to a previous state of existence was she who became his mother in the present life. As soon as possible after his dream he secured some tail feathers of this sort of eagle, which he kept constantly with him, and when he attained to manhood he built a house like the one in his dream. He was 80 years old when relating this story, and said the house in which he then lived, though quite a new house, was like the one in his dream. He said that because of the eagle and its assistance he achieved success in war, and because of the house in his dream he had during his whole life been able to

---

[45] " Aviation " in dreams is frequently mentioned by writers on this subject.

know of important events that took place in his home when he was absent. On one occasion, after he had married and had established a home of his own, he was absent for three days, and on the third night he dreamed that one of his children was dead. He had left them all in good health, but he at once told his companions that he must return, and when he reached home he learned that one of his children had died. He also had a prescience of circumstances other than those connected with his home. Thus he was once with a war party which approached a Sioux village and made a camp preparatory to attacking the village in the morning. During the night "it came to him" that the village was empty. His companions discredited his statement and they made the attack, but found the Sioux village deserted. Niskigwun attributed these powers to the fact that he had faithfully fulfilled the requirements of his dream and had lived a good life.

The eagle of his dream once became visible to his friends in a remarkable manner, the circumstances being as follows: It was very important that he should eat nothing "unclean," but once he was hungry and ate a piece of moose that a woman had stepped over, rendering it unclean according to the Chippewa custom. He became violently ill and a "juggler" (*djasakid*) worked over him. After a time a live eagle came out of him. The medicine man asked his mother if the bird should be put back in him. His mother said, "No; it may make him sick again." The medicine man said in that case he would keep it himself, so he swallowed the live bird. Even this could not deprive him of the *spirit* of the bird which, he said, had remained with him during his entire life.

His subsequent dream also indicated his belief in the power of a dream article, as well as the making of an article in accordance with a dream. Niskigwun said that in a later dream he saw a horned animal, and in accordance with the dream he made for himself a cap with short horns on it. He wore this cap when he felt it necessary to increase his strength, and said that he once wore it almost constantly during an entire winter, wearing it while in the house. During the summer of 1917 he transferred this cap to the writer. A year later she went to his house and inquired concerning his health. He replied that he had lost much of his strength since parting with his horned cap. In response to an expression of regret he said this did not come as a surprise to him, neither did he feel sorry that he parted with the cap. He said that he did not need much strength, as he was an old man and had not long to live, but that he valued his cap very highly, and it was a comfort to him to think it was where it would be safely preserved. Niskigwun died in 1921.

(c) *Dream narrative by Ajawac.*—The dream name given to this informant by her namer is explained on pages 80 and 81, and is, as stated, the name by which she is commonly known. She also received a name in the following dream but asked that it be omitted from the narrative.

Ajawac said that in her youthful dream she saw a winged figure, and that ever since her dream she has carried a representation of the figure, believing that she has secured supernatural guidance from its presence. The representation (pl. 33) is 6 inches long and is made of black cloth, the edges of which are bordered by white beads. She said that in this article she had tried to delineate as closely as possible a strange figure that appeared to her in all her youth whenever she fasted and went to sleep asking for a dream. When the figure was coming toward her it looked like a bird, but when it alighted on the ground beside her it was in the shape of a winged man about 4 feet high, the entire figure being a soft gray color. He always brought her the same message, saying that she would have a quiet, peaceful life and many blessings. He would touch her hair and say, "You will live until your hair is white." In her dreams she seemed to be in a frame house, though she had never seen one. The flying figure paused to alight upon tall poles that stood in a long line like the telephone poles that are now a familiar sight on the reservation. The poles seen in her dreams had crossbars on which the flying figure alighted. It always came from the west and she could see it a long way off coming toward her. The name given her by this mysterious visitant is omitted. His message, she said, has "come true," for she has had a peaceful, happy life. When in doubt she has "always seemed to have a mysterious guidance" that has led her to a successful solution of her difficulties. Long before learning the story of her dream the writer had noted the peculiar gentleness of her manner and the serenity of her eyes. She said that she occasionally made a new figure of the winged man but seldom went far from her house without taking it with her. When giving this information she took the cloth figure from a bag in which she carried her small belongings.

MÏDE'WÏWÏN (GRAND MEDICINE SOCIETY)

(a) *Beliefs and teachings.*—The three principal informants on this subject were Gage'wĭn, Maïŋ'gans, and Na'waji'bigo'kwe, all of whom were members of the Mïde'wïwĭn, and were in good standing at the time of giving their information. The study extended over a period of 14 years and data were obtained on five reservations. Gagewin said, "The Midewiwin is not so much to worship anything as to preserve the knowledge of herbs for use in prolonging life. The principal idea of the Midewiwin is that life is prolonged by right living, and by the use of herbs which were intended for this purpose by the Mide manido." Odinigun, also a member of the society, said, "In the old days the Indians lived out the full length of life." Gagewin did not use the term "Gijiĕ'manido'" ("kind spirit"), which has been used by missionaries to denominate God. None of the informants used the term "Gĭ'tcĭ manido'" ("great spirit"). Two informants said that the highest conception of the Midewiwin was of a deity called Mide manido (Grand Medicine spirit). Subordinate to this were four manido, one at each of the cardinal points, and a multitude of lesser manido who assumed the forms of animals. The manido in the form of a bear and of animals who live in the water were most closely connected with the Midewiwin. Gagewin said that the Mide manido "went around the earth and taught medicine to the Indians. This manido looked like a man and lived on earth about 100 years. He went among the old men, teaching them to use the remedies which are still used by them." It seems probable that he referred to the same tradition as that related by Nawajibigokwe, who said that the East manido came to the earth, assumed the form of an Indian, and taught the people how to treat the sick and to raise the dead.[45a] He also taught the power and the practice of the Midewiwin, together with many of its songs. Gagewin said that "the Midewiwin has always had the idea of a cross connected with it." According to Hoffman "the cross is the sacred post, and the symbol of the fourth degree of the Midewiwin." [45b]

The ethics of the Midewiwin are simple but sound. They teach that rectitude of conduct produces length of life, and that evil inevitably reacts on the offender. Membership in the Midewiwin does not exempt a man from the consequences of his sins. Respect toward the Midewiwin is emphasized, and respect toward women is enjoined upon the men. (See p. 60.) Lying, stealing, and the use of liquor are strictly forbidden. The Mide is not without its means of punishing offenders. Those holding high degrees in the Midewiwin are familiar with the use of subtle poisons which may be used if necessary. Gagewin said that the men were taught to be moderate in speech and quiet in manner, and not hasty in action. This directed the writer's attention to the gentle voices, the patience, and the courtesy of the old people who had been trained in the Midewiwin. The rite of initiation is supposed to inject a certain "spirit power" into the candidate who is expected to "renew his spirit power" by attending the annual ceremony of the society. This is held in the summer, and if there are candidates for initiation another ceremony is held in the fall. The "spirit power" is injected by "shooting"

[45a] Bull. 45, Bur. Amer. Ethn., pp. 21–23.
[45b] Seventh Ann. Rept. Bur. Ethn., p. 155.

it from the medicine bags of the members. On receiving this spirit power the candidate falls to the ground unconscious. The spirit power is conveyed by means of a small white shell, which is said to appear on the surface of a lake when the action of a manido causes the water to seethe. These shells are carried by members of the Midewiwin in the bag with their medicines, and when the candidate regains consciousness one of these shells is said to come from his mouth. The words of the following initiation songs illustrate this action (Bull. 45, Nos. 52, 63, 59) :

> Here it is
> The weasel skin (medicine bag)
> Through it I shoot the white shells.

> It never fails
> The shell goes toward them
> And they fall.

> My Mide.brother is searched
> In his heart is found
> That which I seek to remove
> A white shell.[45b]

Members of the society are also " shot " with the " spirit power " and appear to become unconscious.[45c] It is believed that initiation will benefit or cure the sick.

The organization of the society comprises eight degrees, and members advance from one to the other by receiving certain instructions. A candidate for initiation is given instructions of a moral nature and taught the names and uses of a few simple herbs which he is expected to procure and carry in his Mide bag. In the higher degrees the instructions pertain to the mysteries of the Mide, the properties of rare herbs, and the nature of vegetable poisons. Each degree has its special songs, and a certain sort of Mide bag. (See p. 93.) The instructions given to members of the Midewiwin, as well as the records of the society, were recorded on birch-bark rolls. It seems to have been customary to illustrate the instructions by means of diagrams that were not, like the writings on the rolls, a combination of somewhat familiar figures. An instruction on the Path of Life was illustrated by Figure 11, explained as follows by Maiŋgans (Bull. 45, p. 24) :

" This diagram represents the path of life from youth to old age, the tangent which appears at each angle representing a temptation. There are seven of these temptations.

" The first tangent represents the first temptation which comes to a young man. If he yields to it he will not live long.

[45b] According to Hoffman (Seventh Ann. Rept. Bur. Ethn., p. 191), the shell used in the Midewiwin is Cypraea moneta L.
[45c] In 1925 the writer witnessed this procedure at a similar ceremony among the Menominee.

"The second tangent represents the second temptation, and the penalty for this also is that he will not live long.

"With the third temptation the element of religious responsibility appears, and the man (supposedly a member of the Midewiwin) is asked: 'How did you act when you were initiated into the Midewiwin? Were you respectful to the older members, and did you faithfully fulfill all obligations?'

"The fourth tangent is placed beyond the angle of the line. It represents a temptation coming to a man in middle life.

"With the fifth temptation the man begins to reflect upon his own length of days, and asks himself: 'Have you ever been disrespectful of old age?'

"The sixth temptation returns to the religious idea, and asks whether all religious obligations have been fulfilled.

"The seventh temptation is said to be the hardest of all, and if a man can endure it he will live to the allotted age of man. At this

FIG. 11.—Mide diagram of the Path of Life

time an evil spirit comes to him, and if he has even so much as smiled during a Mide ceremony, he must reckon with it then."

Similar tangents appear on a Mide roll figured by Höffman who states,[46] "The short lines * * * indicating departure from the path of propriety, terminate in rounded spots and signify, literally, "lecture places," because when a Mide feels himself failing in duty or vacillating in faith he must renew professions by giving a feast and lecturing to his conferees, thus regaining his strength to resist evil doing—such as making use of his powers in harming his kinsmen, teaching that which was not given him by Kitci Manido through Mi'nabo'zho, etc. His heart must be cleansed and his tongue guarded."

(b) *Birch-bark rolls.*—The records and teachings of the Midewiwin are inscribed on birch-bark rolls made of heavy bark and either rounded at the ends or strengthened by horizonal strips of wood, one being placed on either side of the bark and securely fastened in place. The characters on the rolls are engraved with a bone stylus and the lines filled with vermilion. The inner side of the roll contains the records or teachings, and the outer side usually

---

[46] Seventh Ann. Rept. Bur. Ethn., p. 176 and Pl. IV.

shows a number of large circles corresponding to the number of "lodges" or degrees of the society represented in the teachings. Thus the circles are in the nature of an index to the roll. The average length of a roll is about 30 inches and the width about 12 inches. The characters inscribed on the roll are crude delineations of animals and human beings together with certain symbols. (See picture writing, pp. 175–176.) The significance of these characters lies in their combination, which produces a sequence of ideas. The devices on Mide rolls are evolved from the teachings of the society, and their significance singly and in combination is taught to initiates.

Concerning these birch-bark rolls Colonel Mallery states: "To persons acquainted with secret societies a good comparison for the [Midewiwin] charts or rolls would be what is called the trestle board of the Masonic order, which is printed and published and publicly exposed without exhibiting any of the secrets of the order, yet is not only significant, but useful to the esoteric in assistance to their memory as to degrees and details of ceremony." [47]

Gagewin said: " The use of the roll is this: If an old man is to present a young man for initiation into the Midewiwin he shows him this roll and explains its teaching to him. Or if a child is to be initiated the old men show this roll to the child's parents and explain its teachings to them."

The roll herein illustrated (pl. 34) was first owned, as far as known, by Black Hawk, who left it to his son Mountain, who in turn transferred it to his son Gagewin, from whom the writer obtained it in 1918. Gagewin was more than 60 years of age at the time and died a year and a half later. This roll represents four degrees of the society; eight degrees are possible, but the teachings would be a repetition of those here indicated. The teaching for each degree is given separately but a man may wait a year or longer before progressing to the next higher degree. The roll (fig. 12) is translated as follows, beginning at the reader's right, with the instructions for entering the first "lodge" or degree:

In taking this degree the candidate provided one dog, which was killed and laid at the entrance of the lodge. He was obliged to step over this dog in entering. (B) represents the bear tracks leading up to the door of the lodge. It was said that the bear preceded the candidate for initiation throughout the ceremony.[48] (C) are the guards at either side of the door.[49] (D) is the old man who acts as leader of

---

[47] Col. Garrick Mallery, U. S. Army, in a paper entitled " Recently Discovered Algonkian Pictographs," read before the American Association for the Advancement of Science, at Cleveland, 1888. (See Hoffman, p. 287.)

[48] A Mide song, said to be one of the oldest, contained the words, " We are following the bear path, my Mide brother." (Bull. 45, Song No. 89.)

[49] The belief of the Mide is that a guard is placed wherever there is danger to life, and that a person who heeds the advice of these guards will live to old age.

the ceremony. (*E*) is the sacred stone, and (*F*) is the sacred pole.

It is believed there are "evil spirits" outside the lodge who try to influence the candidate. They are represented by men (*G*). Before the candidate enters the lodge he is addressed by one of these men who urges him not to enter. During the ceremony these men try to distract his attention and divert his mind. The doorkeeper does not allow them to enter the lodge. It is believed that the life of the candidate will be shortened if he is diverted by these men or shows any discouragement because of their taunts. Within the lodge are four men (*A*) who constantly advise him as to his conduct in the lodge, telling him to look at the sacred pole and to pay no attention to those who try to distract him. They also instruct him to lead a quiet, moral life and to speak gently. These men "throw the shell" into the candidate during his initiation.

A candidate for the second degree must provide two dogs, which are killed and placed at the entrance. (*H*) represents two water spirits and (*I*) two beavers which step aside and allow the candidate to pass through the door which they g u a r d

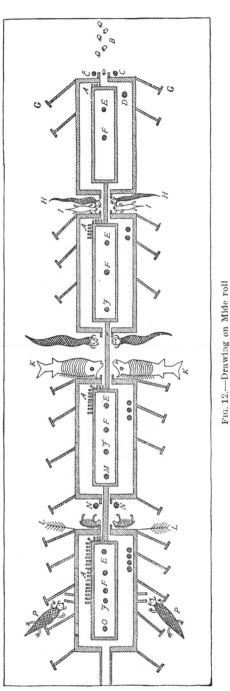

Fig. 12.—Drawing on Mide roll

against others. *F* and *E* represent the sacred stone and the sacred pole as in the first degree, and there are two old men instead of one at

(D). (J) represents a second sacred pole at the top of which is a wooden representation of a large bird said to be a kind of hawk. The men stationed at (A) are more in number than in the former degree, and their counsel relates to success and long life. The efforts to distract the man's attention are more than in the former degree.

Proceeding to the third degree, the principal guard at the door is (K), a very influential water spirit, a large, strong fish. There are three poles in this lodge, and the new one has a wooden representation of an owl at the top (M). (A) and (G) are as before, and there are three old men stationed at (D). The candidate is expected to provide three dogs for this degree.

For the fourth lodge the candidate provides four dogs, and there are four old men and four poles, the new pole having a crossbar. At the entrance are two more poles, marked (L). These have no branches, though such would appear to be the case from the drawing. At (N) are "flattened poles," seeming to be thicker in one dimension than the other. The fourth lodge has four entrances, and the number of temptations or distracting elements is greatly increased. The fourth pole is marked (O). (P) represents the guards at the fourth entrance.

(c) *Mide lodge.*—In 1921 the writer visited a typical Mide lodge on the Lac Court Oreilles Reservation in Washington. The rites of the Midewiwin had been celebrated in this lodge by about 200 Chippewa a few weeks previously. Near the lodge were to be seen the frames of the sweat lodge and the wigwams occupied by those who attended the ceremony from a distance. The Mide lodge (pl. 35, a, b) was constructed of white birch saplings thrust firmly into the ground and interlaced at the top. Pine boughs about 3 feet high were placed around the edge of the lodge with the tops placed downward. This lodge was about 200 feet long, 13 feet wide, and 7 feet high, with openings approximately north and south at the ends of the structure.

Three poles had been set in the lodge, but the middle pole had been (according to an informant) taken away by a person initiated at the last ceremony. One pole was placed about 33 feet from the south entrance, another 22 feet from the north entrance, and the other was midway the length of the lodge. Between the south entrance and the first pole were six stones, about equally distant from each other. Between the first pole and the middle of the lodge (the location of the second pole), were two stones, about 3 feet from each other, between this and the third pole were two stones, and between that pole and the south entrance were four stones. The remains of a fire could be seen near each entrance. No covering is placed over the lodge unless the weather be rainy. The movements of persons

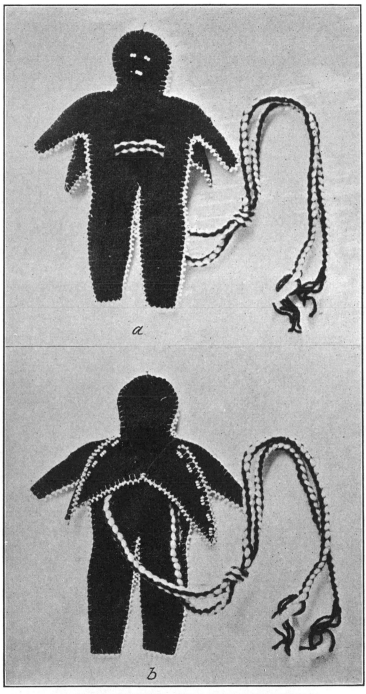

a

b

"FLYING MAN," DREAM REPRESENTATION

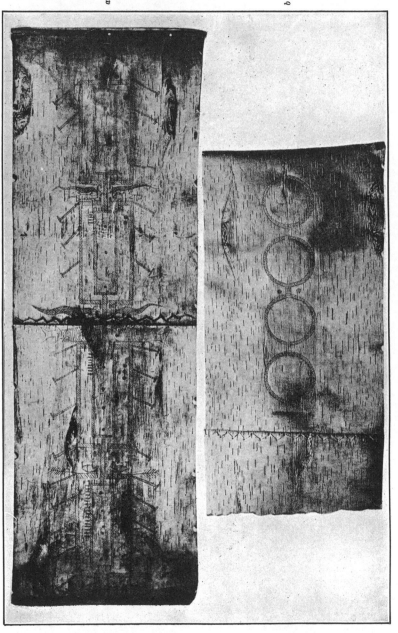

MIDE ROLL. *a*, INSIDE; *b*, PORTION OF OUTSIDE

a

b

FRAME OF MIDE LODGE, LAC COURT OREILLES RESERVATION, WIS.

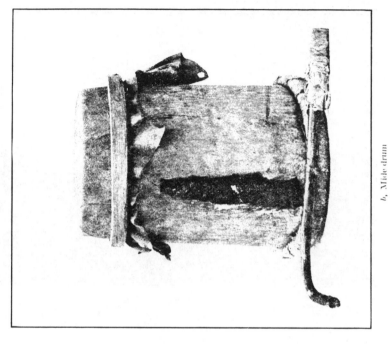

b, Midē drum

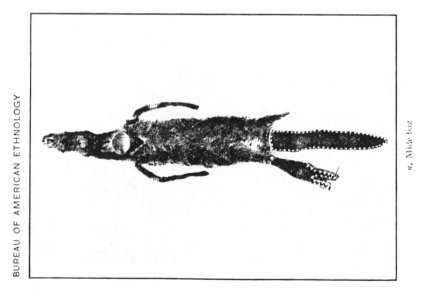

a, Midē bag

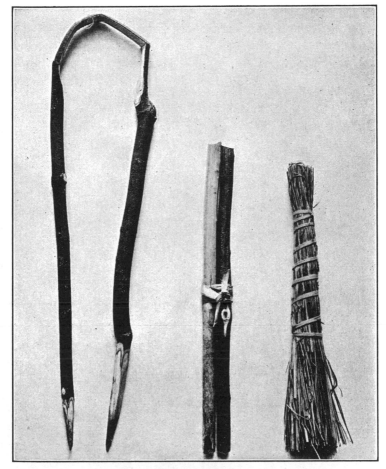

a, Implements

b, Stones used in Mide sweat lodge

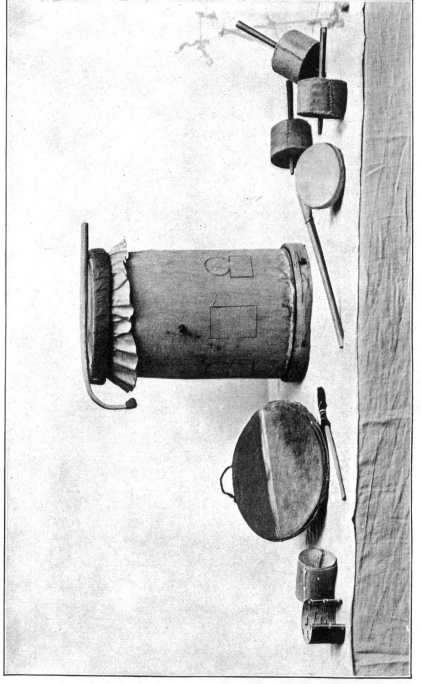

MUSICAL INSTRUMENTS

(Reprint from Bull. 45, Bur. Amer. Ethn.)

in the lodge are visible to outsiders but the significance of these movements are known only to those initiated in the mysteries of the society.

(*d*) *Face painting.*—According to Hoffman (op. cit., pp. 182, 183, and Pl. VII), each of the four first degrees of the Midewiwin had its special form of face painting, the first and second degrees being designated by one and two red stripes across the face, the third degree having the upper half of the face green and the lower half red, and the fourth degree by painting the left half of the face green with red spots and wearing eagle feathers painted red.

(*e*) *Mide bags.*—Each member of the society possessed a bag made of the skin of a bird or animal. This bag was one of his most valued possessions and usually was buried with him. In this bag were carried the medicinal herbs and charms which the person had been taught to use, and also a few of the *migis*, or white shells, which were "shot into the candidate" and into members of the society at a ceremony of initiation. Each degree in the society had its special sort of bag, which thus served as a distinctive badge showing the degree attained by its owner. The custom of carrying these bags and the manner of their use was derived from a tradition connected with the origin of the society. This tradition relates that the four Mide manido with the colors of the dawn painted on their foreheads came out of the eastern sky, each carrying a live otter in his hand. They used these otters as the Mide bags are now used in ceremonies of the society, and by this means they restored to life a young man who had been dead eight days. They instructed the Indians to continue this custom. It is interesting to note that in the Mide songs the bags are sometimes represented as speaking. Thus a song for initiation into the first degree contained the words, "Weasel, thou art calling me," [50] this being said to refer to the weasel-skin bag carried by a member of that degree. Another initiation song contains the words, "There comes a sound from my medicine bag," [51] while in another song an owl-skin medicine bag is represented as saying, "I am the one who is trying to fly. He is making it (the medicine)." [52]

The bags used in the Mide included those made of weasel skin, mink skin, the hide of a wildcat paw (up to the elbow), the paw of a bear, and the skin of a rattlesnake. A bear paw Mide bag is shown in Plate 49, *b*. A rattlesnake bag, seen at Leech Lake in 1910, was made of the skin of a rattlesnake mounted on red flannel. It was worn over the shoulder, the body of the snake hanging down the owner's back and the head projecting over the shoulder in such a manner that he could "shoot" with it during the initiation. A mink-skin bag is shown in Plate 36, *a*. This was given to a child on her

---

[50] Bull. 45, Song No. 60.   [51] Bull. 45, Song No. 13.   [52] Bull. 45, Song. No. 81.

initiation into the Midewiwin and carried by her during her entire life. She gave it to her daughter, who was about 45 years of age when transferring it to the writer. It was said to have been old when given to the child. When in use it was filled with packets of medicine. One packet remains in the skull of the animal. A little stone bowl is with the bag, and it was said that the former owner was accustomed to put food in this dish, it being her belief that if she kept this little bowl filled with food when she made requests of the bag she would never lack for anything. The placing of a dish in a Mide bag is in accordance with instructions given by Winabojo.

(*f*) *Sweat lodge.*—Before a meeting of the Midewiwin it was customary for the old men to go into the sweat lodge, this being considered an important part of the ceremony. The implements comprised four stones, a basin or pail of water, a bunch of grass used in sprinkling the water on the stones, a bent stick used in lifting the principal stone, two sticks used in adjusting the principal stone and called the " arms of the stone," and used also in " drumming " on the stones during the songs. (Pl. 37, *a.*) Four stones which have been used in a sweat lodge (pl. 37, *b*) were placed in proper position by Maïŋgans. The three smaller stones were flat on some surfaces so as to support the larger stone, which was as nearly spherical as could be procured. This stone was regarded as their messenger to the Mide manido.

Four men usually went into the sweat lodge at a time, and the lodge was of the smallest dimensions possible for their use. The lodge consisted of a framework of bent poles closely covered with blankets. No air was allowed to enter, and it was said that men sometimes were almost suffocated and fell asleep in the lodge. Maïŋgans indicated the probable size of the lodge, and it was found to be about 41 inches in diameter. A sweat lodge of this size which had recently been in use was seen by the writer at Lac Court Oreilles, Wis.

The stones were heated in a fire outside the lodge. The three smaller stones were first heated and placed in position in the middle of the lodge. The men then entered the lodge. The larger stone was heated " as nearly red-hot as possible " and brought in. As it was brought in one of the men said, " They are bringing the messenger; be careful he does not fall." The stone was placed in position with great care, but another man usually took the " arms of the stone " and adjusted it to a better position. A leader of the Mide might be invited to the sweat lodge, and if so, the two sticks, water, and bunch of grass would be put before him and he would speak. " He smoked and then thought a while." When he was ready he dipped the bunch of grass in the water and sprinkled it on the upper stone, saying with the action, " We-e-e-e, ho-ho-ho." He did this three times, the other men responding, " Ho-ho-ho." What was said or sung was not a ritual, but with the first sprinkling of the water the man usually said, "Now this messenger is about to depart to deliver our message to Mide Manido." The ascending steam was regarded as an evidence of response on the part of the stone. When the man sprinkled the water for the third time he usually said, "Well, he has given our message to Mide Manido, which is a prayer that he will help us in our undertaking." While the stone was steaming, he "talked and sang," sometimes extending his hand over the stone, moving it slowly in a circle. While he sang some one usually pounded softly on one of the lower stones, using for the purpose one of the blunt sticks which had been used in adjusting the larger stone. The men usually sat with their eyes closed. When the first man had finished all he wished to say he pushed the basin of water to the man next him. This man smoked for a while, then he might say, "I desire this messenger to say to Mide Manido that we desire health and long life." He sprinkled the water three times with the same ejaculations as the first man, the others responding as before, "Ho-ho-ho." When this had been done by all the men in the lodge, the cover was removed from the entrance. There was no subsequent "rubbing" of their bodies, as was done if the sweating were for medicinal purposes. It was said that the men "wiped their faces and soon asked for a little water to drink." The man who first asked for water poured a little on the larger stone before drinking any. The stones were placed at the side of the lodge for safe-keeping.

(g) *Songs.*—This subject has already received extended consideration. (Bull. 45, pp. 14–118.) In no class of Indian songs observed by the writer are the words so forced into conformity with the melody as in the Mide songs. This is accomplished by the addition of meaningless syllables, either between words or parts of words. The words may even be slightly changed but the idea of the song remains the same. Each degree of the society has its own songs, which are used at initiations into that degree. The Mide songs are recorded in mnemonics on strips of birch bark, the figures or characters being described in the section on picture writing. These establish the identity of a song among widely separated members of the tribe, a phase which was tested on three reservations. Certain songs are grouped in series of 8 or 10, the members of the society dancing during the last half of the series. In addition to the ceremonial songs there are songs connected with the use of medicines. Two small birch-bark scrolls containing mnemonics of songs are shown in Plate 38.

(h) *Musical instruments.*—Drum: The drum used in the ceremonies of the Midewiwin and by members of the society when singing its songs in private is called a mĭtĭg'wakĭk, meaning "wooden kettle." It is commonly known as a "water drum" for a reason which will be noted. The drum is made by hollowing out a basswood log, about 16 inches long, the wood being charred and scraped until a cylinder is formed. A thin wooden disk is fitted in the lower end and a small hole is drilled part way up one side. A wooden plug is fitted in this hole. The head of the drum is of heavy tanned deer-skin, about 18 inches in diameter. Water to the depth of a few inches is poured into this receptacle when the drum is to be used, the head is wet, wrung out, laid over the top, and stretched by pressing down a hoop made of a willow sapling which frequently is wound with cloth. The hole and plug make it possible to empty the water without removing the top of the drum. If the head becomes too dry it may be moistened by "splashing" the water in the drum, or by dipping the hand in water and passing it over the surface of the deer hide. If too damp it may be held toward the fire or placed in the sun for a short time, the warmth tightening the deer hide. The water in the drum causes the sound to be heard a long distance while it is not so loud near at hand. This type of drum is decorated with colored bands indicating the degree held in the Midewiwin by its owner. The same decoration appears on the pole in the Mide lodge, indicating the degree into which a candidate is to be initiated.

Two of these drums have been in the writer's possession. The first came from Wabaciŋg and its sound had been heard at Red Lake Agency, a distance of 10 miles across the water. It was decorated with a blue band at the base, four heads representing the four Mide manido, and an oblong outline said to represent a bag containing yarrow, which signifies life. The heads were outlined in red and the bag in blue. This drum was 16½ inches high, 10 inches in diameter at the base, and 8½ inches in diameter at the top. (Pl. 38.) The second specimen was similar in size and construction and was decorated only with blue bands. This, with the loon drumming stick, was obtained from Gagewin. (Pl. 36, b.)

Drumming stick: It is said that a Mide drum stick is more valuable than the drum, and frequently is older. Some of the drumming sticks represent the owl, but that representing the loon is regarded more highly. The loon was the first bird selected to form part of the Mide beliefs, and the end of the stick which strikes the head of the drum is carved to represent the head and eyes of the loon. Gagewin said, "The Mide stretch their hands toward the western ocean, where the loon rises from the water and gives a signal that he responds to their call." A new drumming stick with curved end, covered by a cushion of deer hide, was included with the first Mide drum obtained by the writer. It appears probable that the original drumming stick was retained by the owner of the drum. (See pl. 38.)

Rattle: Four Mide rattles were obtained with the first-mentioned drum and were said to constitute a set. These differ in pitch according to their size and the quantity of pebbles or shot they contain.[53] Three consist of small wooden cylinders, each with a sewn cover of hide, containing small stones or shot and pierced by a stick which forms the handle. These rattles are used also in the "shooting of life power" during a ceremony of the Mide. The fourth rattle is made on a frame of bent wood. The end of the wood is curved to form a hoop which is covered with rawhide and contains small shot or stones. (Pl. 38.) These rattles are not decorated. A similar rattle made of wood and sewed with roots was obtained a few years later. The flat, thin rattle (pl. 38) is a "doctor's rattle" and belonged to Odinigun. He used it as a drum when recording his healing songs.

STORIES AND LEGENDS

Apart from the little stories told for the amusement of children, the stories or legends of the Chippewa may be divided into three classes: (1) Stories concerning the "first earth and its inhabitants," (2) stories concerning the adventures and doings of Wi'nabo'jo, and (3) the a'dizo'ke, or "fairy stories," which were told solely for amusement, and were based partly upon material obtained from the white men, adapted to please the native taste and be understood by the Indians. Such stories were learned from traders and missionaries, one informant saying that the wives of missionaries often told these stories to the Indian children.

The stories of the first earth include the story of the primal ocean and the "creation of the world" from a bit of earth which was brought from beneath the water in the paw of a small animal. Winabojo is the same personage as Nanabush and Nanabojo, being known by several unrelated names among Algonquian tribes. Stories concerning him are told and retold by the old people around the winter fire, and as many of them are amusing there has arisen an impression that Winabojo was a fantastic deity. This, however, is a popular misunderstanding, as Winabojo in the mind of the old Indian was the master of life—the source and impersonation of the lives of all sentient things, human, faunal, and floral. He endowed these with life and taught each its peculiar ruse for deceiving its enemies and prolonging its life. His "tricks" were chiefly exhibitions of his ability to outwit the enemies of life. He was regarded as the master of ruses, but he also possessed great wisdom in the prolonging of life. It was he who gave the Indians their best remedies for treating the sick and who taught the animals the varied forms of protective disguise by which their lives can be extended. His own inherent life

---

[53] The old Chippewa used several hand drums together, selecting those which "chorded."

was so strong that when he apparently had been put to death he reappeared in the same or a different form.

Concerning this character, J. N. B. Hewitt states: "Nanabozho is apparently the impersonation of life, the active quickening power of life—of life manifested and embodied in the myriad forms of sentient and physical nature * * *. He impersonates life in an unlimited series of diverse personalities which represent various phases and conditions of life, and the histories of the life and acts of these separate individualities form an entire cycle of traditions and myths which, when compared one with another, are sometimes apparently contradictory and incongruous, relating, as these stories do, to the unrelated objects and subjects in nature. The conception named Nanabozho exercises the diverse functions of many persons, and he likewise suffers their pains and needs. He is this life struggling with the many forms of want, misfortune, and death that come to the bodies and beings of nature."[54]

The stories concerning the first earth and Winabojo herewith presented were related by Odinigun (pl. 21):

(a) *Story of the first earth.*—The first earth was called Ca'ca. It was in this part of the country. The people who lived there were not wise. They had no clothing, but they sat around and did nothing. Then the spirit of the creator sent a man to teach them. This man was called ockabe'wĭs (messenger). Some of those early people lived in the south where they did not need any clothing. But the people around here were cold and began to worry about what they should do. The ockabewis saw the southern people naked and homeless and left them to themselves. He came farther north where the people were suffering and in need of his assistance. He said, "Why are you sitting here with no clothing on?" They replied, "Because we do not know what to do." The first thing he taught them was how to make a fire by means of a bow and stick and a bit of decayed wood. (This is the method described on p. 142.) Then he taught them how to cook meat by the fire. They had no axes, but he took a pole and burned it in two over the fire. He taught them to boil meat in fresh birch bark. It was a long time before they had things as he wanted them, but after a while they were made comfortable by his help. They had no minds or ideas of their own, only to do as the ockabewis told them to do. This was long before Winabojo.

The ockabewis told them that they must fast and find out things by dreams and that if they paid attention to these dreams they would learn how to heal the sick. The people listened and fasted and found in dreams how to teach their children and do everything. The young men were taught that they must regulate their lives by dreams, they must live moral lives, be industrious, and be moderate in the use of tobacco when it should be given to them. They were especially taught that their minds would not be clear if they ate and drank too much. Tobacco and corn were given them, but it was the ockabewis who taught them how to use them. After a while Winabojo was born, but he had to do as the natives did.

---

[54] "Nanabozho," Handbook of American Indians, Bull. 30, Bur. Amer. Ethn., pt. 2, p. 19.

(b) *Winabojo and the medicine man.*[55]—Winabojo lived after the earliest Indians. He was married, a fact which is not generally stated. He took an Indian wife and had three children, one a baby girl. His wife's parents lived with them and the family lived a long time in the Indian village.

There was an old custom that when two bands of Chippewa played a certain game together each band put up a person for a wager, this person being adopted by the winning band. Once Winabojo's band lost in such a game and refused to give up the wager. One morning Winabojo got up early and went into the woods. He saw a great many men with clubs and asked what they were doing. They replied, "We are going to get the boy that your people wagered in the game; you had better join us or you will be killed." Winabojo decided to do this in order to save his family. When they attacked the village he was so eager that he went right to his own lodge and began to kill his family. He killed the old people and the two boys and was about to kill the baby girl when some one stopped him. Then he was like some one waking from a dream and felt very sorry for what he had done. He took the baby and started to carry it to his grandmother. It was a long way but he reached there at last. The baby was crying, but he did not tell his grandmother what was the matter.

She said, "Why did you bring the baby here? Is its mother coming? I can not quiet this baby."

Winabojo said, "I made a terrible blunder. I joined an attacking party and killed all my family except this baby."

His grandmother said, "It is no use for us to stay here. The people will come and kill us. They will know that you joined an attacking party."

This was the worst thing that Winabojo ever did, and he took his final departure from the earth at this time.

He got some pods from the trees. They were shaped like little balls and he made them grow big. Then he put the baby in one and his grandmother in the other. He stood on the shore and tied them tight, then he put them in the water and asked the water to carry them all away. So they floated off and went clear across a great water toward the setting sun. There is another earth beyond this earth and Winabojo lives there now with his grandmother.

When the traders and the white people came among the Chippewa their manner of life changed, but they remembered Winabojo. Ten men decided to go and talk with Winabojo.[55a] They fasted and took a long time to prepare for the journey. They made a strong canoe and skirted along the edge of the great lake, camping at night. One man had a dream telling where Winabojo was living, and after they had traveled a long time they saw an island. They said, "That must be the place where he lives." They reached the island and went ashore. It was the home of Winabojo. They saw footprints on the shore and a trail leading inland. The men followed the trail and came to a large, firm lodge. They did not dare go near the lodge, but they stood around where they could see it.

---

[55] Other stories concerning Winabojo were related by Mrs. Razer. A collection of stories regarding this hero may be found in Jones's Ojibwa Texts (ed. Truman Michelson), Vol. VII, Pt. II, Publications of the American Ethnological Society. The works of Schoolcraft, Radin, De Jong, Skinner, and George E. Laidlaw should be mentioned in this connection.

[55a] See another form of this story in "Seneca Fiction, Legends, and Myths," Thirty-second Ann. Rept. Bur. Amer. Ethn., pp. 607–632.

Finally one man heard a voice say, " Well, well, my uncle; come in if you want to see me. Don't stand out there." (This was the voice of Winabojo.)

The man who heard the voice went and told the rest of the party. Each had a present for Winabojo. They went into the lodge and had the presents on their backs and in their arms and hands. Winabojo shook hands with them and they all sat down. There was absolute silence.

Beside the door was a stump overgrown with moss. After a while a voice came from this stump saying, " Why don't you speak to your uncle? When we were on earth we talked to our relations." (This was the voice of Winabojo's grandmother.)

Winabojo replied, " I am just thinking what to say. I will talk to our relations. If we are to follow the custom of the place they came from, we must give them food. They must be hungry."

In stories about Winabojo when he was on earth it is always said that he carried his lunch in a bag on his back. This bag still stood there, and in it were bones of bear, deer, and other animals. He had eaten the meat and put the bones back in the bag.

Winabojo got up on his knees, put his hand in the bag, and happened to take out the bone of a bear's foreleg. He threw it in front of them, and it became a bear. It was almost dead, and he told them to kill it and take it to their camp, saying they would find a big kettle there. The men killed the bear and dragged it to their camp. They cooked enough for one meal. It was greasy and there was a great deal of nice broth. When the meat was ready two men took the kettle on a stick and set it before Winabojo.

Winabojo lived with his grandmother. His daughter had grown up and lived in another lodge. He told his daughter to bring wooden dishes and spoons. She came bringing the dishes and spoons. She was very beautiful and wore a red sash. The men had their feast and took the kettle back to the camp. They had come to ask favors, but they decided to wait until the next day.

They went to Winabojo on the following day, and he said, " You have come to ask favors. I will do what I can for you."

One man said, " I have come to ask you to give me a life with no end." Winabojo twisted him around and threw him into a corner, and he turned into a black stone. Winabojo said, " You asked for a long life. You will last as long as the world stands."

Another man gave Winabojo a present and said, " I have come to ask for unfailing success and that I may never lack for anything." Winabojo turned him into a fox, saying, " Now you will always be cunning and successful."

The others saw what was happening to these men and they became frightened. They decided to ask for one thing together, so they asked that they might have healing power in their medicine.

Winabojo put some medicine in a little leather bag and gave it to each man. He said the others had asked so much that they had failed, but that he had given these eight men the real success. He said, " I have given you this medicine. Use it sparingly. When it is gone your power will also be gone." Then he said : " Ten men came to see me. Two made bad requests, and will never get home. The medicine I have given you will not last forever, but I will give my daughter to you. Do not approach her until you get home, then one of you may take her for his wife. She is to be the means of keeping up the power of medicine among men."

They started the next day, and Winabojo said, " I want my daughter to go back, for she is human. Protect her until you get home, then select one of your number to marry her, otherwise she will return here and you will lose the power of your medicine."

So they started; she sat in the middle of the canoe. They went across to the mainland and made a camp for the night. She cooked for them and had her camp at some distance from the rest of the party. It was necessary to camp three nights. All went well until the last night, when the men started a discussion as to which should be her husband. One said: "I suppose she knows which she wants. I will go quietly and ask her." All were watching as this man went and sat down a little distance from the girl's camp. He asked which one of them she would select for her husband if she had her choice. There was no reply. He came back and reported to the others. Then another man said he would go and would say a little more than the first had said. He thought he would say that she could have her choice. So he went toward the girl's camp, but she was gone. They had lost her.

The men felt very, very badly. They realized that a wrong had been done to the world, as her medicine would have been a benefit to the whole race.

(c) *Winabojo's camping around.*—There was once an old man who had eight sons. They lived quietly in the deep woods and were very industrious. The old man kept the camp and his sons went hunting to secure food for them. One day a little boy came to the camp. He was a short, fat boy and was wandering in the woods. They took care of him and later he repaid them by guiding them and making them strong.

After a long time a girl came to the camp. The old man was alone. He asked the girl where she came from and she said that her parents had been killed by an enemy and that she was wandering around.

The old man said, "Come in, live here, and help me take care of the place." She proved to be a woman controlled by an evil spirit, but they got along.

At length one son said to another, "Do you notice that she never eats? She cooks the food for us but refuses to eat any herself. We had better ask our father about her." The other son said that he also noticed it.

A third son said that he would pretend to be sick and would see if he could find out anything. He lay down in another part of the wigwam and pretended to be very sick indeed. His father went out and dug roots, but the medicine did him no good. Then his father went out and dug more roots, but still the son was very sick. The woman also went in and out of the wigwam and the boy noticed that she often brought in a bundle, hiding it behind her belongings. When she was outside the boy jumped up, opened the bundle, and found a human arm. Then he lay down as before.

That night he told his father and brothers when the woman was outside and they said, "We must leave here." The next evening when one of the boys came home he said, "I have killed a deer." According to the custom she went to get the deer, but the boy had hung it so high that it took her a long time to get it.

While she was away the father said, "An evil spirit is here. We must get away. Call on your dreams to help us, for she will follow us. You are young and can get away. I am old and she will probably overtake me. She probably knows by this time that we are going away." So they started in the night. They had the old man go ahead and did not go any faster than he could travel.

As they were going along they heard a voice say, "No matter how fast or how far you go, I will follow and overtake you. Even if you go to the ends of the earth you can not get away from me."

The old man said, "Her voice is getting nearer. Do something; have dreams given you anything that will help us?"

52738°—29——8

Finally the fat boy said, "I dreamed something that will help us. We will go to a certain river. She can not cross that, and if we can get across she can not reach us. This was my dream." This boy was a "wonder child." He said, "After we cross the river I will make a bog on her side of the river, and I will put prickles in her way before she gets to the bog." The man and the boys crossed the river, but soon they saw the woman coming through the bog.

The old man said, "Call on your dreams.[55b] Have you nothing that will help us?" They answered, "We have nothing."

The old man said, "In my youth I dreamed of a river with a waterfall. Below the waterfall there were rapids, and on a rock sat two pelicans. They said they would always help me. I am calling on them to help us."

The man and his sons came to the waterfall and the rapids, then to the smooth water below the rapids. There they saw a rock with two pelicans sitting on it. They could hear the woman approaching and saying that she would get them. The old man wished that the river would be very wide between them, and it was so. The woman raved and called on the pelicans to help her. One pelican said he would take her across on his back. They got half way across and she beat him, saying, "Go faster, go faster." This made the pelican very angry. He called on the other pelican and they threw her into the water. She was drowned and floated away. She went over a waterfall and her body went into a whirlpool below the fall.

So the men were saved. The woman had called upon Winabojo, who heard her and hastened to see what was the matter. He was staying with his grandmother at the time. Winabojo followed the course of the river on the same side that the woman had traveled. The river was so mighty and terrible that even Winabojo could not cross it. As he stood on the shore he saw a little fish and said, "Little brother, can't you get me across this swift river?"

The fish said, "I am too small."

Winabojo said, "I will make you big." So he made the fish big and the fish took him across. In return for this he decorated the fish with spots and made his belly white. (This was a pickerel.) The fish told him that the woman's body was in a whirlpool below the falls, so Winabojo went there, guided by the fish. He saw the woman and tried to get her, but it was of no use. He got a long pole and finally dislodged the body and pulled it to the edge of the water. He snatched it and drew it ashore.

Then he began to talk to her as if she were alive and he had saved her. He said, "What shall we do?" And he answered for her, "Well, you had better think of something for us to do." He said, "If you are willing, I will put up a wigwam and hunt and get food for you." He answered for her, "Do whatever you think best."

He made lots of basswood-bark twine and carried her in a pack on his back. He would carry her until he was tired, then he would put her down, go on, and make a wigwam. He saw that she was in a trance and hoped that she would revive. He finished the lodge, went hunting, and brought food to her, as he would to a living person. So he camped in one place after another. When he went hunting he hid her in case anyone came to the camp. He was very successful with his hunting and lived in this way for a long time. When he had cooked the food he shook her, set her up, and tried to feed her; but it was of no use. He could get no sign of life.

[55b] Cf. section on dreams, p. 81.

Winabojo made three camps, carrying the woman's body from one camp to another on his back. Then he got tired of it and said, "If she is going to die she might as well die now." So he cut off her head and left her there.

This story is called "Winabojo's camping around." [56]

(d) *Winabojo's diving for a wager.*—Winabojo was always wandering around through the woods. He walked many miles, following streams and gathering berries. Once as he was going along he saw a lot of loons at the other end of a lake. They had a wager as to which could start at the end of the lake, dive, swim the farthest, and come back again. They were playing in a wide, open space of water, but below this space the water was rapid and filled with rocks.

When Winabojo appeared suddenly to the loons they were frightened and started to fly away, but Winabojo said, "Don't go. We are all friends." He called them, and they came to him in flocks. He said, "We will have fun. I will dive, too. Let us put up a wager and see who can stay longest under the water. Your play is too easy for me. Let us make the space longer; go down with the current and come back again." The loons had put a stake under the water. The plan was that when a loon reached this stake he should move it farther down the stream, the one who followed him did the same, each proving that he could swim farther by moving the stake. Winabojo was the last to start, and the loons were all under the water when he was ready to dive. The loons swam with their eyes open, but Winabojo told the Indians that they must always close their eyes when they went into the water. Winabojo said, "Now I am ready," filled his lungs, threw himself into the water, and, as he supposed, swam toward the stake, but his eyes being closed, he lost the direction. Instead of swimming toward the stake he hit a great rock. It stunned him and cut a gash in his forehead.[57] The loons saw him strike his head and float away. They said, "Winabojo can not be killed. He will come to life and do us some harm. He is so foolish that he will probably blame us."

Winabojo drifted down the stream until he came to some bushes. Then he revived and felt of his forehead. He took some clay and put it on his forehead to stop the bleeding. One of his teeth was gone. He stayed there until he felt better. After a while he got up and said he would go to his grandmother who could cure him. His grandmother scolded him well for his heedlessness but she healed him with an herb.

This story is called "Winabojo diving for a wager."

The stories of the classes previously described were tribal traditions, handed down for many generations, and the telling of them was a rather dignified matter, a request being accompanied by a gift and the story telling preceded by a feast. In the adizoke, however, the story teller was given scope for his imagination. The examples here presented will be recognized as containing adaptations of Hans Anderson's Fairy Tales and of Uncle Tom's Cabin, together with other fanciful ideas entirely foreign to Indian life. Such stories would naturally be listened to attentively and greatly enjoyed by the old-time Indians.

---

[56] It is a custom of the Indians to withhold the title of a story until its conclusion. A similar custom in regard to the name of the principal character is noted in connection with the narrative of Nawajibigokwe on page 183.

[57] The narrator added, " I suppose, wherever he is, he carries that scar."

The following story was told the writer one cold winter night by Little Wolf, a man proficient in story telling. This narration was made possible by the courtesy of Mrs. Charles Mee, who acted as interpreter, and who asked the man to come to her home for the night. The entire story comprised about 1,600 words and was told without hesitation. It was followed by a shorter story, the entire story telling continuing until after midnight. A portion of the story is given in the words of the interpreter, the remainder being summarized:

(e) *Adizoke* (*fairy story*).—The story begins. It is in a large city. There were two great men in this town and they built a stone house. After this big house was done there was a son born. This child was raised in a tunnel or cave under the house. The great man, every night and morning, went to the cave and kissed his son. The child never saw daylight except through a small window. He was never outside. When he was large enough they brought him a small black-and-tan dog. When the boy was 4 years old he played all the time and his only companion was this dog. At 6 years old he had never been outside. When he was 9 years old, just outside the window a friend of his father's began to build a boat. It was a large boat. On the boy's tenth birthday the boat had been finished and they built a platform out to the boat. This boat was made of gold and silver and inside it there were stores of all kinds. The two men told all the people in the city that the boy was to see daylight for the first time. It is impossible to describe the people who thronged both sides of the platform to see him. They had never seen such a great man's child. Rows of soldiers guarded, and thousands came to see.

The day had come. He was to be taken out at 9 in the morning. They had many cannons ready and the doors were thrown open. On each side were his parents, each holding one of his arms. As soon as he put one foot out a cannon was fired. At every step a cannon was fired. It took their breath away to see this wonderful child. He got into the boat. The little dog was with him. The boat started and he did not know in what direction it was going. The boy and his dog were running from door to door, playing, in the boat. The boy went to turn around and saw his shadow on the wall. He could see it go before him. He wished his boat to travel on the earth, and when he found it was running along the earth he looked ahead and saw a lake. He said, " I wish my boat to go safely to the lake." He kept on playing. He looked out and saw his shadow still running along beside him and he talked to his shadow. He saw something shining in the water ahead. The boy spoke to the boat again. " Go ahead. If that shining thing is a house, you must stop in front of it." The boat suddenly shook. The boat went in front of the house. The boy saw a door and rapped on it. The door opened and a man was there who was very glad to see him and said he was alone in the house as the boy was in the boat. The boy said, " Come in my boat and you shall be part owner." So the man locked the door and got on the boat with his new friend. Now there were three on the boat. The boat started and they began to play around again. The boy was so happy, playing from one corner of the boat to another. Suddenly the boy stopped, looked out, and noticed how fast they ran in the water. He said, " My boat, go back as you came." Then he went on playing. He looked out and the boat was on dry land. They played some more, then they looked out and saw some one sitting on the land.

The boy said to his friend, "Who is that?" The man said, "It is some one sitting there." The boy said to the boat, "You must go where those people are and stop near them." He forgot that he had told the boat to stop and did not notice until the boat shook and stopped. He opened the door. The dog jumped out before him. Both started to run toward the figures. The man went, too. They found some men sitting in a circle. They sat close together. Each man sat cross-legged with his left hand on his knee and an awl in his right hand which he held up as high as his head. All were looking at something on the ground. The boy said, "My friends, what are you doing with those awls?" The boy looked on the ground and it was all glistening with beautiful rings. They said it was a game they were playing. They threw the awls to see which would hit the center of a ring. The boy said, "My friends, can I buy those rings? I will give the contents of my boat for them." They said, "Is that true?" "Yes; give me the rings and I will give you what is in my boat."

He took a ring and put it on his finger. Then the men went and began to unload the boat. The boy gave them all the money in the boat. The boat turned around and started home with the boy and his party in it.

The boy's father was watching for him in the city. They were watching for him with spyglasses. One day when they were looking they saw a speck like a mosquito. It was the boy in the boat. The boat did not move as when it started. The boy's father said, "Our son's boat looks *light* in the distance." Then they began to fire cannons. The boy was listening and heard the cannons. Then they reached his father's city. When they reached the landing his father asked, "Where are the goods?" "I bought this ring." His father said, "All right." The boy said, "I have a friend with me." "All right, if you have a new friend." The boy went right back to the cave, and every step he took they fired off a cannon, the same as when he came out for the first time.

The second section of the story is concerning a second trip of the boat, in which the boy was accompanied by his dog and the man. They heard a noise, the boat went toward it, and they saw a negro "whipping a woman with a great pine tree." When this woman looked at the boy he saw that she had a beautiful face.

The negro stood with uplifted whip. At some time there had been a war with colored people, and this beautiful girl was an officer's daughter and was captured, and the negroes treated her in this way.

The boy bought the woman with the contents of his boat and returned as from the first trip, being greeted in the same manner. The party all lived together in the cave. The girl was lonely, and in reply to questions by the boy's father she said that her father was a great officer and that he lived across the ocean. The narrator continued: "The man said, 'My son, take her across the ocean to find her friends. To-morrow you will start in a large boat like a war vessel with two flags and two cannons. You will take 10,000 men with you and 8 officers and 500 sailors who know all about the ship, in case you get into war.' The boy was delighted. It did not take long to make this great boat. The little boy's room was on one side of the boat and his friends were on the other side and there was a stairway in the middle. This was the first time the boy discovered that he was an officer. When the time came to start he was dressed in officer's clothes and got on the boat with his friend, the dog, and the girl."

As already stated, there were eight officers on the boat. After they had been on the ocean a long time four of these officers became envious of the captain's beautiful wife, and they gradually turned two of the others against the captain. After a time they won another to their side. Finally the eighth joined the mutiny and the captain was thrown overboard. After the boy-captain had lain a long time at the bottom of the sea he was rescued by a spirit bird who restored him to his wife. On one of his trips in the boat the boy had bought the body of a dead man which was really the spirit bird in disguise. He found that his wife had borne a son. The spirit bird told him to kill his son with his sword. The captain took the sword and was just going to strike the child when the bird said, " Stop! Now I know you pity me, for you were willing to kill this child for me. Bring up this child. I see your pity. You bought my body after I had been killed. Although I had money—a trunkful—I believe you did it from pity. Now I am going to leave you."

The story ends with the triumphant return of the boy to his father, with cannons firing at every step. His father received him with unbounded joy and he lived in the stone house with the cave under it until he was 100 years old.

In the above story we can readily trace the influence of biblical teaching, current history, the tales of travelers from across the sea, giving details concerning the construction of ships, and, strongest of all, the influence of European " fairy stories," with their mention of castles and of unlimited gold and silver. The game with the gold rings is, of course, the "awl game" of the Chippewa (p. 118) played with a vast number of gold rings. The ship that moved without being propelled by oars or paddles was doubtless suggested by a steam vessel, and the officer with the sword may have been English, or possibly an officer of the United States Army. We see in it a medley of ideas, but the form of the story contains elements of construction which are worthy of observation. We note the repetition of one incident with variations and steadily increasing interest in the repeated voyages of the boat. We note the cumulative phase—the boy, then the boy and his dog; then the boy, dog, and man; then the boy, dog, man, and girl; also the four mutinous officers, with the other four yielding to entreaty, one at a time. After each acquisition to the ranks of the mutiny the narrator said, " Now there were three officers who stayed by the captain," or, " Now there were two left with him." A cohesion is given to the story by the appearance of the spirit bird, who was in reality the body of the dead man bought by the boy, and, according to the story, supposed to have turned into five $100 gold pieces. The division of the story into sections by the boy's return to the cave between his voyages and " playing around as before," is admirably suited to hold the attention closely for a time, then let it relax, then call it up again with increased fascination of plot.

This brief comment shows that the structure of the story, or entertainment, is in accordance with many of the accepted standards of story writing and of dramatic production.

MUSIC

This subject has received such extended consideration by the writer that repetition seems unnecessary. The drum is the only accompanying instrument except in the Mide and djasakid songs, when a rattle is sometimes used. The wooden flute in former times was played by the young men. In addition to Mide songs and those connected with the treatment of the sick, either by Mide or djasakid, there are songs of social dances, game songs, war songs, love songs, and little melodies for the entertainment of children. There are also songs connected with many of the old stories, including some of those concerning Winabojo.

DANCES

The Chippewa, like other tribes, danced before they went to war and celebrated their victories in the scalp dance. Among their social dances were the begging dance, in which they went from house to house, or tent to tent, begging food for a feast (Bull. 53, pp. 229–233), and the woman's dance, in which many gifts were exchanged (Bull. 45, pp. 190–196). Dancing formed an important part of the initiation ceremonies of the Midewiwin.

CHARMS

The Chippewa, more than many other tribes, believed in the use of "charms." Constructively these were of two classes, i. e., charms that comprised several units or materials and charms consisting only of herbs. The first of these classes included charms using figurines, outline drawings, or a hair or part of the clothing of the person to be affected, together with certain herbs. Into both classes there entered the belief that the supreme test of the power of a substance was its ability to act independently of its material presence. Thus an herb applied externally might cure the bite of a reptile, but it was considered evidence of great power if an herb carried in a packet could protect a man so effectively that he would not be bitten by the reptile. The old-time Chippewa appear to have believed that matter has two sorts of properties—one tangible and the other intangible. The medicine men, through their dreams, learned the intangible as well as the tangible properties of matter, their use of the former being designated as "charms," or included in the general term of "medicine."

Certain herbs were believed to cure the sick and also to act as "charms." Among these is *Lathyrus venosus* Muhl., the roots of which were used as a dressing for wounds and were also carried on

the person to secure safety and success. Evil as well as good was
said to be accomplished by these means and the Chippewa had certain antidotes to counteract evil charms. Some of the antidotes
acted by material presence and others acted independently of such
contact. Figurines were used in many of these and ranged from 1
inch to 6 or more inches in height.

This subject will be considered under the following classification:
(a) Love charms, (b) charms to attract worldly goods, (c) charms
to insure safety and success, (d) charms to influence or attract animals, (e) protective charms, (f) charms to work evil, and (g) antidotes for evil charms.

(a) *Love charms.*—(1) The most common form of love charm
consisted of two figurines made of wood representing a man and a
woman. (Pl. 39, a.) These were about an inch in height and were
tied together with a hair or a raveling from the clothing of the
person to be affected. With the figurines was tied a tiny packet of
"love-charm" medicine, one of the usual ingredients being the seeds
of *Onosmodium hispidissimum* Mackenzie. The figurines thus prepared were placed in a little bag and carried by the person wishing
to create the influence. It was said this charm would attract a person from a considerable distance, and that it could be prepared with
special herbs in such a manner that "in four days the man to be
influenced will suffer a headache so severe as to cause nosebleed."
Medicine was sometimes placed on the lips of the figurines. It was
said that "a wife who feels that the heart of her husband is being
alienated may place medicine over the heart of the male figurine,
wear the charm, and regain his affection."

(2) Another form of love (or "attraction") charm was shown to
the writer by an informant. It consisted of a little dust or powder
in a buckskin packet. The powder was colored vermilion and in it
were little shining facets resembling quartz. The amount was about
what could be lifted on the end of a penknife. The owner had paid
$5 for it, and said that "when she was to meet anyone whom she
wished to influence she rubbed a little on her cheeks and the person
always spoke kindly to her."

(3) *Onosmodium hispidissimum* Mackenzie (false gromwell): The
seeds of this plant were said to have power as a love charm and were
used alone or in combination with other substances, one example of
the latter use being with the figurines already noted. The seeds are
tiny and round with a luster like that of pearls. They were said to
be "magnetic" and to adhere to a needle thrust among them. Numerous other herbs were supposed to have power as love charms.

(b) *Charms to attract worldly goods.*—(1) An elaborate charm
of this sort (pl. 39, b, c, d) was obtained from one of the writer's in-

formants who said that she " wore this bag at her waist when she attended dances and always received many presents from other women." The charm consists of a bright red velvet bag decorated in a flower pattern and bordered with shining glass beads. In the bag is an embryo rabbit and a piece of paper on which are inscribed in picture writing the figures of two women, one of whom has received from the other a shawl, a calico dress, and a gift of money. These are closely tied in a small piece of blue silk. It was said these embryo were sometimes found among the intestines of rabbits and were highly prized as charms. The informant said she found three in the body of a rabbit that she was cleaning, and would not part with this one if she had not the other two in her possession. She said further that " when a man found one of these he usually gave a feast and told everyone about it and they decided how it should be used."

(2) The " magnetic " seeds described in connection with love charms were also used to attract wealth. It is not unusual for a Chippewa to carry a few of them tied in a cloth. The writer has seen them carried in a purse "to attract money."

(c) *Charms to insure safety and success.*—(1) *Lathyrus venosus* Muhl (wild pea) : A piece of the dried root carried on the person was believed to effect a happy outcome of any difficulties. The following incident was related concerning its use: "A man while in a drunken rage had killed his wife. His relatives hastened to Na-wajibigokwe and asked whether she had any *mi'nisino'wūck.* She gave them a small piece of the root, which the man carried in his pocket. The writer is reliably informed that the man is alive and free to-day, although it is well known that he killed his wife." [58] This is one of the most highly valued herbs of the Chippewa. In addition to its power as a charm it is said to be a powerful curative agent, being used as a remedy for convulsions.

(2) *Polygala senega* L. (Seneca snakeroot) : The root of this was carried to insure safety on a journey. It was also supposed to improve the general health of a person who carried it constantly. Like the preceding, this was used as a medicine, and was supposed to have special value as a tonic.

A typical bag for a small quantity of medicine was cut from one piece of buckskin, the strip with which the bag was tied being part of the bag itself. Such a bag was opened and the pattern cut (fig. 13). The medicine was put in the middle, the edges gathered up, and the strip wrapped around it and tied.

(d) *Charms to influence or attract animals.*—(1) A charm to make a watchdog faithful was used by the Chippewa. Hairs were cut from the lips of a puppy and placed with charcoal in a birch-bark

---

[58] Bull. 53, Bur. Amer. Ethn., p. 66.

packet, which was hidden in the owner's personal belongings. The informant who brought the specimen said that she had used it with success, and at the present time had a particularly competent watchdog as a result of this charm.

(2) Herbs used to attract animals and fish. *Hepatica triloba* (hepatica). An informant said that her father used this, together with other roots, in the following manner: He chopped the roots and put them in the center of a small fungus which he had scooped out, the skin of the fungus forming a little bag. This he placed on or near the traps which he set for fur-bearing animals. His rise to a high position in the tribe was attributed to his knowledge of this medicine. When he was a boy he was very poor and had only one trap. After a while he was able to buy a second trap. Then an old Mide told him about this medicine. He used it, and soon was trapping more successfully than any other man. "Because of this he rose to be head chief and had credit at any trader's, for they all knew he could always get enough furs to pay for his goods." This man was Nagan'ab, chief of the Chippewa at Fond du Lac, Minn.

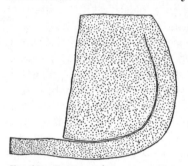

FIG. 13.—Pattern for bag to contain a small amount of medicine

Cornus alternifolia L. f. (dogwood): This was used in the following manner to attract muskrats: A steel trap was set below the water near one of the muskrat houses and a hazel twig was placed upright in the jaws of the trap. The twig was usually about 10 inches long and the adjustment was such that about 1 inch of its length projected above the water. This portion of the twig was cut into splinters and the chewed root of the above-named plant was placed among the splinters. (Pl. 45, *b.*) The muskrats were attracted by the odor, and the attraction was so strong that if one muskrat was caught in the trap the others would devour its body in their attempt to reach the medicine. Only a small amount of the root was required for this purpose. The plant was also used as a remedy for sore eyes.

Eupatorium perfoliatum L. (boneset); *Asclepias syriaca* L. (common milkweed): The small root fibers of the first plant were chewed with the root of the second and applied to a whistle used in calling deer. (See p. 129.)

Aster novae-angliae L. (aster): The root, dried and powdered, was smoked in a pipe to attract game. The smell of the smoke was said to be like that of a deer's hoof. It was said that "when the hunters see a deer track they sit down and smoke this root, then go

a, Love charm; *b*, *c*, *d*, Bag and articles placed therein, constituting a charm; *e*, Bead chains
worn as a charm

IMPLEMENTS USED IN GAMES

a, Snake game; *b*, Stick game; *c*, Counter; *d*, Bone game; *e*, "Bunch of grass" game;
f, Awl game; *g*, Plate game

a little farther, sit down and smoke again, and so on as they follow
the deer's track. Often the deer will come toward them, sniffing
the air." (See p. 129.)

Arctostaphylos uva-ursi (L.) Spreng. (bearberry): The root of
this plant was used similarly to the preceding. It also had a medicinal use and was used as a remedy for headache.

Aster puniceus L. (aster): The fine tendrils of this root as found
in the autumn were smoked in a pipe with tobacco to attract game.

Acorus calamus L. (calamus); *Aralia nudicaulis* L. (wild sarsa-
parilla): The roots of these plants were dried, grated very fine, and
a decoction made of the two. This was sprinkled on fish nets and
allowed to dry before the nets were put in the water. The amount
of powdered roots needed for one application was less than half a
teaspoonful. Both plants had several medicinal uses; among these
uses the former was considered a remedy for "humor in the blood,"
and the latter for sore throat and toothache. (See p. 125.)

(*e*) *Protective charms.*—Many protective charms were carried
secretly by the Chippewa. A personal fetish was usually a crude
representation of an object seen in a dream, either by the wearer
or by someone who transferred it to him, together with the powers
or benefits accruing from the dream. Instead of being a direct representation, the object might be symbolic of the dream. For instance,
a woven or plaited cord, supposed to insure safety when crossing
water, was given to an adult, together with the name "A'jawac,"
meaning "Wafted-safely-across-the-water." (Pl. 31, *d.*) This cord
was smoothly woven of yarn in colors commonly worn by the person
to whom it was given. The instructions were that the cord be kept
among the owner's personal belongings and taken in this manner
on ordinary journeys, but that if the owner were in danger when
crossing water the cord be tied around the waist, next the body,
thus insuring absolute safety. Other instances are noted in the
section on dreams.

A charm that was worn openly consisted of a somewhat similar
cord that was hung around the neck. The same sort of cord was
made of strings of beads. Two forms of this cord or chain are
shown in Plate 39, *e*. The pattern of the first represents a striped
snake, and the chain is supposed to be a protection from the bite
of that reptile; the second is a similar protection from the spotted
snake. These chains also act as a protection against any form of
evil. The woman who made these chains said she could remember
when her mother "often sat up all night to make chains for a war
party that was going into the Sioux country where snakes were
numerous. Almost every man wore one of these chains." The colors
were not important and the usual length of the chains was about 42

inches. There appears to have been no significance in the design of cord or chain supposed to secure protection from sickness.

The following herbs were used as protective charms:

(1) *Plantago major* L. (plantain): The powdered root was mixed with vermilion and carried on the person. This was not only a protection against the bite of snakes but prevented their appearance. The leaves of this plant were used as a remedy for external inflammation.

(2) *Acorus calamus* L. (calamus): A decoction of the root was "sprinkled around to keep rattlesnakes away." This was used in a decoction placed on nets to attract fish; it was also used as a remedy for "humor in the blood."

(3) *Lathyrus venosus* Muhl. (wild pea): The dried root in considerable quantities, rolled in birch bark, was carried as a general protection by warriors and hunting parties. A special use of this herb is noted on page 109.

Protective medicines of various sorts were mixed with vermilion and applied as paint on the bodies of warriors.

(4) *Apocynum androsaemifolium* (dogbane): The root of this was chewed by a man at a dance "if he feared that some one might use bad medicine against him." Dancers were said to use "charm medicines," rubbed on their limbs, which enabled them to dance without weariness but produced the opposite effect on those who danced behind them or "crossed their footprints." This is used as a remedy for headache.

(5) *Agastache anethiodora* (giant hyssop): The whole plant was used, and was said to act as a protection "if the person ahead were carrying medicine to strengthen him." This was used as a remedy for coughs and for burns.

The following narrative illustrates the belief in protective medicines or charms. The incident was related by Niskigwun, whose war-medicine songs are recorded in a previous work.[59] Niskigwun said that he was once on a war party with Odjibwe and they engaged in a fight near the present site of Minneapolis, Minn. During the fight Odjibwe suffered a sudden and complete collapse. Certain men carried powerful stimulants, and Odjibwe, who was not provided with protective medicines, had "passed over their tracks." Friends came and told Niskigwun, who asked, "Have you no medicine?" They replied, "no." It was Niskigwun's custom to carry stimulating medicine in a pouch made of the tail of a buffalo. He took some roots from this pouch, chewed them, and sprayed the medicine from his mouth on Odjibwe's limbs. It was necessary to "take Odjibwe under the arms and hold him up," but Niskigwun

[59] Bull. 53, Bur. Amer. Ethn., songs Nos. 6 and 7.

struck him with the buffalo tail, literally whipping him with it until he was able to walk. Niskigwun said "he was saturated with the medicine and regained his entire strength."

(6) Even infants were provided with protective charms. Examples of these are the "spiderwebs" hung on the hoop of a cradle board. These articles (pl. 24, *a*) consisted of wooden hoops about 3½ inches in diameter filled with an imitation of a spider's web made of fine yarn, usually dyed red. In old times this netting was made of nettle fiber. Two spider webs were usually hung on the hoop, and it was said that they "caught any harm that might be in the air as a spider's web catches and holds whatever comes in contact with it."

(7) Miniature representations of dream objects were frequently hung on a child's cradle board, the child deriving a benefit connected with the nature of the dream. Such articles were usually given the child by the person who named it, and were in accordance with the namer's dream. (See p. 58.)

(8) A charm which was believed to cause an approaching thunderstorm to recede consisted of a spherical stone. This specimen was obtained from Mrs. Razer and had been in her possession 14 years, and had been used successfully by her. The stone appears to contain bits of quartz and was admired for its "shining in the sunshine." Mrs. Razer said that "the thunder bird likes this stone as a hen likes the egg she has laid and will not hurt it." She said that if a thunderstorm threatened, the proper procedure was to put this stone, with a little tobacco, on a birch leaf, anywhere out of doors. She had used this with a "common leaf," but the birch was the proper leaf to use, as the birch tree was believed to be under the protection of the thunder bird. This charm stone measures 2¼ and 1⅝ inches in its two diameters and weighs 7 ounces.

(*f*) *Charms to work evil.*—No herbs intended for use in evil charms were collected and no specimens of such charms were sought, but the following methods of working such charms were described by reliable informants:

(1) A figurine larger than those used in the love charms was suspended from the branch of a tree by a very fine thread, it being said that when the thread broke and the figurine fell the person whom it represented would die.

(2) A space of earth was cleared and smoothed. The person working the charm then drew on the bare ground an outline of the person to be influenced by the charm and put "bad medicine" on the part of the body to be affected. It was said that "the person will have a sharp pain in that part of his body to which the medicine man points when he is working the charm."

(3) "Medicine" was mixed with water and sprinkled on the clothing of the person to be affected, or was put on the ground where he would come in contact with it. The person would become paralyzed unless someone came at once who had the proper medicine to counteract that which had been used against him.

(4) "Medicines" were given to produce insanity in various forms.

(5) "Medicine" was given a pretty young woman which would cause an eruption to appear on her face.

(6) The skin of an owl was removed, dried, and filled with "medicine." It was said this was sent through the air to the lodge of the person to be affected.

An instance of the sending of an owl skin filled with medicine has been recorded, together with the song which was sung by the Mide when sending the owl.[60] It was said that the Indians "could get no food after the owl went to the camp," and that they nearly starved. A recent informant said that many years ago her uncle shot an owl that alighted on the tipi poles. He found it was a dried owl skin and had medicine on its face; then he knew it had been sent to cause starvation in his lodge. He threw the owl skin in the fire and they experienced no harm from it.

(g) *Antidotes for evil charms.*—The Chippewa believed there was an antidote for every evil charm or "bad medicine," and that the affected person could be saved if the person having the proper antidote could be found in time. In this, as in the practice of curative medicine, the knowledge of special plants often was limited to certain individuals.

Artemisia gnaphalodes Nutt. (white mugwort): The dried flowers of this plant were used to counteract the effect of "bad medicine" placed in a person's path. In using it the person took the coals of hard wood, put the dried flowers on the coals and stood over the fumes in such a manner that his limbs and feet were saturated. It was said that "his legs would swell up if this were not done."

It is interesting to note that a fumigation of the head and hands with this herb was performed by those who had cleansed the dead. The herb was also burned in the lodge during a case of contagious disease.

GAMES

Two classes of games were played by the Chippewa: (1) Games of chance, including the moccasin, hand, plate, snake, and stick games; and (2) games of dexterity, including the bone, bunch of grass, awl, woman's, and la crosse games.

(a) *Moccasin game.*—This game, which is still played by the Chippewa, consists in the hiding of four bullets under four moc-

---

[60] Bull. 45, Bur. Amer. Ethn., pp. 105, 106.

casins, one of the bullets being marked. The other implements of the game are the "striking sticks" of oak, which are used in "making a guess," and 20 counting sticks made of ironwood. Four men usually play the game, each "hiding" player having a partner who sings and pounds the drum while the opponent guesses the location of the marked bullet. Any number of people may watch the game, placing their wagers on one or the other pair of players.[61] As indicated, one player hides the bullets under the moccasins and his opponent guesses under which moccasin the marked bullet is hidden. A variant of the game, not mentioned in the previous account, is the hiding of the marked bullet in one of the player's hands instead of beneath a moccasin. A "guess" concerning this position is indicated by moistening with the tongue the tip of the guesser's finger, this finger corresponding to the opponent's next which he believes the marked bullet to be hidden.

(*b*) *Hand game.*—This game consists in the concealing of two small objects in the hands of a player, the opponent guessing in which hand one or both objects are concealed. The articles used in the hand game are not of an arbitrary sort, but those most frequently used in old times were a "gun worm," a small piece of horseshoe nail wound with string, or a small stone sewed in a bit of cloth. The number of players varied from two to any number, and the score was kept by means of sharpened sticks, which were stuck in the ground beside the players.

A slight variation of this game was noted among the Canadian Chippewa who had four possible hiding places for the articles, two in player's hands and two under the edge of a blanket which was laid on the ground. It was customary to play the game with a flint and a gun worm, the score being made by guessing the position of either article, according to an agreement made before the beginning of the game. A majority of the other games mentioned in this section were played by the Canadian in the same manner as by the American Chippewa.[62]

(*c*) *Plate game.*—This and the two games next following are forms of dice games. The name of this game shows its relation to the "plum-stone game" of the Plains tribes,[63] the word by which the game is designated being *bŭ'gese'wĭn*, from *bûge'san*, meaning "plum," with the termination *wĭn* which denotes action. The implements comprise a shallow bowl made of wood and a number of small figures cut from bone. The manner of play consists in tossing

---

[61] See Bull. 53, Bur. Amer. Ethn., pp. 210–213, and Culin, Stewart, Twenty-fourth Ann. Rept. Bur. Amer. Ethn., pp. 335–351.

[62] Culin, Stewart, Games of the North American Indians, Twenty-fourth Ann. Rept. Bur. Amer. Ethn., Washington, 1907, pp. 267–346.

[63] Ibid., pp. 97–101.

up the bowl containing the figures, the effort being to have certain of the figures stand upright when the bowl is returned to a quiet position.

The set of figures made for the writer (pl. 40, *g*) comprises five round disks, and others called " men, the sun and a dog." In counting, if a " sun " is upright the count is three, if the men or the dog are upright the count is 10 for each. A score is also made on the position of the round disks, which each count one if falling with the white side uppermost. The keeping of the entire score is complicated.

(*d*) *Snake game.*—The implements of this game consist of four wooden snakes and several sticks used as counters. (Pl. 40, *a, c.*) The wooden snakes made for the writer were about 10 inches long and the counters 9 inches long. The snakes were scorched brown on the side which represented their backs; two were unpainted on the reverse side and two had an undulating red line the length of their bodies. The mouths of all were painted red. The counters were five in number if the players numbered less than five; if more than that number were engaged in the game the number of counters was increased to 10. The players were seated around a blanket spread on the ground, the order of playing being from right to left. The manner of play was as follows: The player held four wooden snakes in his right hand and dropped or threw them on the blanket, the score being determined by the position in which they fell. The counters were laid at one side of the blanket until appropriated by the players; when all the counters were in the hands of players a person making a score was entitled to take the counters from the other players. The score was as follows: If all the snakes fell right side up or all fell wrong side up, the player was entitled to one counter and another play. If he scored on his second play he was entitled to a third play. If two snakes fell right side up and two showed the white side without the red line the player was entitled to one counter and another play. If two snakes fell right side up and the other two showed the white side with the undulating red line, the player was entitled to two counters and another play. This was the highest score. If he made the same score on his second play he again received two counters, and if he succeeded in making the same score on his third play he returned the four counters which he then held, giving them to the player who held the one remaining counter and receiving that one in exchange. Thus his score was 6, represented by 5 and 1.

(*e*) *Stick game.*—The implements of this game resembled those of the snake game and comprised four sticks about 10 inches long and several counters. The sticks were marked with diagonal lines, a sharp hot iron being used for the purpose. (Pl. 40, *b.*) The manner of playing was the same as in the preceding game.

(*f*) *Bone game.*—Success in this and the four games next following depends chiefly on dexterity. This type of game is characterized by Culin as the " ring and pin." It is widely distributed among the Indian tribes and is analogous to the well-known European game of cup and ball. Various forms of game implements are illustrated by Culin, including a string of the toe-bones of the deer.[64] One of these bones was sometimes used by the Chippewa to give weight to the string of dewclaws. (Pl. 41, *a.*)

The implement used in the game consists of the dewclaws of the deer strung on a narrow strip of deer hide, at one end of which is an oval piece of the leather pierced with a number of small holes, and at the other end is a needle-like piece of bone taken from the leg bone of a young doe. Ten is the usual number of dewclaws used in the game, this being the number obtained from one deer. In recent times a brass thimble has been used instead of a bone next the bit of leather, and a darning needle has replaced the sharp bone at the other end. Much of the success of the game depends on the " balance " of the game implement, this being determined by the relative weight of the bones and their order on the string The heaviest bone is placed next the bit of leather. The number of holes in the bit of leather is not arbitrary, but is usually about 25. The vertebra of fish are sometimes used instead of dewclaws in making the implement for this game.

If a considerable number are to play this game, they are divided into two sides. Each side has a leader who chooses the men who are to play on his side. Before the play begins they decide how many points shall constitute a game and how many points shall be scored by the most difficult play in the game, which is known as " catching the bone next the tail." A player continues his play as long as he scores, passing the game implement to his opponents when he fails to make a score.

The manner of play is as follows: A player holds the needle between the thumb and forefinger of his right hand, he then extends his right arm, the needle pointing upward, and the bones falling below his thumb. He then takes the bit of leather in his left hand and draws it backward toward his body until the string of cones is in a horizontal position. With a quick motion of his hands he releases the bit of leather, swings the string of bones forward, and catches one or more of the bones on the needle, the object being to hold a series of bones in an erect position on the needle.

The score is as follows: To catch the bone next the needle and hold all the bones erect on the needle counts 10; to catch any bone in the

⁶⁴ Culin, op. cit., pp. 527–561.

series and hold only that bone counts 1, the number in every instance corresponding to the number of bones held erect on the needle. To catch the bit of leather secures a score corresponding to the number of holes in the leather, and to catch the heavy bone or the thimble next the bit of leather counts the value decided upon before the beginning of the game. The number of points in a game is frequently 100, though any number may constitute a game. It is said that the score is "shouted by everybody," so there is no need of counters. The games are indicated by sticks placed upright in the ground.

(g) *Bunch of grass game.*—The game implement is a bunch of grass tied by a short cord to a pointed stick. (Pl. 40, *e.*) The manner of play was similar to the preceding, but less skill was required, as the purpose was simply to catch the bunch of grass on the stick. This game was usually played by women. The material for making the game implement was readily available and the playing of the game was in the nature of a pastime. A smaller game implement of the same sort was made for the use of children.

(h) *The awl game.*—The implements of this game consist of a ring and a sharp metal point set in a wooden handle, an ordinary awl being commonly used for this purpose. The ring may be made from the leg bone of an animal or it may consist of a narrow strip of basswood bark, firmly wound with thread or with the fine fibers of the bark. (Pl. 40, *f.*) The manner of play is as follows: The ring is laid on the ground and the awl is thrown toward it, the purpose being to have the awl strike inside the ring and stand upright in the ground.

(i) *Woman's game.*—Concerning this game Culin says: "The game of double ball throughout the eastern United States and among the Plains tribes is played exclusively by women, and is commonly known as the woman's ball game.[65] The implements for the game consist of two balls or similar objects attached to each other by a thong, and a curved stick with which they are thrown. The balls vary in shape and material. Among the Cheyenne two small slightly flattened buckskin balls are used. Among the Sauk and Foxes and other Algonquian tribes the balls are oblong, weighted with sand, and frequently both, with the connecting thong, are made of one piece of buckskin.

As played by the Chippewa, each player has a pair of rather long slender sticks with which she attempts to catch and to carry the two short thick sticks or billets tied together with a thong. The billets are made of heavy wood, oak being commonly used for this purpose. Only the swiftest runners joined in this game, which was played in an open field, often about 300 feet in length, at either

---

[65] Culin, op. cit., p. 647,

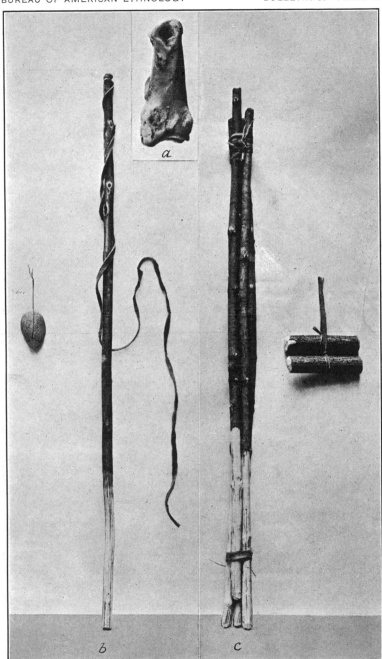

a, Bone of deer toe, used in game implement; *b,* "Spinning stone" game; *c,* Implements
used in "woman's game"

PORTRAIT OF NODINENS

end of which was a "goal stake." The players were divided into two sides, each of which had a leader. The play was opened by the leader of one side who tossed the pair of short sticks into the air. All the players rushed forward attempting to obtain it and carry it through the opponent's line to the opposite goal. The score was made by striking the pair of sticks against a goal post, and the side making the score had the privilege of tossing the pair of sticks when the play was resumed. The implements used by the Chippewa are shown in Plate 41, *c*.

(*j*) *Lacrosse game.*—In this game a ball is tossed with a racket which is made by bending a sapling so as to form a small loop at one end, this loop being filled by a pocket of network. In former times the ball was made by charring a knot of wood and scraping away the charred portion until the ball was of a satisfactory size and shape. A ball covered with deerskin is commonly used. A large number of players take part in the game and are divided into opposing sides. Back of each group of players is a goal consisting of two upright poles and a crossbar. Each player has a racket (or "lacrosse stick") and his aim is to catch the ball and carry it to the goal back of his opponents.[66] The writer witnessed the playing of the moccasin game, woman's game, and lacrosse at large gatherings of Chippewa.

THE INDUSTRIAL YEAR

(*a*) A narrative covering the entire cycle of the year is herewith presented and is followed by a detailed description of the several Chippewa industries, each of which had its appropriate season. The narrator is Nodinens (pl. 42), a member of the Mille Lac Band of Chippewa, who was 74 years old when giving this information. The narrative is given practically in the words of the interpreter. She said:

When I was young everything was very systematic. We worked day and night and made the best use of the material we had. My father kept count of the days on a stick. He had a stick long enough to last a year and he always began a new stick in the fall. He cut a big notch for the first day of a new moon and a small notch for each of the other days. I will begin my story at the time when he began a new counting stick. After my mother had put away the wild rice, maple sugar, and other food that we would need during the winter she made some new mats for the sides of the wigwam. These were made of bulrushes which she had gathered and dried. She selected a nice smooth piece of ground and spread them out.

I, as the oldest daughter, boiled basswood bark, and made cord, and grandmother made the bone needles that we would use in weaving the mats. When the rushes were ready, we laid a cord on the ground and measured the right

---

[66] Culin, op. cit., pp. 562–569.

length for the mats. My mother knew just how long they should be to go around the wigwam, and we made five long ones, four of middle size, and two small ones. The long ones were two double-arms' lengths, and the middle-sized ones were about one and a half double-arms' lengths. (See terms of measurement, p. 137.) We laid the rushes two layers deep on the ground with the ends resting on the cord, and then fastened the ends of the rushes to the cord, after which we fastened the cord to the pole that was the upper, horizontal part of the weaving frame. (Cf. section on weaving mats.) My grandmother directed everything, and she had a large quantity of the thorns from the thorn-apple tree in a leather bag. She had been gathering these all summer, but she made sure she had plenty. We all three worked hard getting ready for winter. When my mother had finished the bulrush mats she made more mats for the floor, using either fresh reeds or some that she had gathered during the summer, and she made more of the woven-yarn bags in which we kept our belongings.

My home was at Mille Lac, and when the ice froze on the lake we started for the game field. I carried half of the bulrush mats and my mother carried the other half. We rolled the blankets inside the mats; and if there was a little baby, my mother put it inside the roll, cradle board and all. It was a warm place and safe for the baby. I carried a kettle beside my roll of mats. We took only food that was light in weight, such as rice and dried berries, and we always took a bag of dried pumpkin flowers, as they were so nice to thicken the meat gravy during the winter. There were six families in our party, and when we found a nice place in the deep woods we made our winter camp. The men shoveled away the snow in a big space, and the six wigwams were put in a circle and banked with evergreen boughs and snow. Of course, the snow was all shoveled away in the inside of the wigwam, and plenty of cedar boughs were spread on the ground and covered with blankets for our beds, the bright yarn bags being set along the wall for use as pillows. In the center was a place for a fire, and between it and the floor mats there was a strip of hard, dry ground that was kept clean by sweeping it with a broom made of cedar boughs. The wigwam looked nice with the yellow birch-bark top and the bright-colored things inside. Outside the door there was a little shed made of cedar bark in which we kept the split wood for the fire, so it would not get wet and so we could get it easily in the night. Sometimes there were many of these sheds around the door of a wigwam. The men brought the logs and the women chopped the wood, and put it in the sheds ready for use.

There was a big fire in the middle of the camp, and all the families did their cooking around this fire if the weather was not too cold, but we always had a fire in the wigwam in the evening, so it would be warm for us to sleep. We always slept barefoot, with our feet toward the fire, and we loosened our other clothing. I wore a dress of coarse broadcloth, with separate pieces of the cloth to cover my arms, and I had broadcloth leggings that came to my knees, but I wore no other clothing except my moccasins and blanket. The big rack for drying meat was over the fire in the middle of the circle. During the day the women kept this fire burning low and evenly to dry the meat. When the men came home at night the rack was taken off the fire, for the men put in lots of light wood to dry their clothing. They sat around it, smoking and talking. If a snowstorm came on we spread sheets of birch bark over the meat. We did not dry it entirely—only enough so that it would keep— and the drying was finished in the sun when we reached our summer camp. The fire blazed brightly until bedtime, and then the men put on dry wood so it would smolder all night. The women were busy during the day preparing the meat, attending to their household tasks, and keeping the clothing of the men in order. Each man had two or three leather suits which required considerable mending, as they had such hard wear. We snared rabbits and partridges for food and cleaned and froze all that we did not need at the time.

My father was a good hunter and sometimes killed two deer in a day. Some hunters took a sled to bring back the game, but more frequently they brought back only part of the animal, and the women went next day and packed the rest of the meat on their backs. It was the custom for a man to give a feast with the first deer or other game that he killed. The deer was cut up, boiled, and seasoned nicely, and all the other families were invited to the feast. Each family gave such a feast when the man killed his first game. (Cf. " First fruits " feast.) The men were good hunters, and we had plenty of meat, but every bit of the deer that was not eaten was dried for carrying away, the extra meat, the liver and heart, and even the hoofs. I remember that once a hunter heard an owl following him. When he returned to camp he said: " You must preserve every bit of deer. This is a bad sign, and we will not get any more game for a long time." The hunters went out every day, but could find nothing. We stayed there until we had eaten almost all that we intended to carry away. We were so hungry that we had to dig roots and boil them. My father was a Mide, and one day, when the provisions were almost gone, a young man entered our wigwam with a kettle of rice, some dried berries, and some tobacco. He placed this before my father, saying: " Our friend, we are in danger of starving; help us." This man was the ockabewis who managed and directed things in the camp, and his arms were painted with vermilion.

My father called his Mide friends together and they sang almost all night. The men sang Mide songs and shook their rattles. No woman was allowed to go in that direction. The children were put to bed early and told that they must not even look up. My mother sat up and kept the fire burning. My father came in late and sang a Mide song, and a voice was heard outside the wigwam joining in the song. It was a woman's voice, and my mother heard it plainly. This was considered a good omen. The next morning my father directed that a fire be made at some distance from the camp. The ockabewis made the fire, and the Mide went there and sang. They put sweet grass and medicine on the fire, and let the smoke cover their bodies, their clothing, and their guns. When this was finished, my father covered his hand with red paint and applied it to the shoulders of the men. They took their guns and started to hunt, feeling sure they would succeed. No woman was allowed to pass in front of the hunters when they were starting. The ockabewis killed a bear that day and every man got some game. They killed plenty of deer and bear, and each person boiled the breast of the animals in a separate kettle from the rest of the meat. There was a feast, and they brought these kettles to my father's lodge, and the old men ate there, sitting by themselves and eating from these kettles. After that whenever we were short of game they brought a kettle of rice to my father and he sang and the luck would return. He was so successful that we had plenty of food all that winter.

The hides were tanned with the hair on and were spread on the cedar boughs along the edge of the wigwam. Father gathered us children around him in the evening and instructed us as we sat on these soft hides. (Cf. section on government of children.) He instructed us to be kind to the poor and aged and to help those who were helpless. This made a deep impression on me, and I have always helped the old people, going into the woods and getting sticks and scraping their kinnikinnick[67] for them. During the winter my grandmother made lots of fish nets of nettle-stalk fiber. Everyone was busy. Some of the men started on long hunting trips in the middle of the winter, and did not get back until after the spring work was done; then they rested a while and started off on their fall hunting and trapping.

Toward the last of the winter my father would say, " one month after another month has gone by. Spring is near and we must get back to our other work." So the women wrapped the dried meat tightly in tanned deerskins and the men packed their furs on sleds or toboggans. (See pp. 43, 136.) Once there was a fearful snowstorm when we were starting to go back and my father quickly made snowshoes from the branches for all the older people. (See pp. 148, 149.) Grandmother had a supply of thorn-apple thorns and she got these out and pinned up the children's coats so they would be warm and we started off in the snowstorm and went to the sugar bush.

When we got to the sugar bush we took the birch-bark dishes out of the storage and the women began tapping the trees. We had queer-shaped axes made of iron. Our sugar camp was always near Mille Lac, and the men cut holes in. the ice, put something over their heads, and fished through the ice. There were plenty of big fish in those days, and the men speared them. (See section on fishing.) My father had some wire, and he made fishhooks and tied them on basswood cord, and he got lots of pickerel that way. A food cache was always near the sugar camp. We opened that and had all kinds of nice food that we had stored in the fall. There were cedar-bark bags of rice and there were cranberries sewed in birch-bark makuks and long strings of dried potatoes and apples. Grandmother had charge of all this, and made the young girls do the work. As soon as the little creeks opened, the boys caught lots of small fish, and my sister and I carried them to the camp and dried them on a frame. My mother had two or three big brass kettles that she had bought from an English trader and a few tin pails from the American trader. She used these in making the sugar.

We had plenty of birch-bark dishes, but the children ate mostly from the large shells that we got along the lake shore. We had sauce from the dried cranberries and blueberries sweetened with the new maple sugar. (Cf. section on sugar making.) The women gathered the inside bark of the cedar. This can only be gotten in the spring, and we got plenty of it for making mats and bags.

Toward the end of the sugar season there was a great deal of thick sirup called the "last run of sap," and we had lots of fish that we had dried. This provided us with food during the time we were making our gardens.

The six families went together, and the distance was not long. Each family had a large bark house with a platform along each side, like the lodge in which the maple sap was boiled. We renewed the bark if necessary, and this was our summer home. The camps extended along the lake shore, and each family had its own garden. We added to our garden every year, my father and brothers breaking the ground with old axes, bones, or anything that would cut and break up the ground. My father had wooden hoes that he made, and sometimes we used the shoulder blade of a large deer or a moose, holding it in the hand. (Pl. 53, e.) We planted potatoes, corn, and pumpkins. These were the principal crops. After the garden was planted the Mide gathered together, made a feast, and asked the Mide manido to bless the garden.

[67] This is a common expression and refers to tobacco and red willow. *Kinikinige* means " he mixes together things of different kinds." Cuoq, J. A., Lexique de la Langue Algonquine, Montreal, 1886, p. 168.

They had a kind of ceremony and sang Mide songs. Old women could attend this feast, but no young people were allowed. Children were afraid when their parents told them to keep away from such a place. The gardens were never watered. A scarecrow made of straw was always put in a garden.

In the spring we had pigeons to eat. They came in flocks and the men put up long fish nets on poles, just the same as in the water, and caught the pigeons in that way. We boiled them with potatoes and with meat. We went to get wild potatoes in the spring and a little later the blueberries, gooseberries, and June berries were ripe along the lake shore. The previous fall the women had tied green rice in long bundles and at this time they took it out, parched and pounded it, and we had that for food. There was scarcely an idle person around the place. The women made cedar-bark mats and bags for summer use. By that time the reeds for making floor mats were ready for use. They grew in a certain place and the girls carried them to the camp. We gathered plenty of the basswood bark and birch bark, using our canoes along the lake and the streams. We dried berries and put them in bags for winter use. During the summer we frequently slept in the open.

Next came the rice season. The rice fields were quite a distance away and we went there and camped while we gathered rice. Then we returned to our summer camp and harvested our potatoes, corn, pumpkins, and squash, putting them in caches which were not far from the gardens.

By this time the men had gone away for the fall trapping. When the harvest was over and colder weather came, the women began their fall fishing, often working at this until after the snow came. When the men returned from the fall trapping we started for the winter camp.

(b) *Making maple sugar.*—The first and one of the most enjoyable events of the industrial year was the making of maple sugar.[68] Each group of relatives or friends had its own portion of the maple forest, known as its sugar bush. There the birch-bark utensils needed in making sugar were stored from year to year in a small lodge, near the large lodge where the sap was boiled. The sap kettles were kept boiling all night and the season was a busy one for all in the camp. The sap was boiled to a thick sirup, strained, replaced in the kettles, and heated slowly. When it had thickened to the proper consistency it was transferred to a "granulating trough," where it was "worked" with a paddle and with the hands until it was in the form of granulated sugar. If "hard sugar" was desired, the thick sirup was poured into little birch-bark cones, dishes, or other receptacles, including the upper mandible of ducks' bills, which formed a favorite confection for children. In Plate 43 two women are "graining" sugar, one with a paddle and the other with her hands. A paddle used for this purpose is shown in Figure 14, a.

Maple sugar was used in seasoning fruits, vegetables, cereals, and fish, being used more freely than the white race uses salt. It was also eaten as a confection, and dissolved in cold water as a summer drink. It was frequently mixed with medicine to make it palatable, especially for children.

---

[68] Cf. extended account in "Uses of Plants by the Chippewa Indians," Forty-fourth Ann. Rept. Bur. Amer. Ethn.

(c) *Offering of first fruits.*—A custom which began with the season of making maple sugar and lasted throughout the industrial year was that of offering a portion of the first fruit or game to

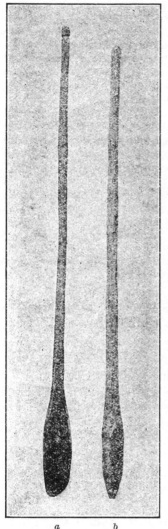

manido. This was done by giving a feast at which the host " spoke to manido," and offered petitions for safety, health, and long life. The speech and prayer on such an occasion depended on the person giving the feast, and often was quite lengthy. Everyone was given a little of the " first fruit " and then partook of the feast. Some of this special food was usually put on the graves.[69] Persons strict in observing old customs kept a kettle especially for cooking the first fruit or game, but this was not necessary. A small brass kettle which has been used for this purpose by five generations is now the property of Mrs. George Walters, of White Earth.

(d) *Making gardens.*—As indicated in the foregoing personal narrative by Nodinens, each family had its own portion of the ground for its garden. Among the earliest tools used in gardening by the Chippewa were three wooden implements described by Tom Skinaway, of Mille Lac, who made small models of two of them. These are a short, broad hoe, and an implement for grubbing roots, made from the crook of a tree root which gave it strength. The third wooden implement resembled a crowbar. The Chippewa state that they had squash and pumpkin before the coming of the white man, and that these, as well as other vegetables, were cultivated by them in gardens.

a   b

FIG. 14.—*a,* Graining ladle for maple sugar; *b,* pestle for pounding wild rice

(e) *Fishing.*—This was an industry which continued almost the entire year. Under some circumstances the people moved directly from the sugar camp to their gardens, but more frequently they went from the sugar camp to a place where they could fish. Sometimes

[69] Cf. puberty customs, p. 72; mourning customs, p. 75; and narrative, p. 121,

MAKING MAPLE SUGAR AT MILLE LAC, MINN.

PHOTOGRAPH BY MINNEAPOLIS JOURNAL

SPREADING FISH NETS TO DRY

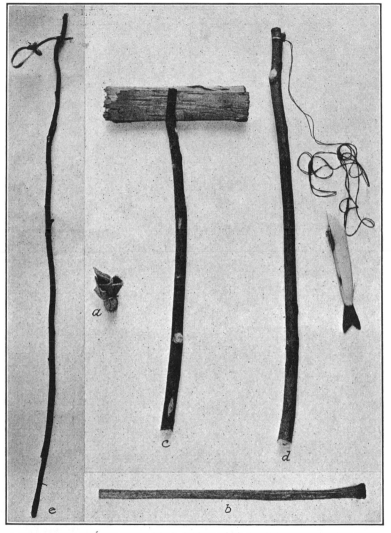

a, Packet of "medicine" to attract fish; *b*, Stick on which "medicine" was placed to attract muskrats; *c*, Model of fishing torch; *d*, Decoy for fish; *e*, Bark noose used in catching partridge

BIRCH-BARK MAKUKS FOR GATHERING AND STORING BERRIES

this was near the site of their summer camp, and they remained there until it was time to plant their gardens. The autumn was a special fishing season, as it was during that time they secured the supply of fish for winter use. It was said the fish "seemed to come near shore in November, just before the lakes froze." At that time the women set their nets. Sometimes they took up the nets in a snow-storm, and sometimes the net full of fishes froze so that it was necessary to take the net into the house and thaw it before taking out the fish. Much care was taken with this industry, as fish, both fresh and dried, constituted an important food of the Chippewa.

Fish were secured by the following means: (1) By the use of seines; (2) by spearing at night with a torch; (3) by spearing through the ice with a decoy; (4) by traps; (5) by the use of bait; (6) by fishhooks; and (7) by trolling.

(1) The use of seines was the general method of obtaining fish, as it secured the largest results in both number and variety of fish. The manner of making nets and their size are noted on page 154. If the water were shallow the net was attached to stakes at the corners, but if the water were deep the upper corners were fastened to canoe paddles which floated on the surface of the water, the lower corners being weighted with stones, tied with basswood fiber. The nets were thoroughly washed after being taken from the water and were sometimes dipped in a decoction of sumac leaves to destroy the odor of fish, it being said that the fish would not approach a net with the slightest odor upon it. The placing of "medicine" on the nets to attract fish is considered in connection with the use of charms on page 111. The packet shown in Plate 45, a, contained enough "medicine" for one application to a fish net, the amount being less than a teaspoonful.

Fishing, except in the coldest winter, was the work of the women, who placed the nets in the water at night and took them up in the early morning, spreading and drying them. Every camp had a pole over which the nets were hung for the spreading of the meshes, and a row of tall stakes on which the nets were hung to dry. (Pl. 44, a, b.) After drying they were gathered in a long bundle which was tied in the middle and hung in the lodge or in some safe place. The writer witnessed the taking in of a seine and the drying of the nets. (Pl. 20, a, b, c.)

(2) Spearing at night with a torch: The larger fish were speared and were best secured at night. The torch used in night fishing consisted of a stake about 4 feet long which was split at the end, strips of birch bark about 6 inches wide and 18 inches long being placed in this slit and fastened in such a manner that, the stake (or pole) being upright in the canoe, the birch-bark strip extended

over the water and threw a light on the water. By this the occupant
of the canoe could see the fish and spear them while he himself
remained invisible. Extra strips of bark were carried to replenish
the torch. A miniature of such a torch is shown in Plate 45, c.

(3) Spearing through the ice with a decoy: The decoy fish were
made of wood with a tail of birch bark and body weighted with
lead. (Pl. 45, d.) Some skill was required in making these
so that their equilibrium in the water was perfect. When using
them the Indian cut a hole in the ice and lay flat beside it with his
face over the opening. His head and shoulders were covered by a
blanket, which frequently was supported by a tripod or frame of
sticks. With his left hand he guided the decoy so that its movements would be as lifelike as possible, and in his right hand he
held the spear ready to strike at the proper moment.

(4) The use of traps: These were of two sorts, the small traps used
in catching small fish and a large form of trap known as a "sturgeon
rack" for catching the large Lake Superior fish. The small traps
were made of twigs and branches of trees and were placed in shallow water where the current would carry the fish into them. In
describing the "sturgeon rack" Mrs. English said:

> When I was a child we lived near a place where two deep rivers met and
> flowed into Lake Superior. In the spring, as soon as the ice went out, the
> sturgeon 5 or 6 feet long came from Lake Superior and went up these
> rivers. In order to catch them as they returned to the lake the Indians con-
> structed a framework across the river. This was made by sinking heavy
> poles like piling not far apart. On top of these they placed timbers strong
> enough for persons to sit upon, and between the poles they strung basswood
> cord back and forth until it formed a stout netting through which the fish
> could not pass. When the fish came down the river the Indians, seated on the
> framework, caught them with hooks and killed them with clubs.

(5) The use of bait: The Chippewa caught bullpouts (catfish)
by means of a line. They tied a piece of old blanket with a sinker
to the end of a string which they let down into the water. The fish
took this in his mouth and was drawn up by the line.

(6) Fishhooks: The earliest fishhooks were made of deer bone.
In later times the Chippewa made fishhooks from wire, using them
with lines of nettle-stalk fiber or basswood twine. An interesting
"fishline bobber" consisted of a large cork pierced by a large quill
about 6 inches long which extended only part way through the cork.
Inside this was a smaller quill which projected at the top, extended
through the cork, and was bent in a loop below it. The fishline was
inside the smaller quill and thus was held in a vertical position
several inches above the water. The motion of this upright quill,
as well as that of the cork, readily indicated a "nibble" on the hook.

(7) Trolling was accomplished by twisting a line around the wrist and then around the canoe paddle, which moved the line through the water.

(*f*) *Gathering berries.*—This was usually done by the women and older children, and as the country of the Chippewa abounded in berries of many varieties it formed a summer industry of some importance. Like other industries it was pleasurable, and a berry party was enjoyed by the Indians. A woman usually carried at her belt a small birch-bark makuk in which she placed the berries as she gathered them. This differed from other makuks in being larger at the top and having wigup strands for fastening it to the belt. From this the berries were emptied into a very large makuk with the white of the birch bark left on the outside. (Pl. 46.) This was somewhat of a temporary container, large at the top and without a binding of root to hold the upper edge firm. A berry party often carried an ax to cut the higher boughs of cherry or similar trees. In old times the low-bush cranberries were gathered by hand. Later a box was used. This was open at the end, with the lower edge cut like the teeth of a rake. It was operated as a scoop, taking off the tops of the plants with leaves and small stalks as well as the berries.

Blueberries, chokecherries, and June berries were always dried whole on frames made of slender reeds. These reeds were identified as *Phragmites phragmites* (L.) Karst. Four makuks of fresh berries usually made one makuk of dried berries. Chokecherries were pounded, stones and all, after they were dried. Raspberries were "boiled down" and then spread in little patches on sheets of birch bark, which were laid in the sun until the water had evaporated from the cooked fruit. The little cakes were then piled one upon another and tied in packets for storing. Cranberries (low-bush variety) were usually eaten while fresh.

(*g*) *Gathering medicinal herbs.*—While herbs for medicine might be gathered at any time, it was customary to give special attention to this work in August, when the plants were fully developed and most varieties were in blossom. Roots were gathered in the spring and fall, and bark in summer "when the sap was in the tree." Tobacco was always placed in the ground before roots were dug, the tobacco being first offered to the cardinal points, the zenith, and the earth. The same procedure was followed before removing the bark from a tree or taking flowers or leaves for medicinal use. The person gathering the substance talked in a low voice, saying the substance was intended for a good purpose, that no more was taken than was necessary, and asking that its use might be successful.

The writer has seen this done on two occasions, once by a man and once by a woman who used herb remedies in treating the sick.

The plants were dried and each variety was tied by itself.

(*h*) *Gathering wild rice.*—The rice camp in the autumn was the close of the season in which the people worked in groups, and corresponded somewhat to the maple-sugar camp of the early spring. Each group of relatives had its share of the rice field as it had its share of the sugar bush, and this right was never disputed. The women established it each year by going to the rice field in the middle of the summer and tying a small portion of the rice in little sheaves. The border of each tract was defined by stakes, but this action showed that the field was to be harvested that year.

When the rice was ripe the people made their camp on the lake shore and prepared for work.[69a] The rice was harvested by the women, the procedure being as follows: A canoe was "poled" through the rice, this being often done by a man. The implements used in the harvesting were two sticks about 24 inches long. The woman seated in the stern of the canoe bent down the stalks with one stick and knocked off the ripe kernels with the other, continuing until her canoe was full of rice kernels. The rice was evenly dried on sheets of birch bark, parched in a kettle to loosen the husk, and then pounded with long wooden pestles (fig. 14, *b*) in a barrel sunk in the ground, several people combining in this part of the work. The rice was then winnowed to remove the husks, after which it was "trodden" in a small wooden receptacle, partly sunken in the ground. The treading was done by a man wearing clean moccasins. A pole was placed on one side (or both sides) of the receptacle and he leaned on this pole so that the entire weight of his body did not rest on his feet, the motion being not unlike that of a dancer.

Rice was stored in bags woven of bark and sewed across the top, a layer of hay being placed over the rice. (Pl. 64, *c*.)

(*i*) *Hunting.*—The principal game animals were the deer, moose, fox, and wolf. The deer and moose were hunted with lights, the "deer call," and the use of "medicine." Three kinds of foxes were shot, the red, black, and silver gray. These were swift of foot, but got out of breath readily when pursued. Three kinds of wolves were shot, the timber wolf, the large prairie wolf, and a small prairie wolf said to be like a mongrel dog and to be an inferior animal. The Chippewa shot the large wolves and chased the small ones until they were out of breath and could be easily shot. A Canadian Chippewa said he remembered hearing his grandfather tell of killing

---

[69a] Gathering rice is described in detail in " Uses of Plants by the Chippewa Indians," Forty-fourth Ann. Rept. Bur. Amer. Ethn.; in " Wild Rice Gatherers of the Upper Lakes," A. E. Jenks, Nineteenth Ann. Rept. Bur. Amer. Ethn.; also in "Material Culture of the Menomini," Alanson Skinner, Indian Notes and Monographs, 1921, p. 142.

deer with bow and arrow. At that time the Indians used flint arrow points set in a shaft and tied with sinew, but fastened lightly so that the animal running through the brush would break off the shaft. This left the arrow point in the animal's body. The Indian followed the animal and waited until it bled to death. This sometimes took an entire day. He said he had heard of arrow points made of the heavy sinew [70] from the neck of a buffalo, and also made of bone, but said the latter were too easily broken. According to the Chippewa, it is the habit of a deer to jump, then trot, and then walk in a circle when it is trying to evade a hunter, but a deer never crosses its own trail when it has completed the circle. Knowing this, a Chippewa hunter circles outside the circle traveled by the deer, then closes in, and frequently finds the deer tired out and lying down near the place where it began its circle.

A hunter carried his knife in a sheath attached to a braided belt made of basswood bark. If snow were on the ground he often carried a small toboggan on his back for use in bringing home the game. A pitch torch was used (see pp. 149, 150) in hunting deer and moose, also an instrument called a " deer call." (Pl. 47, *a*, *b*.) This consisted of two hollow sections, each made of a piece of wood cut in two cones. The two sections fitted together, making a very tight joint. A single-beating reed was in the upper edge of the lower section, the upper section forming the mouthpiece, and the lower section being sufficiently large to permit the free vibration of the reed. It had no lateral openings. In blowing this instrument the hands were held cup-shaped over the end, one hand being opened as the sound was emitted. This action affected the tone, producing a sound like that of a fawn calling the doe. It is said that the doe always came toward this sound and thus was secured by the hunter.

Three herbs were used as "hunting charms," these being identified as *Aster novae-angliae* L., *Arctostaphylos uva-ursi* (L.) Spreng., and *Aster puniceus* L. The powdered roots of the first and second and the fine root tendrils of the third were smoked in a pipe, usually with tobacco or red willow, some hunters preferring one and some another of these herbs. The smoke of the first was said to resemble that of a deer's hoof and to be very penetrating. As the hunters followed a deer's track they occasionally sat down and smoked one of these herbs, and it is said that before long the deer came toward them sniffing the air.

In time of special anxiety a man blackened his face before going to hunt, signifying that he had eaten nothing for a time before going and intended to eat nothing while he was away. He told his wife to have the children fast while he was gone, and to blacken

---

[70] This was used by the Sioux for the handle of an awl.

their faces. It was said that a man was usually successful if the children fasted as well as himself. If he returned successful, he would say it was because of the good will of a spirit and because his children had fasted. If a man went out expecting to get bear or moose and secured none, he would try to bring home some small game like rabbits or partridges for his children because they were fasting for him. But if it were necessary for the father to return empty handed, they would "eat their supper cheerfully and without repining." The mother always reserved some food in a birch-bark dish so they would have something to eat whatever might be the result of the hunt.

Mr. Henry Selkirk stated that he was once hunting with his uncle and a party of men. They got no game the first day. That evening they had nothing to eat except rice and dried blueberries, so they made an offering to manido by putting part of their food beneath the ashes of their fire. They scraped the ashes away and laid the food there. The next day his party saw a bear and killed it.

(j) *Trapping.*—The principal informants on this subject were Star Bad Boy and Joseph Sharrett, who is a veteran of the Civil War and an experienced Indian trapper.

An outfit of a trapper might comprise four otter traps and about 20 smaller traps. The trappers were busy all winter going to watch their traps, moving some to more favorable places, studying the habits of the game, watching for fresh tracks, and removing the animals caught in the traps. These traps were distributed over a wide stretch of country to catch the various sorts of animals.

Otter: Before traps were used to catch otter the Indians used nets made of nettle-stalk fiber. These nets were made particularly strong, with wide meshes, and were stretched directly across a stream where the otter traveled. When steel traps were used they were placed in the water where the otter were accustomed to land, and were so arranged that when the otter rose to put its front paws on the land its hind paw was caught in the trap. About 15 feet of cord secured the trap, and when the otter felt itself caught it started to swim back to deep water and was drowned.

Beaver: In order to catch this animal, a poplar pole was laid on the bottom of a lake or stream where the water was 2 or more feet in depth. Steel traps were put about 2 feet away from this pole. The beaver nibbled the pole, stepped back as it ate, and was thus in a position to be caught by the trap.

Mink, marten, and fisher: The latter animal was plentiful in the Chippewa country. Two types of trap were used for these and other small animals. One type consisted of a wide board, released at one end by the nibbling of the bait and falling and crushing the animal. This was said to have been " adapted from traps made by white men."

(Pl. 47, c.)   The native "fall trap" was made with a little stockade of upright poles.   The entrance to this stockade was about 7 inches wide and the bait was at the farther end.   A string extended from the bait to a heavy stick at the entrance of the little stockade, and the nibbling of the bait released this stick, thus catching the animal. (Models of both these traps were made by Gagewin.)

Rabbits: These were snared by means of nettle-fiber nets, or caught with traps like those used for mink.

Bears: The black bear was caught in the vicinity of White Earth. It is said that the cinnamon bear (known as the "prairie bear") sometimes came to Otter Tail, and that some were killed there. The brown bear was very rare, even in the old days.   The trap used to catch bear consisted of a pole laid across their path and another suspended by one end above the path, this being the same general type as that used for small animals.   The bait was beneath the log. The trap was so adjusted that the weight of the bear released the suspended log which struck its back and pinned it down.   It was the custom to visit these traps every two days.   Bear traps were set along the streams as the bear came to the streams to catch "suckers," of which they were very fond.   The traps were baited with cooked fish, mashed and mixed with fish oil, or occasionally with maple sugar.

Partridges: These were caught by means of a loop of basswood fiber at the end of a stick.   It was said that the partridges were such silly birds that they would sit on a branch while a boy came up behind them and dropped the little noose over their heads.   When they started to fly away he captured them.   A specimen of this device was made by John C. Carl.   (Pl. 45, e.)

CHIEFS

According to the Handbook of American Indians "a chief may be generally defined as a political officer whose distinctive functions are to execute the ascertained will of a definite group of persons * * * and to conserve their customs, traditions, and religion.   He exercises legislative, judicative, and executive powers delegated to him in accordance with custom for the conservation and promotion of the common weal." [71]

The following information on the subject was supplied by Ĕn'dûsogi'jĭg (pl. 48), an hereditary chief at Mille Lac.   He said that a chief was respected for his personal characteristics, and that anyone who wished to join his band was at liberty to do so.   His father's band comprised about 100 persons of various totems.   He

[71] Bull. 30, Bur. Amer. Ethn., pt. 1, p. 263.

said that some totemic groups were larger than others, but that none were considered better than the rest.

The duties of a chief included the presiding at councils of his band, the making of decisions that affected their general welfare, and the settlement of small disputes. He represented the band at the signing of treaties, the payment of annuities, and any large gathering of the tribe.

Associated with the chief were two "head men" who acted as his protectors. They were selected from among the warriors.

At a large council the men of a band always sat near their chief.

RIGHT OF REVENGE

It was a custom among the Chippewa that the relatives of a murdered man could avenge his death by killing the murderer or, if they wished, could adopt the murderer into their family. The chiefs did not interfere with this custom.

Mr. Henry Selkirk related the following instances which came under his personal knowledge. A man killed a young man, and was taken before the young man's father, who announced that he would spare the life of the murderer and adopt him. Beside the old man sat his adopted sons. When the murderer was being led away to the old man's wigwam they shot him. No one could dispute their right, though the old man had forgiven him.

On another occasion a murderer was similarly arraigned before the father of the man he had killed. The old man made a long speech, walked four times around the murderer, and then shot him. A large assembly of Chippewa watched this and concurred in the judgment.

CUSTOMS PERTAINING TO WAR

Warning: A flute was used in giving a signal of danger to the village. It was played by a warrior, the intervals and manner of playing being different from that of the young men.

Summoning of warriors: A warrior who wished to lead a war party sent a messenger with tobacco to ask the warriors to join the expedition. The messenger went to each village and requested the warriors to assemble; he then explained the purpose of the expedition, filled a pipe, and holding the bowl of the pipe, offered the stem to one warrior after another. All who were willing to join the expedition signified this willingness by smoking the pipe. In a short time the warriors assembled and camped near the lodge of the leader, who gave a feast, explaining more fully the proposed expedition, and receiving the final pledge of the warriors.

a, b, Deer call; *c,* Trap for marten or beaver

PORTRAIT OF ENDUSOGIJIG

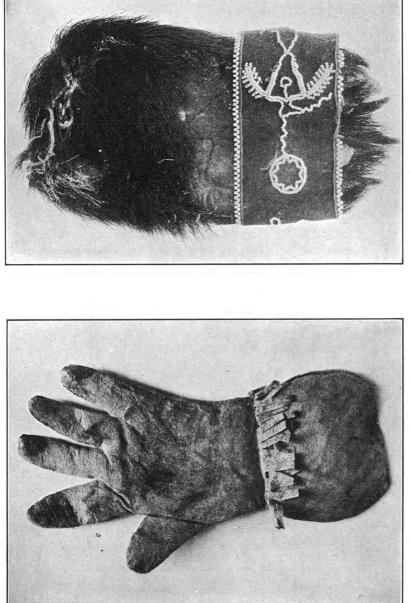

b, Bear-paw Mide bag

a, Buckskin "hand" sent as war summons

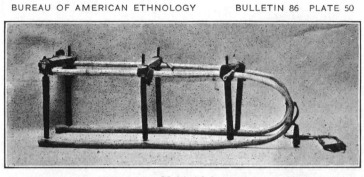

a, Model of sled

b, Model of sled made of branches, for immediate use

If the matter were of great importance the messenger might carry the representation of a hand with which the Chippewa were accustomed to seal important agreements. (See p. 173.) The use of such a representation was described by an old warrior, Niskigwun, and the "hand" (pl. 49, *a*) was made under his direction. It is a replica of a hand, which, according to his statement, was used in summoning the Chippewa to the expeditions which drove the Sioux out of western Wisconsin and northern and eastern Minnesota, and resulted in the distribution of the Chippewa over a large part of the conquered territory. Niskigwun took part in this expedition. The "hand" is life size, made of buckskin, and lightly filled with moss. There is an opening at the side of the wrist in which tobacco was placed, and the "hand" is smeared with red paint to represent blood. When sent to the warriors a pipe was laid across the palm of the hand, the fingers were folded over it, and the whole was wrapped securely in cloth or buckskin.

The occasion for sending the buckskin hand was as follows: Many years ago the Chippewa and Sioux made a peace agreement at La Pointe, Wis., and for a time the Sioux remained near the Chippewa, living in harmony with their former enemies. At length they withdrew to the country which they then inhabited and which is now the State of Minnesota. One of their number who had married a Chippewa woman remained among her people. For a time he treated her kindly, but later he beat and finally killed her. This angered the Chippewa so deeply that they resolved to break their peace pact with the Sioux and fight them to a bitter end. Accordingly, a buckskin hand similar to the one illustrated was made and sent to all the Chippewa villages. Those who accepted the tobacco and smoked the pipe, sent with this hand, signified in that manner their willingness to join the expedition. Thus a bloody war was instituted, a war that did not cease until the Sioux were driven out of Minnesota, and a final peace was consummated by the United States Government at Sisseton, S. Dak.

As the Chippewa drove out the Sioux they made Chippewa settlements where the Sioux camps had been. At that time the Sioux lived in mud or clay houses with an opening at the top for the smoke to escape. These houses had entrances that were larger at the base than at the top. The Chippewa killed most of the Sioux inside their houses. The Chippewa had been in contact with the whites and had secured gunpowder. When fighting the Sioux they wrapped gunpowder in a cloth and let it down through the hole in the top of the Sioux dwelling. The fire was directly beneath this hole. The Chippewa let down the bag of powder and ran away. Then there was a great explosion that killed all the Sioux in the house. This was the way that the Chippewa succeeded against the Sioux who had no gunpowder. The Sioux fought with bows and arrows, using chiefly arrows with bone heads.

Departure of warriors: The gathering that preceded the departure of the warriors has already been noted. Dances were held every night from the time of the assembling of the warriors to their departure. At these dances the leading warriors related their deeds of valor, enacted former exploits, and sang their personal war songs. Numerous songs concerning former victories over the Sioux were sung at these dances.[72] A war drum and a turtle shell were obtained from Maïngans, who said they belonged to his grandfather. The drum has two heads and is about 20 inches in diameter and 4 inches in thickness. Both of these articles were used in the gatherings that preceded a war expedition. Maïngans said that after the leader of the war party had finished drumming he placed the drum on the ground and on it laid a turtle shell filled with tobacco and red willow. The warriors sat around the drum and the leader passed the tobacco to them. When all had begun to smoke the leader made a speech, telling how honorable a thing it is to go to war; then he drummed again and sang. A large stone was in front of him, and he lifted it up as though it were exceedingly light in order to show his great strength. Then he offered a petition for the safety of those who were to go to war with him. None were allowed near except those who were to go with the warriors.

The final event before the departure of the war party from the village was the dog feast. The head alone was eaten, and only the men who were going with the expedition partook of it. Participation in this feast was considered equivalent to a pledge that the warriors were prepared to meet the full fortune of war, whether death or worse, at the hands of the enemy.

If the war party traveled on foot, the women walked in front of them for a short distance, walking to and fro before them and singing a song of farewell. (Bull. 45, No. 150.) After a time they separated and stood in two lines, between which the men walked, going forth without farewells. The women returned to the village, still singing the same song, which is translated:

> Come,
> It is time for you to depart,
> We are going on a long journey.

If the war party went in canoes, the women, in canoes, escorted them a short distance.

---

[72] Chippewa war songs and customs are considered in Bull. 53, Bur. Amer. Ethn., pp. 59–137.

Return of warriors: News of the return of a land expedition was usually brought by runners. A party returning in canoes announced their return by firing guns. The women then went in their canoes and "zigzagged" back and forth in front of them, escorting them in this manner.

If scalps had been secured they were presented to wives or mothers of men who had been killed by the enemy. A woman who received a Sioux scalp from Odjibwe once sang a song with these words, "Odjibwe our brother brings back." The scalps were put in hoops set on poles and carried from one village to another. When all the scalp dances were finished the poles bearing the scalps were usually planted in the grave of a man killed by the Sioux. They remained there undisturbed until wind and weather completed the victory.

It was said that "the leader of a war party gets all the credit if it is successful." This is in accordance with the Indian precept that a man must earn whatever honor is bestowed upon him. The man who secured scalps of the enemy was honored, but the man who simply went with the war party and did not distinguish himself in any way does not seem to have been lauded for that action.

TRANSPORTATION

As the Chippewa lived along the lakes and watercourses their summer transportation was by canoe. The size of the canoes varied from the small canoes used by children or young people in going along the shore on such small trips as gathering berries up to the large canoes which transported a family and all its possessions. In loading such a canoe the bottom was first loaded heavily and then the children alternated with the bags of clothing and household equipment in the middle of the canoe. There were always two paddles, one for the man who sat in the front and the other for the woman who sat in the stern. When "portaging" a canoe the Indian ties the paddles inside to the thwarts. There are two thwarts near each end of the canoe. He then puts the canoe above his head, the paddles resting on his shoulders with the blades toward the front. Held in this position the curve of the paddle blades helps support the canoe.

In old times the winter transportation was by dog team and toboggan or sled. Three dogs constituted a team and were harnessed by means of a collar made of a piece of flat rawhide with a hole cut in it. This was wound with blankets or soft hide so it would not chafe the dogs' necks. To this were fastened the straps for dragging the sled or toboggan, and the collars were slipped over the dogs' heads, resting against their shoulders. They traveled one behind another and were able to go 40 or 50 miles a day. Supplies for the American Fur Co. and the Hudson Bay Co. were sometimes shipped by way of St. Paul, Minn., and in winter such consignments were carried to the distant trading posts by dog teams, the trader sending down furs and receiving the goods as the dogs made their return trip. In summer such consignments were carried in Red River carts made entirely of wood and drawn by oxen.

Two types of winter carrier were used, the toboggan and the sled. The former was the older and was especially adapted for traveling through the woods. The French called this a traineau, and the Chippewa called it nobûgidaban (nobûg, flat; daban, drag), a word from which the English word toboggan is derived. These carriers were made of hard wood, cut during the winter when there was no sap in the trees. The end was turned by exposing the wood to the heat of a fire or placing it in hot water. Cleats were placed along the side and also across the toboggan, and the load was secured by means of cords passed beneath the side cleats and back and forth across the load. The toboggan was drawn by a cord passed from the floor of the toboggan to the upward-turned front portion. A toboggan drawn by dogs required only the width of a footpath, and its load was close to the ground, making it convenient in traveling through the woods. To the rear of the toboggan was fastened a strap which acted as a brake, and if the team descended a steep hill the driver or his companion walked behind the toboggan holding this strap to keep it from running on the dogs.

A rawhide covering was sometimes placed over the front part of a toboggan and was called a " shoe " because of its resemblance to the toe of a shoe. This afforded a protection to the limbs of the occupants. If necessary, several men pulled a toboggan, passing the straps across their chests. A hunter frequently carried a small toboggan on his back and used it in bringing home part of his game. When the Chippewa obtained horses they made large toboggans, which were commonly called " horse traineaux."

Rev. C. H. Beaulieu described the horse traineau used by his father when inspecting his inland trading posts, his father being at that time the trader at Fond du Lac, Minn. The front part of the traineau was covered by the " shoe " already described. Back of the seat was a space for his luggage and for an attendant who traveled with him. This man rode only part of the time, running behind the toboggan or sitting on the luggage. Another type of carrier was used near Lake Superior and near Mille Lac, both places having stretches of ice or open country. These carriers were large sledges with high poles at the sides, and were made of ash, which bends but does not break. In making them a long strip was bent so as to form a runner and one side of the floor of the sled. Horizontal bars connected the two sides of the sled, and across these the load was placed.

Perpendicular posts connected the runners with the floor of the sled, extending high above it and holding the load in place. (Pl. 50, *a*.) In loading either the sledge or toboggan a blanket or hide was spread on the ground. Articles were placed on it and the blanket or hide securely folded over them. A number of such packets were made.

A sled for immediate use might be made of rough branches tied together with green bark. This was made of branches of ash, the joinings being effected by splitting the branch, turning back the two sections, and binding each securely with green bark to the desired position. Such a sled might be made by a man in the woods and used to bring home game he had shot. (Pl. 50, *b*.) This was similar to the snowshoe in Plate 54, *d*.

METHODS OF MEASURING TIME, DISTANCE, AND QUANTITY

The native terms for these measurements are given on pages 17–19. By examination of these it will be noted that they are usually expressed in reference to the human body or to some manifestation of nature rather than in arbitrary terminology. Thus linear measurements are designated by the thumb, hand, and arm. Measures of small quantity are referred to the handful or to a " swallow." Measures of distance are referred to a man's endurance or convenience in traveling from place to place. The terms for day are referred to the sun and moon, and the divisions of the year are designated according to the progress of the seasons, or man's relation to them, as October, the falling (leaf) moon, and April the month in which something is boiled and evaporated, understood to refer to the making of maple sugar.

The Chippewa studied the heavens at night, and could tell the time of the night and the season of year by the stars. They had names for some of the constellations, such as the " bear head " and the " bear back."

EXCHANGE OF COMMODITIES WITHIN THE TRIBE

The Chippewa were surrounded by sources of supply that were abundant for their needs, but among them, as in any community, some persons made better use of opportunities than did their companions. If a family had more than enough for their needs, they frequently made gifts or exchanged with others in a friendly manner. It was considered beneath the dignity of an Indian to " dicker " or trade with a view of getting an exact equivalent. This did not arise until the traders came and traded for furs, placing a definite price upon commodities.

An example of specialized industrial work is afforded by the statement that there was an old lame man who "had knives and could cut and scrape anything." It was said that he could carve ladles and put native dyes on them. So skillful was this old man that "people would travel miles to get his work, and he supplied the whole reservation with pipestems."

PAYMENT OF ANNUITY

Previous to the treaty of 1854 the Chippewa went to Madeline Island in Lake Superior to receive their annuities. The supplies to be distributed were brought in sailing vessels, the only vessels on Lake Superior at that time being the *Algonquin* and the *John Jacob Astor*. The coin was shipped from Washington in boxes, each of which contained $1,000. From this custom arose the use of a Chippewa word meaning "a little box full," in referring to one thousand dollars. The tops of the boxes were screwed down and the top of each screw was covered with sealing wax. The Chippewa term for annuity means "the paying."

The Chippewa to the number of many thousands came from over the entire territory now comprised in northern Wisconsin and northern Minnesota, traveling on foot or in canoes. The annuities were given early in September, and the Indians came some time before that. They were brought from the mainland to the island in great bateaux, and received rations while waiting for the annuities. In later years the annuities were paid at Fond du Lac, and still more recently at the various agencies on the reservations.

A few days before the payment of an annuity the chief of each band with his leading warrior went to the issue clerk and reported the number of families in that band, the persons comprising the families, and any special needs they might have. The articles were wrapped in great bundles and prepared before the day they were to be distributed, several clerks being necessary to tear off the lengths of cloth and sort out the articles. The blankets were of three colors, white, red, and green.

Each chief personally received a little more than the Indians, this being called the "surplus." As a matter of fact, the quantity of goods required for the chiefs was taken out first, each receiving according to the size of his band, and the remainder was divided pro rata among the Indians.

A man usually received—
> A three-point blanket.
> Broadcloth for breechcloth and leggings.
> Calico or linsey-woolsey for shirt.
> Knife.

Gun (flintlock).

Comb.

Lead bars for making bullets. (These bars were about 16 inches long and the thickness of a man's thumb, and could be broken in short pieces with an ax.)

A woman usually received—

A two-and-a-half point blanket.

Calico or linsey-woolsey for dress.

Flannel.

Comb.

Broadcloth torn in dress lengths.

Needles, thimble, thread, scissors (thread in skeins).

Tin dishes.

For a child there would be given a one-point or two-point blanket and cloth for a dress, or other needed articles.

The principal articles of food distributed were flour, pork, and saleratus.

After the goods had been distributed the Indians were given money, the payment being in silver and amounting to three to ten dollars per person.

The issuing was done expeditiously. The agent's interpreter usually acted as roll keeper. He called the name of a chief, and the chief stepped forward and stood beside him. The interpreter then called the names of the members of that band and the number of shares to which each was entitled. The chief was ready to identify the men if necessary, and to see that each was given his share. The man spread his blanket on the floor, put the articles in it, tied the corners together and threw the pack over his shoulder, giving place to the next man. The "shares" corresponded to the number of persons in his family.

Traders were allowed inside to collect accounts, bringing a list of the charges against individuals. Frequently an Indian would give the trader all his payment money, and the trader would take out the amount of the charge, or, at the Indian's request, would keep the entire amount. In such an event the Indian would later go to the trader and ask how his account stood. If the balance was in the Indian's favor the trader would ask whether he wanted cash or trade. If the Indian wanted trade he would tell the trader what articles he desired and the trader would make out a list to the amount of the credit. The Indian would hand the list to the trader's clerk and receive the goods. Rev. C. H. Beaulieu said that he remembered an Indian at Fond du Lac who had all his payment money in the corner of his blanket, and who gave it without counting to Rev. Beaulieu's father, then trader at that point.

Mrs. Julia Warren Spears gave the following account of a payment at Madeline Island. The account was in manuscript, written by her at the age of 88.[73]

In the summer of 1847, when a girl, I was staying with my brother's family at the old fort * * * in the southern part of Madeline Island. The old fort was the first building ever built on the island; built by my grandfather, Michel Cadotte, his home and trading post. After a few years my father * * * built a home there, a number of buildings at the same time, so it was quite a village. There were strong cedar posts put all around the buildings as a protection for the Indians. The Indian payment was to be in the month of August. The Chippewa were arriving every day from all parts of Wisconsin Territory, and the island was very crowded when they all arrived. Their agent was James P. Hays; he was a good man. My brother, William W. Warren, was the interpreter. They were both well liked by the Indians. That year the Indians received $10 a head, and each family got a very large bundle of goods. * * * They had rations issued out to them during payment. * * * The day before they would start for their homes they had a custom of going to all the stores and houses and dancing for about one hour, expecting food to be given them. They went around in different parties of about 25 or 30. A party came to our house at the old fort. We were prepared for them. The day before we had cooked a lot of "Legolet bread," a lot of boiled salt pork, and cookies to give them. They came dancing and hooting. They were naked, with breechcloths, their bodies painted with black, red, yellow, vermilion, with all kinds of stripes and figures. They were a fierce-looking crowd. They were all good dancers. After they were through they sat down on the grass and smoked. We gave them their food, and they were well pleased. They thanked us and shook hands with us all as they left.

TRADERS AND TRADING POSTS

French and English traders came among the Chippewa at an early date. It is probable that the French traders came first, during the time that preceded the taking of Canada by the English.

The oldest trading post of the American Fur Co. among the Chippewa was at Mackinaw Island, and a secondary post was established about 1825 on Madeline Island in Lake Superior. This post was in charge of Michel Cadotte, maternal grandfather of Mrs. Mary Warren English, Mrs. Julia Spears, and William W. Warren, author of the "History of the Ojibways." Madeline Island was also the point where annuities were paid to the Chippewa. Later a trading post was established at Fond du Lac, Minn., known as the post for the Department of Fond du Lac. This post was in charge of Clement Beaulieu, father of Rev. Clement H. Beaulieu. There the inland traders from the various parts of the present State of Minnesota obtained the stock of goods which they traded with the Indians for their furs. The traders started in the early fall, the goods being

---

[73] Practically the only changes in this manuscript are those in punctuation and capitalization.

put in packs weighing 75 pounds each, this being half the load of a man in portaging. One pack was strapped on his back, the other being thrown on top of it. They went in canoes, following the various watercourses. With them were men from the trading post who paddled or poled the canoes. These men acted as *coureurs du bois* in the Indian country, and at the end of the season they paddled or poled the canoes on the return trip to the post at Fond du Lac.

At each inland post the "post trader" had his warehouse and dwelling. On their return from Fond du Lac the Indians hastened to make the principal purchases of the year and to "outfit" for their hunting expeditions. Usually they were allowed to have their purchases charged to their account, the trader's books being kept by pictures of articles purchased, and when furs were placed to a man's credit, by pictures of the various sorts of furs. This bookkeeping was called by a Chippewa word meaning "he pictures."

The Indians who lived near the post were able to deal directly with the trader, bringing in their furs and having them placed to their credit or taking their value in goods. Those living farther away had their dealings chiefly with the *coureurs du bois*, who were outfitted by the trader. They usually went singly and might be gone a longer or shorter time. They carried packs on their backs or on toboggans, going out laden with trader's goods and returning with quantities of furs.

The traders carried a stock of staple articles and also trinkets. Broadcloth of several qualities and "list-cloth" were sold. (See section on clothing.) The trader measured this cloth from his ear to the end of his fingers. Some measurements were made by spreading both arms. Among the larger articles in the trader's store were blankets, shawls, kettles, and pans. Traders also sold nets of "gill twine," and the cord for making these nets.

Among the trinkets offered for sale were beads for necklaces and for beadwork, silver armlets, ribbons, and colored worsted braid, large brooches of pierced silver often measuring more than 2 inches in diameter, two of these being worn on the front of a woman's dress. There were also huge "ear bobs" of silver, the Indians piercing their ears and wearing sometimes several of these heavy ornaments. Similar heavy ornaments were worn in the nose, which was pierced. Nose rings so large that they extended down over the mouth were also worn. Silver and "gilt" rings were sold, also thimbles, all these trinkets being purchased most liberally in the spring when the Indians brought in their furs. A bear hide was worth not more than the equivalent of $10 in trade. The value of other furs varied according to their size and quality.

The trader had a frame in which he packed his furs. This frame was about 30 inches long and 2 feet wide, and had four corner

posts and a bottom or floor raised a little above the ground. Before
the trader began to pack the furs he laid three cords across the
bottom of the frame, these cords being long enough to tie over the
bale of furs when the frame had been filled. The trader then packed
the furs, placing the largest at the bottom, and folding the sides if
they were too large. Bearskins were usually placed at the bottom,
then smaller skins laid flat. The hides dried on a frame (see section
on tanning) were shipped as they were taken from the tanning frame.
The bale was topped with a bearskin if this was available, otherwise
a wolfskin was used at the top. Each bale was numbered and its
contents listed. When the frame was filled the cords were tied
around the furs. The packing usually was done outdoors, and the
trader had a stout frame with a lever so that he could press down the
pack of furs and tighten the cords.

The furs collected from the Indians were usually shipped to
Leipzig, which was then the fur market of the world.

FIRE MAKING AND USES OF FIRE

A Chippewa said: "The greatest wonder that ever came to the
Indians was fire. Like everything else, it came to them through the
Mide. Some one asked, 'What do you want us to do with this?' A
man replied, 'This is for warmth and for cooking.' The Indians
were afraid of it at first, but soon learned that it was useful." They
found that the fire burned them, causing pain, but the Mide provided a "medicine" which they could put on their hands and on
the soles of their feet, after which they could thrust their hands into
the fire or walk in the flames without being hurt. A song was sung
when this "fire-charm" was used. (Bull. 45, No. 86.)

Three methods of obtaining a spark of fire were used among the
Chippewa. The simplest was the striking together of two stones,
the "punk" being held in the same hand as one of the stones. Next
in probable development may be placed the striking together of
stone and metal, and in later times the obtaining of a spark by
friction between two pieces of wood, the apparatus comprising a bow,
a stick of ash, and a cedar hearth with shredded bark "to catch the
spark." Birch and cedar bark were used, but the latter was considered the more inflammable of the two. (Pl. 51, a, b, c, d.)

The obtaining of fire by the use of flint and steel was the more
common of the three customs above noted. The form of the steel
varied from a broken file to a well-shaped piece of iron, suggesting
the work of a blacksmith. (Pl. 52, h, upper.) The most common
form is the one shown below the first. (Pl. 52, h, lower.) This was
obtained from an old woman who said it belonged to her grandmother.

With the flint and steel was carried a piece of decayed wood, or "punk." A bit of flint appears as *f*, and decayed wood as *g*, in Plate 52.

A Chippewa said, "Fire was the first and best tool that the Indians had."

Before axes were common the Chippewa obtained wood by burning a fallen tree into sections. A log of soft wood was selected and fires were made at intervals beneath it. The fire was allowed to burn only enough so that the log could be broken.

Mide drums and similar articles were hollowed by charring the wood and scraping it out.

The heat of a fire was used in scorching wood as a decoration.

Heated stone or metal points were used in burning holes in pipes, flutes, and other wooden articles.

Heated stones were used in the sweat lodge.

A Canadian Chippewa said that in a winter camp long ago his people obtained water by putting a snowball on the end of a stick and placing the stick in the ground near the fire, slanting over a birch-bark dish. The snow melted and the water fell into the dish.

One or two men traveling in the winter sometimes made a high bank of snow on the windward side of their little camp and slept between the snow bank and the fire.

It was said that a winter traveler sometimes made a fire on the place where he wished to sleep, scraped the embers away, wrapped himself in his blanket, and lay down on the warmed ground. Another informant doubted whether this was a "strictly Indian custom."

In the long winter evenings the fire in the lodge gave light for work and the various activities of the family.

Signal fires were used, especially for signaling across wide expanses of water. The offering of food by placing it in the fire is noted on page 130. (See also p. 145.)

The uses of fire for drying meat, fish, fruit, and vegetables are noted in the sections on these subjects.

PIPES

(*a*) *Pipe bowls.*—Stone pipe bowls were in use among the Chippewa at an early date, and it was said "they used to dig a hole in the stone for the tobacco." The writer obtained a pipe bowl of stone with a simple decoration of straight lines which belonged to the celebrated chief Wadena and had been in his family for many generations; also a pipe bowl of chipped red stone which belonged to Niskigwun. A peculiarity of this pipe bowl is the shape, which fits conveniently between the fingers. These are of hard stone.

Two sorts of comparatively soft stone were widely used by the Chippewa. These were a smooth black stone found in central Wisconsin and a red stone found near Lake Superior. The latter was similar in texture but darker in color than the familiar red pipe-stone of the Sioux. The pipes smoked by women were usually of the black stone and were small. Plate 52 (at the top) shows a typical woman's pipe. Pipes of red pipestone were smoked by the men (pl. 52, *a*), and as the stone was comparatively soft when first quarried it was possible to inlay the pipe with decorations of lead. Bars of lead were given to the Chippewa as part of their annuities, lead being needed for melting into bullets. The pipe decorations took the form of lines and frequently of somewhat elaborate designs. These were cut in the stone and filled with the melted lead, which afterwards was highly polished. The Indians also had pipe bowls made of a material called in English " white lead." This was an alloy containing lead and some harder metal, and was soft enough to be shaped with a knife. Wooden pipe bowls were made from a knot of wood and sometimes were carved. The openings were burned with a hot iron. Small pronged deer horns were also used as pipe bowls. The stem and pipe were separated when put into the pipe bag, and the tobacco was removed from the bowl by means of a sharpened stick called a " pipe cleaner " (pl. 52, *e*), which was also carried in the pipe bag (pl. 52, *b*).

(*b*) *Pipestems.*—Any wood with a pith was used for round pipe-stems, hazel being a favored material. A straight slender stick was selected and carefully split lengthwise. The pith was then removed and the stick glued together again. The glue commonly used was obtained from the sturgeon. If glue were not available they sometimes used pitch, which was said to be " very sticky when applied warm." These had the mouth end " slightly flattened." The pipe-stems in common use by both men and women were about 7 inches long. Longer pipestems were used on formal occasions, and were sometimes decorated by scorching the wood. (See pp. 171–172.) Flat pipestems were made in a similar manner and usually were about 1½ inches wide. The simplest decoration consisted of brass tacks, the wood usually being scorched to give a brown color. Sometimes a portion of the wood on either side of the bore was cut out, giving an ornamental openwork pattern. Occasionally the entire stem was carved in an openwork pattern, the flue extending down one side of the stem.

The stems of ceremonial pipes were frequently more than 3 feet long and were elaborately decorated.

(*c*) *Materials for smoking.*—The materials smoked by the Chippewa in earliest times were said to be the dried leaves of the bearberry (*Arctostaphylos uva-ursi* (L.) Spreng.), and the dried, powdered root of a plant identified as *Aster novae-angliae* L. The latter

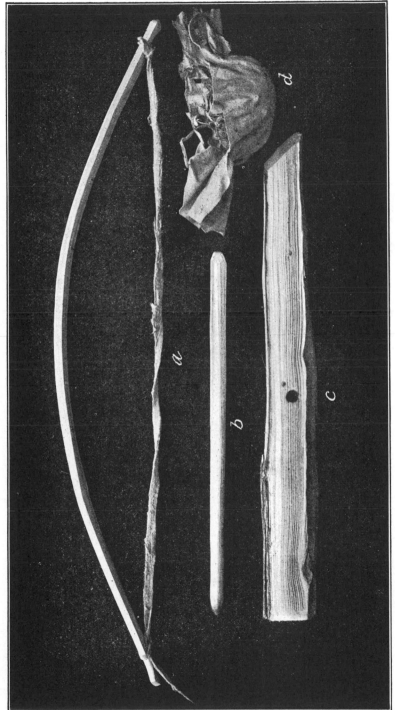

FIRE-MAKING OUTFIT, CONSISTING OF BOW, STICK, HEARTH, AND SOFT BARK

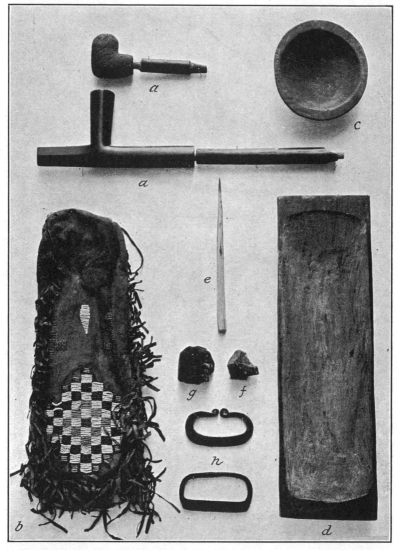

a, Typical woman's pipe and stone pipe; b, Bag for carrying pipe and tobacco; c, Bowl for
cutting tobacco; d, Tray in which tobacco and willow are mixed; e, Pipe cleaner

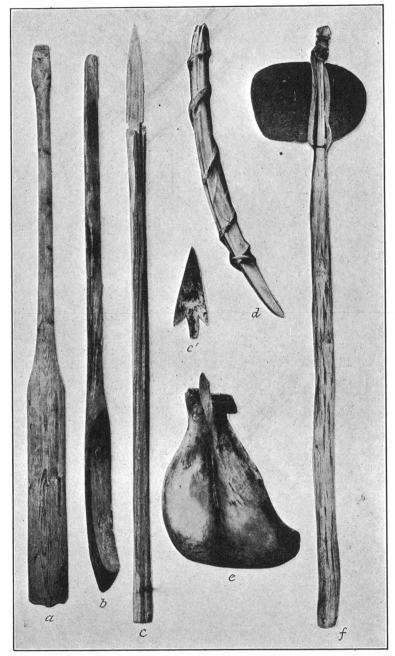

a, Canoe paddle; b, Snow shovel; c, Arrow shaft, with point set lightly; c', Arrow point;
d, Two knives made of bone; e, Shoulder blade used as hoe; f, Stone club

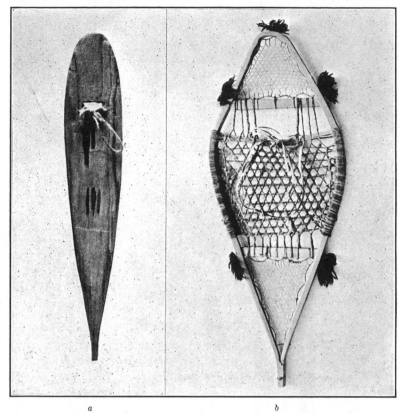

a   b

a, Model of wooden snowshoe, used in Canada; b, Snowshoe

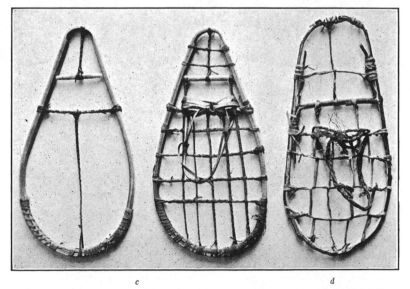

c   d

c, "Bear paw" snowshoe (unfinished and finished); d, snowshoe made of branches, for immediate use

was also smoked as a "charm" to attract game (pp. 110, 111). Two sorts of bark were smoked, one being known as "red willow" (*Cornus stolonifera* Michx.) and the other as "spotted willow" (*Cornus rugosa* Lam.). The manner of preparing the bark is as follows: The sticks are gathered in bundles, the outer bark is removed and discarded, and the inner bark is scraped off, the man drawing his knife toward him when removing it. He then takes one of the sticks and splices another on it so as to form a letter "Y," after which he laces narrow strips of basswood or other fiber back and forth between the upper branches of the frame, making a sort of netting. This is his "toaster" when preparing his material for smoking. He puts the scraped bark on this little framework and holds it over the fire until the scrapings of bark are crisped or toasted to the desired degree. He takes a little of this material in his hands, and holding his hands in a vertical position over a cloth rubs the crisped bark between his palms, letting the resultant powder fall on the cloth. It is then tied in a cloth or wrapped in leather and kept for use, or may be put loose in a man's tobacco bag. A plug of the white man's tobacco or a "twist" of native tobacco is kept in the same bag, and when a man wishes to smoke he slices a little tobacco, puts the powdered bark on the little pile of tobacco and mixes the two. The usual proportion is 2 parts of powdered bark to 1 part of sliced plug tobacco. In the old days a much smaller proportion of tobacco was used, as it was difficult to obtain and was made to last as long as possible. A small wooden bowl is used for cutting the tobacco, which may be mixed and offered in an oblong tray if a number are smoking. (Pl. 52, *c*, *d*.)

The above, of course, represents only the most typical custom, which varies widely in usage. Thus some men cut the bark finely and use it without scorching, and others use the white man's "smoking tobacco" instead of the plug tobacco.

Men usually carried dry cedar chips wrapped in buckskin with their flint and steel so that a light for the pipe could be obtained at any time.

Tobacco was regarded as a gift from the manido, and for this reason it was supposed to have "magic power," in that it increased the efficacy of a request and made an obligation or agreement more binding. Thus a gift of tobacco accompanied a request and its acceptance signified a promise to grant the request. The smoking of tobacco by both parties was an essential part of the making of a treaty. Tobacco was put in the water by those who desired that a storm should subside, and it was put in the fire if a storm were feared on land, this action being performed by someone who was qualified by his dreams to make the request from the proper manido.

Thus, if a party were in danger from a storm it was not sufficient for any member of it to put the tobacco in the water or the fire. This must be done by someone who has had a suitable dream.

BOWS AND ARROWS

The principal informants on this subject were Ĕn'dûsogi'jĭg (pl. 48), a chief of the Mille Lac band, and Tom Skinaway, a blind member of that band. Both had been skillful workers in wood. Endusogijig said that in old days the Chippewa made bows from small trees, scraping off the bark and bending them. Such bows were probably for emergency use, like the sleds and snowshoes that were roughly made when needed. The bows of finished workmanship were made of hickory or ash, the former being preferred for bows used in war or when hunting large animals. The length of the bow varied with the stature of the owner and was equivalent to the measure from the point of the shoulder across the chest to the end of the middle finger of the opposite hand. It was said a typical bow was about 48 inches long, and the largest bows were about three fingers wide.

Chippewa bows were of four varieties: (1) Bow having the outer surface flat and the inner with a ridge or rib. This was particularly strong. (2) Bow with both outer and inner surfaces flat. (3) Bow with the sides cut in scallops, this sort of bow being used when hunting squirrels. (4) Bow with the outer surface rounded and the inner surface flat. This type was a hunting bow and was also used in war. It was said that the bows with both surfaces flat were not strong enough for war and broke if used in that manner. After the bow was shaped it was put in hot water to bend the wood and also to strengthen it. A bow might also be strengthened by charring the inner surface.

The bows were decorated in various ways. The colored juice of roots was formerly used for this purpose. A reddish color was produced by the use of a "black mud" found near a certain spring. They put this mud on the fire and held the bow in the fumes. Lines were also etched with a hot pointed stone or a hot iron and might be filled with red paint.

Only two materials were said to make serviceable bowstrings. These were ze'sûb (nettle-stalk fiber), and the neck of a snapping turtle. One informant included the sinew of moose or deer but the other said this material was likely to break when wet. The nettle-stalk fiber was "waxed" or rubbed with pitch to make it waterproof, this being applied after the bowstring was finished. The preparation of this fiber is described on page 152. In making a bowstring of a turtle's neck the Chippewa cut off the neck of the snapping turtle close to its body, removed the skin and cut it round and round, making a long strip, which they twisted into a cord. This type of bowstring was said to be particularly good as it would neither stretch nor shrink, and lasted a long time.

The arrows used by the Chippewa were not so long as the Sioux arrows, partly because a long arrow was not convenient to use in the woods, and also because the Chippewa often shot "from the knee." The Chippewa war arrow was equivalent to the distance from a little below a man's elbow to the end of his first finger. The shaft was smoothed by a grooved piece of sandstone that was rubbed around the wood. Some arrows were of wood throughout but a majority consisted of a wooden shaft with an arrow point fastened with sinew.

In very old times the stalk of the June berry bush was used for arrow shafts; a notch was cut in this stalk, the arrow point of stone or iron was inserted and held in place by winding the shaft with strips of green bark from the small branches of the June berry. Arrows made of pine or cedar were used in hunting ducks or other water birds, as they would float on the water if they missed their mark, and could thus be recovered. Such arrows had a further advantage in that they did not tear the bird. If arrows with metal points were used in hunting ducks, it was customary to sharpen the metal like a little blade so it would cut the feathers and go through the bird. A special arrow for hunting rabbits had the end tipped with the claw of a mud turtle. This was like a sharp spike and penetrated the fur better than an ordinary arrow point. In old times arrow points of bone were used for shooting deer. These were made of bones that were somewhat pointed and were made sharply pointed for this purpose. A Canadian Chippewa said that his people fastened the arrow point to the shaft so lightly that it became detached as the deer ran through the bushes. Remaining in the animal, it made its death more sure. The earliest iron arrow points were cut from the hoop of a pork barrel and tied in place with sinew. Later they were cut from frying pans or other utensils obtained from the traders. (Pl. 53, c, c'.)

Feathers were tied to the arrow shaft with sinew, the feathers most desired being those of the eagle and hawk. These were frequently dyed in bright colors. Each warrior had his own mark on his arrows, this being a special sort of feathers or a mark on the shaft consisting of lines burned with a hot iron. A good arrow would travel about 500 feet and the "shooting distance" for deer was about 50 feet. Tom Skinaway said that when he was a young man he could make 10 arrows in a day, complete with points and feathers. This was the number that usually comprised an "order" from a worker in wood.

Arrows with sharp points were carried in a quiver of stiff buckskin fastened to a band that crossed the body, passing over the right arm and under the left. The quiver rested on the man's chest, the end of the arrows being in front of his face when he was using the bow, and easily available to his right hand.

SNOWSHOES

Three sorts of snowshoes were used by the Chippewa in the United States, i. e., the round snowshoe, the "snowshoe with a tail," and the snowshoe with the toe turned up. All these consist of a wooden frame with netting in the open spaces. A Canadian Chippewa added a fourth sort, which consisted entirely of wood and was fastened to the foot by a thong across the toes. A model of this snowshoe is shown in Plate 54, a.

The wooden frame of a snowshoe is usually of ash, the wood being bent by heating it. Strips of rawhide were commonly used for the netting below the feet, and twine for the netting at the ends. It was said that horsehide is particularly adapted to this use, as it neither stretches nor shrinks when wet. On the north shore of Lake Superior the Chippewa make the netting under the feet from the intestines of freshly killed moose and use the sinew for the smaller nettings.

The round snowshoe is probably the oldest form and is called "bear-paw shoe" and "old woman's shoe." The shape of these snowshoes is not unlike that of a bear's footprint, and the name also refers to an old legend that the bear once wore snowshoes. The second name is due to the fact that old women usually wear this kind of snowshoes. One of a crude pair is shown in Plate 54, d. Such might be worn by old women or made in an emergency from unpeeled branches, laced with narrow strips of basswood fiber. A pair of bear-paw snowshoes in course of construction is illustrated in Plate 54, c, showing the order in which the braces were adjusted. The netting in snowshoes was done with a wooden needle having the eye midway its length. (Pl. 9, a (c).) The flat snowshoes are excellent for traveling on level country where there are no trees. For use in the woods, however, the snowshoes with the toes turned upward were more practical. These were similar to the flat snowshoes in every other respect. (Pl. 54, b.)

A Canadian Chippewa said that his people had snowshoes with large-meshed netting for use on soft snow and with small-meshed netting for travel on hard snow.[74] An informant at Mille Lac said

---

[74] Cf. Orr, R. B., Snowshoes. Thirty-second Ann. Arch. Rept., App. Rept. Min. Ed. Ont., Toronto, 1920, p. 24.

that neither these nor the snowshoes made entirely of wood were ever used by the Chippewa of Minnesota.

MAKING OF PITCH

A necessary commodity in the economic life of the Chippewa was the pitch used to cover the seams of articles made of birch bark, rendering them water-tight, and also used for torches. The gum of any evergreen tree could be used in making pitch, but Endusogijig said that trees growing near the water had the best gum. It was the custom to go to the woods in summer and scrape the bark from portions of selected trees. The gum would then ooze out and the Indian would return later and gather it. The gum, with the pieces of bark to which it adhered, was put in a bag woven of basswood fiber (pl. 55, *a*), and boiled in a kettle. The texture of the bag was open so that the gum escaped and was skimmed from the surface of the water, the bark and refuse remaining in the bag. The writer saw this process at White Earth. The gum, having been boiled, was placed in a birch-bark dish for storage and a piece of birch bark tied on as a cover. At a subsequent time it was boiled to the proper consistency for use, and when it was almost done a quantity of charcoal was added to make the pitch firm. This charcoal was from cedar chips and was pounded to a fine powder. Pitch is applied to canoes with a paddle or spatula of suitable size and to small articles with a small spatula. (Pl. 55, *c*.)

TORCHES

Birch bark and pitch were the materials used for giving light at night, various forms of torches being made from them.

(*a*) The most common torch was a piece of tightly twisted birch bark. The torch illustrated (pl. 56, *a*) is 15 inches long and it is said would burn while a person traveled about a mile. If it burned low it was brightened by lowering and shaking it a little, after which it was held erect.

(*b*) The women's torches were of the same type. They usually were lighted at the fire and carried by the women on errands about the camp. If a woman's work required a light she stuck this torch on the end of a stick placed upright in the ground. These torches (pl. 56, *b*) are almost the same length as the former torch, but much smaller in diameter.

(*c*) The torch used for fishing was of a different type and is described on page 129. (Pl. 45, *c*.)

(*d*) A pitched torch was used in hunting deer, which were attracted by its light. (Pl. 56, *c*.) This torch was made by taking a stick of hazel brush and crushing it so that the tough fibers were well separated; this was dipped in melted pitch which penetrated between the fibers; it was then wrapped in a thin cloth and the pitch spread thickly over the cloth. The specimen illustrated was 12 inches long, and it was said that it would burn all night. This torch was placed in a socket on the front of a canoe. Behind it was a shield of sufficient size to conceal the occupants of the canoe. In old times this reflector was made of ash bark, bent around, but in later years a board has been used for this purpose.

A tallow torch was prepared like a pitch torch. The "grease inside the body of a deer" was melted in a kettle. A stick of any sort of wood was pounded with a stone at one end until it was mashed into fibers. Butternut was said to be good for this purpose. This end was put in the melted tallow until the fibers were filled with it. Then a cloth was wrapped around it, and it was dipped again, this being repeated if necessary.

CANOES

As the Chippewa traveled chiefly by water, the canoe was an article of great economic importance in the tribe. The size of the canoe varied according to its use, the largest canoes being capable of carrying more than 10 persons. The ordinary length was three double arm spreads, and the width was about 36 inches in the middle. This size would hold about six adults, and if they wished to travel rapidly it would need four men to paddle the canoe. The lines of the canoe varied, some being designed for speed and others for safety in the transportation of commodities. It was said that Winabojo taught them to make canoes, as well as bows, arrows, and all other useful articles. A good canoe maker was highly respected in the tribe, as the work required skill and experience, and the welfare and safety of the tribe was largely dependent on the proper building of its canoes. Young men were allowed to assist in the work, but canoe making was regarded as a craft which "must be learned by observation and experience."

The canoes were made of birch bark which was cut in the early spring, when the bark is most easily removed from the tree. For this purpose a large tree was selected with particularly heavy bark. The tree was felled and the bark was removed.

Cedar was used for the ribs, thwarts, and the piece around the top, and the sewing was done with the split roots of either tamarack or spruce. Much stress was laid upon the proper whittling of the ribs, and it was said that only a few men in the tribe (in old days) could make these of really excellent shape. If these were faulty the canoe was easily upset. A good canoe maker had certain measurements which he used in planning a canoe, the unit of measurement being the "hand spread," or span from the thumb to the end of the middle finger. The details of these measurements are too complicated for present consideration. The principal tool was the curved knife, commonly called a "crooked knife." The "canoe awl" was made of bone several inches long and slightly curved. (Pl. 55, *b*.) This was used in making holes in the bark, through which the split root was passed in sewing together the sheets of bark which formed the body of the canoe, and in attaching the "stay" which formed the upper edge. Over the seams a layer of pitch was applied with a wooden spatula, as noted in a subsequent paragraph.

There were different prices for making a canoe. An informant at Mille Lac remembered an instance in which an old man was paid a blanket and two 10-yard pieces of calico for a canoe. A frequent price was a three-point blanket.

The camp of Joe Brown, considered the best canoe maker at White Earth, was visited by the writer in 1917 and a portion of the process was photographed. (Pl. 57.) Two pairs of short poles were placed upright in the ground, the distance between the pairs representing the width of the canoe. A flat frame, the length and width of the inside of the canoe, was laid on the ground between the rows of poles, and on this frame were laid sheets of birch bark, weighted down with stones. These sheets of bark were to form the body of the canoe. Short stakes were put along the sides of the frame, bending the edges of the birch bark upward, close to the sides of the frame. A piece of wood outlining the upper edge of the canoe was then fastened in place, and the ends of the bark were fastened to this rim. The curve at the ends was shaped by a piece of cedar which was used as a pattern.

Next were put in place the flat pieces of wood which line the canoe. These were very thin, 4 to 6 inches wide, and of different lengths, some being 4 or 5 feet long. These extended the length of the canoe next the birch bark. The ribs were then put in, horizontal, extending from one rim, across the bottom of the craft, to the rim on the opposite side. Then the narrow crossbars were fastened in place, acting as braces to the canoe. If there were enough women to do the sewing a canoe could be "sewed" in one day, the sheets of bark fastened together, and the rim securely sewed to the bark. The canoe was then allowed to dry about four days, and then the seams were covered with pitch. This could be done in one day, but if only one woman were doing the work she took longer for the task, keeping the canoe well protected from the sun and working as she had opportunity. The writer photographed a woman at this work, near the village of Waba'ciŋg (commonly called Ponema, or Cross Lake), on Red Lake, opposite the agency. She had the warm pitch in a small kettle, put it on with a spatula, and smoothed it with her thumb.

A canoe in use at Cass Lake and one made by an expert canoe maker at Mille Lac are shown in Plate 58.

TWINE

(a) *Basswood fiber, commonly called basswood bark.*—One of the most important articles in the economic life of the Chippewa was the twine made from the fiber that lies between the bark and the wood of the basswood tree.

In removing the bark from the tree an incision was made at a point as high as a man could reach, the cut descending straight to the ground, after which the bark was turned back in a sheet. It was then cut in lengthwise strips about 4 inches wide and laid among the reeds at the edge of a lake or pond, being held in place by tying the reeds together above it. There it remained for about 10 days. The writer saw these strips of bark taken from the water, softened and slippery from soaking. The rough outer bark was easily detached and the soft yellow fiber or inner bark heaped in the bottom of the boat. It was cut into narrower strips, wound in coils, and hung to dry. In this form it was ready to store with a woman's supply of birch bark, reeds, and other materials. There were many layers of this fiber, and the entire thickness would be needed for the strips in bags for boiling gum or in making baskets. Somewhat thinner fiber was used for woven bags, and one thickness was sufficient for twine, the fiber being split when the twine was made. In separating the layers of bark an Indian woman begins in the middle of a strip perhaps 6 feet in length and works toward the ends. Slippery-elm bark was similarly used, though less extensively. This bark required no soaking before being used.

The material used for tying sheaves of wild rice in the field was commonly called " rice twine," but was not twisted. It consisted of narrow strips of basswood fiber tied end to end. The day after the bark was taken from the water it was said to be in the proper state for making "rice twine." It was also said the work must be finished that day or the bark would become too dry. The first part of the process consisted in boiling the bark to make it tough and strong. The several layers were separated and the pieces cut into strips about one-half inch wide. Each of these narrow strips was coiled separately and the coils heaped in a birch-bark tray. When this was finished the strips were tied together and wound in a ball, the winding being done in such a manner that the ball was

a, Bag for boiling gum; *b*, Canoe awl; *c*, Pitch spreader

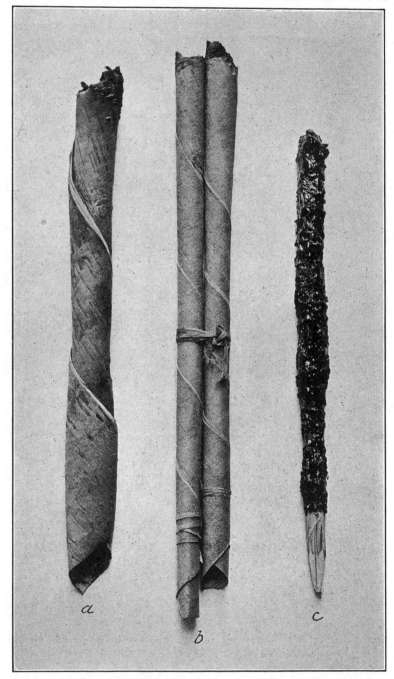

a, "Traveler's torch," birch bark; *b*, "Women's torches," birch bark; *c*, Pitched torch

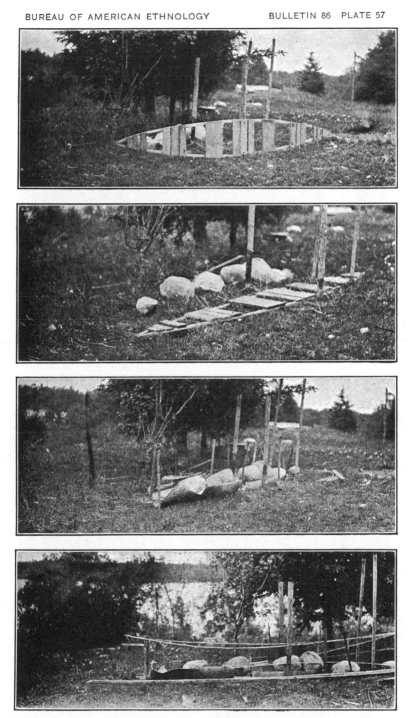

PROCESS OF MAKING A CANOE

CASS LAKE MINN.

BIRCH-BARK CANOES

unwound from the middle. One ball was said to be enough for a canoe load of rice.

Basswood fiber was used in smaller quantities and narrower width for tying the stones on fish nets to serve as sinkers, for sewing the tops on filled makuks and rice bags, and for a multitude of other purposes. Basswood bark was an article in such frequent use that a woman had a quantity of it in all thicknesses at hand and prepared it in various ways as it might be needed. If she wished to tie a small packet, she usually moistened a strip of bark by drawing it between her lips.

The bark to be used for twisted cord was prepared by moistening it, separating it into layers, and tearing strips of the desired width. If the twine is to be very strong the bark is boiled. The woody fibers are detached from one another and the bark softened by drawing the strips of bark back and forth through the pelvic bone of a bear which has an opening of suitable size, the bone being shown in Plate 59, a. This work, in old times, was usually done by children. The process of making twisted twine is described as follows by Doctor Skinner.[75] The woman "takes two of the fibers in one hand and holds them, spread a few inches apart, against her bare shin. She slides the palm of her other hand backward and forward over them until the fibers twist together. At the end of each yard she combs the fibers with her fingers, selects two more, and rolling half an inch of their ends with the ends of the old piece, makes a splice so perfect that it is invisible." The work, as seen by the writer, was done on the flesh of the right leg above the knee, this forming a cushion on which the fibers were readily twisted. The entire process is dexterous and surprisingly rapid. Twine made in this manner was an important article of economic use.

(b) *Bulrushes.*—It is said the vegetable substance first used by the Chippewa in making twine was the outer covering of the rushes used in making floor mats (*Scirpus validus* Vahl). This root covering falls under the water and clings around the root of the plant, making it difficult to secure. The twine was made by twisting two strands of this into a cord and then twisting together two of these cords into a small rope.

(c) *Nettle-stalk fiber.*—The fiber of the wood nettle (*Urticastrum divaricatum* (L.) Kuntze) was as important as basswood bark to the industries of Chippewa women. Cord made from this fiber was fine and strong. The plants that dried in the field were best adapted to this purpose, though freshly cut stalks were sometimes used. The

[75] Skinner, Alanson. Material Culture of the Menomini. *In* Indian Notes and Monographs, Museum of the American Indian, Heye Foundation, New York, 1921, p. 250.

process was the same as that described in connection with basswood bark. The finest cord was used for weaving into cloth. (See p. 30.) Nettle fiber twine was used, among other purposes, for fish nets and snares for rabbits and traps for otter. Plate 59, c, shows in actual size the nettle stalk and the finer and coarser twine made from it.

(d) *Sinew.*—The sinew of deer was used for making bowstrings, two fibers of the sinew being moistened by passing them between the lips and then twisted together as described above.

(e) *Yarn.*—The fine yarn first obtained from the traders was twisted into the coarse yarn desired for weaving bags by means of the distaff. (Pl. 9, a (d).) In using this implement the fine yarn was passed over a nail above the worker's head and wound on the distaff.

FISH NETS

In early time the nets or seines were made of nettle-stalk twine, the lighter twine being used for the fish nets and the stronger twine used for tying the nets to the poles. Manufactured twine for fish nets was issued to the Chippewa with their annuities at an early date. The implements now used in making fish nets are probably the same which have been used for many years and consist of a shuttle, which carries the twine, and a square piece of smooth wood around which the twine is passed before making the knot. With these is used a finger protector of leather, which is worn over the little finger of the right hand, the twine being tightly wound around the hand and pressing against this finger. (Pl. 59, b.) The width of a net was measured by the number of meshes, and the length by the number of "arm spreads" (the distance from the fingers of one hand to the fingers of the other with arms outspread). An average size is 19 meshes wide and 60 arm spreads long. Pieces of light wood about 12 inches long are fastened to the edge of the net as "floaters," and opposite each is a stone "sinker." The distance between these is twice a single "arm length."

WEAVING OF MATS

(a) *Floor mats made of bulrushes* (*Scirpus validus* Vahl).—The rushes were gathered in large quantities and dried on slats in a field or hung from horizontal poles near the worker's house. These poles (seen at Mille Lac) were about 6 feet from the ground, supported by posts, and two long poles were placed side by side. The rushes were tied in pairs of little bundles, each pair connected by a cord a few inches in length. By means of this cord the pair of bundles was suspended across the pole, the rushes hung with the tops downward. They were stored in large bundles when dried and were "boiled up" before being woven. A portion were dyed to form a colored pattern, as described in a subsequent paragraph. At present this decoration is usually in the form of stripes placed at intervals through the entire mat; the writer has, however, seen a woman weaving a mat with flowers effectively spaced on the mat. An older style is shown in Plate 63, the pattern being in the center with a border extending around the mat.

In beginning a mat a length of basswood cord was measured equivalent to the length of the mat. To this cord the end of the rushes were fastened one after another, the ends being turned over the cord and fastened to make a firm edge. (Pl. 60, *a*, *b*, and p. 120.) When this was completed the cord was fastened at intervals, usually being "sewed over and over" to the pole. The next process consisted of fastening the pole to two upright poles at a height above the ground somewhat greater than that of the width of the mat. Thus the rushes hung downward and formed the warp of the mat, basswood twine being passed between them to complete the weaving. This twine was not put on a shuttle, but was held in a little roll in the weaver's left hand, the right hand being used to separate the rushes preparatory to slipping the twine between them. An unfinished mat is shown in Plate 61, *a*.

The weaving of these mats could be conducted in two ways: A woman might have the mat on a light frame which she set up near her house or she might have a building especially constructed for this work. The weaving could only be done when the rushes were slightly damp, and if a woman did her weaving out of doors she was obliged to lay her unfinished work on the grass or to protect it in some manner from the heat of the sun. She could work only in the early morning or late evening when the condition of the atmosphere was such as to moisten the rushes. Her work was a constant care to her as the rushes must not "dry out" before the mat was completed. If they became dry they were brittle and a broken rush was difficult to mend. Plate 1, *b*, shows Mrs. Gurneau of Red Lake, Minn., at work in this manner. The mat is fastened to three poles, one across the top and one on each side, making it portable, and it is leaned against a permanent frame near her dwelling. But she desired to do her work more efficiently and spent part of her time in gathering material for a structure to be used exclusively for weaving. When the writer made her acquaintance she was "packing" a load of jack-pine bark on her back in order to make this structure. The bark was removed from the trees in strips or sheets about 3 feet wide and at a convenient height from the ground. Trees of this sort are of about the same size, being perhaps 9 inches in diameter, which makes the sheets of bark quite uniform in size.

The removal of the bark kills the tree, and it is left to dry, being cut later for firewood. It required 40 packs, which took some time to gather, and meantime she was weaving on the outdoor frame as illustrated. The forty packs were finally secured and her husband made the frame for the structure. The only opening was toward the north so the sun could not shine into it; the sheets of bark made it cool and somewhat damp, and it was closed when not in use. The structure in two stages of its progress is shown in Plate 62. The sheets of bark were fastened to the poles of the framework by narrow strips of basswood fiber. An awl was used to pierce the pine bark on either side of the pole, after which the narrow piece of basswood fiber was passed through from the inside, back again on the other side of the pole and tied securely. This left "stitches" about 2 inches long on the outside of the structure, and held the bark in such a manner that it could not warp away from the framework. Inside the structure there was a permanent frame consisting of a heavy horizontal pole fastened to upright posts that were planted in the ground. The edge of the mat was fastened to the horizontal pole, and as the work progressed the ends of the mat were tied to the upright posts. When the mat was finished the lower edge was "bound off" by turning up the ends of the reeds and fastening them in a manner somewhat similar to that on the edge fastened to the horizontal pole.

As a substitute for a bark structure, a woman may have a cool, dark shed which can be tightly closed when not in use. In this a woman keeps her supply of birch bark, rushes, and strips of basswood bark.

The designs now commonly used in floor mats are narrow stripes of colored rushes combined to form a broader stripe that occurs at intervals through the length of the mat. Colored rushes are sometimes worked in diagonally, forming a pattern in lattice or diamonds. One of Mrs. Razer's mats contained a pattern of a vine with leaves crossing the mat at intervals. She said this was very difficult to make, as the rushes are likely to be broken on a curved pattern. In old times the pattern often covered the entire mat, the center having a design of its own and a border being placed around its edge. (Pl. 63.)

(b) *Floor mats made of cedar.*—In northern Minnesota and Canada, where rushes were not abundant, the floor mats were made of strips of cedar. These mats were woven on a frame similar to that used for rush mats, but the woof, instead of being basswood twine, consisted of cedar strips the same width as those used for the warp. Part of the cedar strips were dyed either black or dark brown, and a pattern was secured by carrying the woof strips over

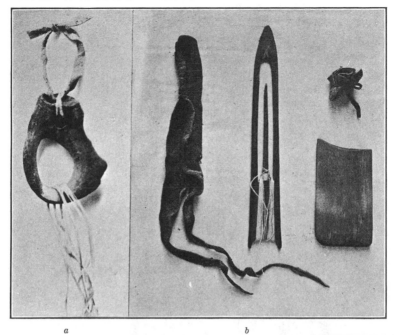

a   b

a, Bear bone, used in softening basswood fiber; b, Implements used in making fish nets, and
packet of "medicine" to attract fish

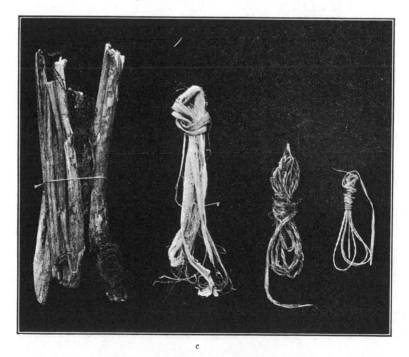

c

c, Nettle stalks, and stages of process of making twine

a, Detail of weaving reed mat

b, Beginning of reed mat

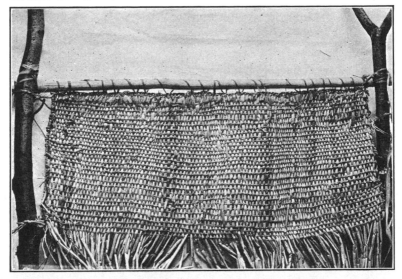

a, Unfinished reed mat on frame

b, Unfinished mat made of strips of cedar bark

a, Frame of structure to be used for mat weaving

b, Partially completed structure to be used for weaving

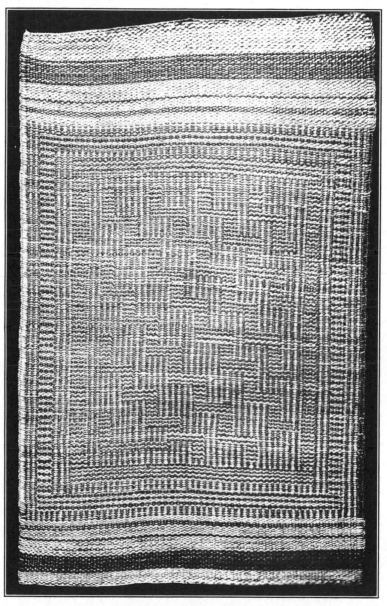

RUSH MAT, OLD DESIGN

c, Bark bag filled with wild rice

a   *b*

a, Lower end of bark bag; *b,* Unfinished bark bag

two or more of the warp strips instead of over one. The strips were about 1¼ inches wide. The black dye was the same as for dyeing rushes, and an informant in Canada said that a dark-brown color was obtained by making a decoction of the dark portion of the bark next the rough outer bark and boiling the strips in this dye. In cedar, as in rush mats, it was desirable to keep the material damp and pliable. A cedar mat on its frame leaned against the shady side of a house is shown in Plate 1, a. In this position the woman could work at it in the morning and evening. The edges of the mats were turned and "sewed over and over" with narrow strips of cedar. A wide variety of patterns are seen in cedar mats, and the effect of the colors is artistic. (Pl. 61, b.)

(c) *Mats for the sides of wigwams.*—These mats were made from cat-tail reeds (*Typha latifolia* L.) and were woven on the same frames as the floor mats. The reeds were turned in the same manner to form a selvedge at the beginning of the work, but the method of work was entirely different. The floor mats, as already stated, were woven with basswood twine, but in these mats the reeds were strung together with strands of basswood fiber which had been boiled to make it tough. This fiber was threaded into a bone needle, which was passed horizontally through the reeds at intervals of 8 or 10 inches. The needle was slightly curved and was usually about 9 inches long. In a majority of instances the "eye" was near one end, but a very old needle was obtained in which the eye was midway the length. This needle was very long. (Pl. 9, a (g).) The ends of the reeds were often left free, so that only one side of the mat had a selvedge. This made it easier to place the mat in an upright position against the side of the wigwam.

(d) *Frames for drying berries.*—The reeds used in these frames were identified as *Phragmites phragmites* (L.) Karst. They were made on a frame like the preceding mats and were woven with basswood twine, but differed from the floor mats in that the twine was placed at intervals of 8 or 9 inches instead of close together, and the twine was knotted between each reed. This separated the reeds, and in the finished mat produced spaces through which the air could circulate, thus assisting the drying of the berries. These mats were about 24 by 36 inches in size.

WEAVING OF BAGS

(a) *Bark.*—In weaving bags the Chippewa used the inner bark of the cedar, basswood, and slippery elm. Woven cedar bags were formerly used for holding personal belongings and for storing wild rice, the latter use continuing to the present day. The strips of inner bark were boiled to make them pliable, the basswood being boiled in a metal kettle which gave it a reddish color. The typical bark bag used for storing rice is woven without a seam, the beginning of the work being done across a short stick which is suspended at the ends (pl. 64, *b*), the work as completed being drawn down and shaped into a square or oblong bag. When the bag is finished the stick is removed, and the corners sewed down. (Pl. 64, *a.*) A barred space is usually left at the upper edge. The bags are filled solidly and laced together with basswood fiber. A different sort of bag was made for boiling the bark from which gum was obtained. It was necessary that the storing bags should be close, but these bags must be open meshed. (Pl. 55, *a.*) Accordingly they were woven somewhat like drying frames for berries. The material for these bags consisted of strips of bark about one-eighth inch wide, fastened together at intervals of about one-half inch with strands of basswood fiber knotted to make a space between the strips of bark. The weaving was in a long rather narrow piece that was sewed up the sides to form the bag. The ends of the strips of bark were left long, so that the bag when in use might be securely tied at the top.

A different sort of bag, woven of fine strips of bark and made at Mille Lac, is shown in Plate 72, *c.*

(*b*) *Roots.*—The material chiefly used in making root bags was tamarack, split and boiled to render it pliable. The manner of weaving was the same as that of the bark bags first described, and the bags were used for storing medicinal herbs and roots as well as wild rice.

(*c*) *Yarn.*—One of the most useful articles in a Chippewa family in former years was the woven yarn bag, about 20 inches square, which served as a container for personal belongings. The first bags of this sort were about 9 inches square but later they were made larger and took the place of bags made of cedar, as household articles. (Pl. 65, *a,* *b, c.*) The material first used was a cord made by raveling a woolen blanket and twisting the threads into a cord and, if desired, was colored with native dye. This was woven with a warp of nettle-stalk twine. The bag shown in Plate 66 is 20 by 24 inches in size and is made of raveled blanket with fiber warp. Many interesting geometric designs are seen on these bags as well as figures of men and animals. The woolen yarn first brought by the traders was white and the Chippewa women dyed it with native dye, continuing the style of patterns used on the bags made of raveled blanket. The frame on which these bags were woven consisted of two smooth sticks about 16 inches long and one-half inch in diameter. These were placed upright in the ground at a distance slightly wider than the width of the bag so that the " spring " of the wood kept the work in place while the weaving was done. (Pl. 67.) The threads were woven diagonally. The upper edge of the work was sewed in a seam, forming the lower edge of the bag, and the lower edge of the work, which formed the upper edge of the bag, was finished with a space of " open work." The bag was closed by sewing the upper edges together with twine.

WEAVING OF BANDS

This industry is considered with reference to the materials used in the work.

(a) *Strips of cloth.*—Every Chippewa woman carefully conserved the cloth obtained from the Government or from the trader, and from strips of old cloth she wove bands which were sewed into rugs for the floor of her dwelling. These rugs are sometimes seen at the present day. Some are round or oval, but the most typical are oblong with the bands extending the length of the rug. The writer saw a Chippewa woman engaged in this industry, her loom and a piece of unfinished work being shown in Plate 68. This woman, Ma'gidĭns by name, was more than 70 years old at the time and said that she learned this work from her grandmother when a child. The loom is of cedar 13 by 13 inches in size, with bars 1 inch wide separated by spaces. Each bar has a hole midway its length. Strips of cloth were passed through the holes and also through the spaces between the bars. The strips were fastened at one end to an iron bedstead, while the other ends were fastened to the belt of the worker, who maintained the right tension for weaving by adjusting her own distance from the bed. As the work progressed she " let out" the strips that were tied to the bed and slipped the finished work through her belt, tying it in place. The loom was placed an easy arm-length from the worker's body and about the same distance from the bedstead. A similar implement from a Salishan tribe is in the City Museum at Vancouver, British Columbia.

The process of the work is like that of weaving rag carpets, except that no shuttle is used. A strip of cloth 3 or 4 yards long is wound in the form of a little roll and used as woof, other strips being added as may be necessary. The worker holds the roll of woof in her right hand, passes it between the warp threads, elevates the weaving frame, and returns the roll of woof with her left hand, the change in position of the frame producing a change in the relative position of the woofs. The pattern is determined by the arrangement of colors in the warp, only one color being used in the woof. A great variety is seen in the patterns. (Pl. 68.) The usual width is about 1½ inches, but much wider braids are frequently made.

(b) *Yarn.*—Similar braids were made entirely of yarn and tied above the bands on cradle boards.

(c) *Yarn and thread.*—Belts were similarly made, using yarn as the warp and carpet warp as the woof, this being a comparatively modern form of the industry. (Pl. 71, *a.*)

(d) *Bark.*—A narrow belt made of soft basswood bark was worn by hunters, the knife sheath being attached to this belt. No loom was required for this purpose, the threads being crossed diagonally. This process was not observed by the writer.

NETTING OF BELTS

Belts made of yarn are the most common and characteristic among the Chippewa, and are usually about 9 inches wide and 2 yards or more in length. One of these belts was woven under the writer's observation, a portion of the yarn being colored with native dye.

The frame on which the work was done consisted of two poles or stakes about 4 feet long, driven firmly into the ground about 3 feet apart. The end of the yarn was tied to one of these stakes and wound around them both, beginning about 2 feet above the ground. The belt which the writer saw on the frame was of red, blue, and yellow yarn in stripes. The red and blue strands were first used, three red and three blue strands being used in alternating colors placed one below another. (Pl. 69, *a.*) Yellow strands were then added, the colors being separated at one side of the frame and inter-mingled at the other side. This portion of the process being com-pleted, the poles were somewhat loosened, permitting the drawing together of the threads into a space the width of the belt to be made. A needle threaded with yarn was then passed in and out between these strands separating the colors. This was made firm by means of a split stick which was slipped over the yarn and tied at either end. This split stick became the bar of a crude loom, holding the threads in position for netting.

The yarn was cut next to one of the poles. The material then consisted of a long skein of yarn, arranged horizontally in colors, held in place at one point by a split stick. This skein was tied around one of the poles about 3 feet from the ground and tied around the other pole at a lower point. The woman then seated herself beside the work as shown in Plate 69, *b.*

The first process in netting was to separate the alternate threads so that the red and yellow threads were above and the blue and yellow threads beneath, the two portions being held in position with the hands when the woman was at work. If she left the work she tied the upper threads with a bit of yarn to prevent their becoming intermingled with the lower threads. The netting was done by using the left thumb in the manner of a hook, the right hand adjusting the threads. By this means an upper thread was constantly placed

a, b, c, Bags woven of yarn or raveled blanket; *d,* Old beaded bag

BAG WOVEN OF RAVELED BLANKET, OBVERSE AND REVERSE

PARTIALLY COMPLETED YARN BAG ON FRAME

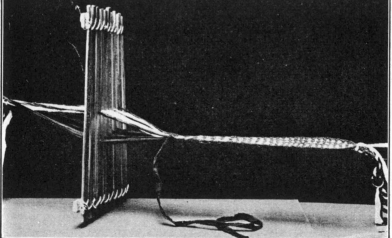

WOVEN BRAID AND HEDDLE WITH UNFINISHED WORK

a, Winding yarn for netting belt

b, Nodinens, netting belt

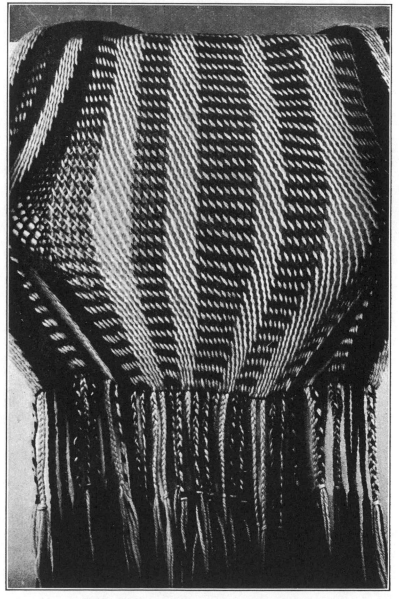

END AND FRINGE OF NETTED BELT

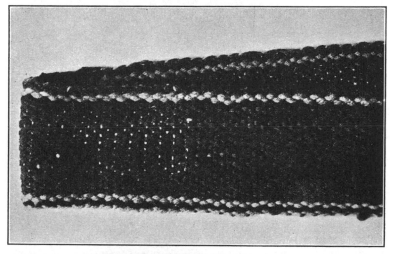

a, Sash woven of yarn and carpet warp

b, "Sturgeon flesh" pattern, woven belt

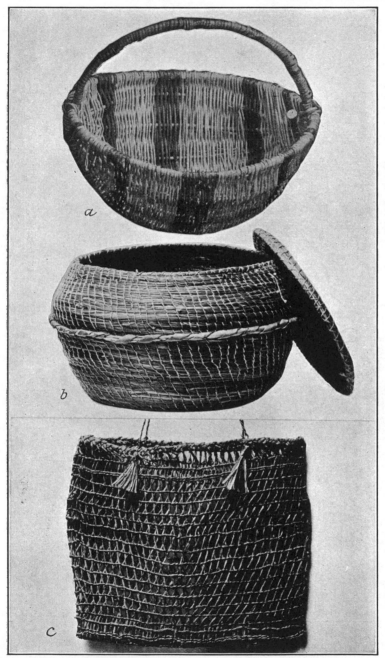

a, "Melon-shaped" basket; *b*, Sweet-grass basket; *c*, Bag woven of fine strips of bark

beneath a lower thread, producing a twisting of the two. The interlacing of the threads near the lower end of the loom was corrected when the completed work was released from the pole behind the worker. One end of the belt being completed, the position of the work was reversed and the other end netted, beginning at the other side of the split stick. When both ends had been netted the split stick and the yarn stitches were removed, leaving no trace on the completed work. The netting was secured at the ends by needle and yarn, at least 12 inches of the yarn being left to form a fringe. (Pl. 70.)

Another pattern of woven belt is shown in Plate 71, *b*.

WEAVING OF BLANKETS OF RABBIT SKIN

Two methods of weaving rabbit-skin blankets were used by the Chippewa in northern and northeastern Minnesota and in Canada. In making one sort of blanket the rabbit skin was cut " round and round " in a narrow strip so that one hide made a continuous strip. Green hides were used and the strips twisted in drying so that they resembled soft cords. The weaving was done on a warp of cotton twine, with a space of about half an inch between the rows of rabbit skin. The blanket was firmly woven as the rabbit skin was tied around each thread of the warp. Such a blanket was seen at Grand Marais, Minn. For making the other sort of blanket the rabbit skins were tanned dry (without removing the hair) and were cut in strips " round and round," after which they were woven like the netting on snowshoes. When made by either method the blanket is alike on the two sides and very thick. A blanket of the latter sort, about 6 feet square, was recently made at Grand Portage, Minn.

WEAVING OF HEAD ORNAMENT OF MOOSE HAIR

A favorite dance ornament consisted of a roach of stiff moose hair which was woven in a long strip and then coiled and sewed into the ornament. In weaving this ornament a woman tied one end of a stout string to a post at a height of about 3 feet from the ground and tied the other end to a stick which she placed under her as she sat on the ground. This held the weaving string taut, and with a second string she fastened the moose hair in place. This weaving was witnessed by the writer. A detail of the process is shown in Plate 16, *c;* but as moose hair was not available, the specimen was made of fine grass.

A similar ornament was made with the hair of the porcupine as the outer row while inside this was white deer hair dyed red and clipped very short after weaving. The porcupine hair used for this purpose was the long hair on the animal's back.

BASKETRY

The making of baskets was not a highly developed art among the Chippewa, as the birch-bark makuk answered the purpose of a general carrier and was made more easily than a basket. It is said, however, that baskets were made of willow branches at an early date. The "melon-shaped" basket was an old form. In the pale yellow part of this basket the willow has been peeled; in the green stripes it is not peeled. The brown stripe is made of branches that have been blighted to a limited degree, and the red stripe is of branches that have been heavily blighted. (Pl. 72, a.) Covered baskets were made at an early date and the willow was sometimes colored with native dye. Baskets were made of stiff strips of the inner bark of basswood, woven in a lattice having the upright and transverse strips the same width. This custom was not observed among the Minnesota Chippewa but was seen at Lac Court Oreilles, Wis., and among the Canadian Chippewa.

"Black ash" is used in making baskets by the Chippewa at Mille Lac. In preparing this wood it is their custom to take a long strip of the wood and pound it with an ax head until it separates into the sap layers. These are cut the desired width, then dyed and woven. The perpendicular and horizontal strips in these baskets are not always the same width and the colors show a wide variety. This entire custom was witnessed among the Winnebago, who said it was revealed to a woman, long ago, in a dream.

Coiled baskets were made of sweet grass but were more akin to bowls, as they had no handles. It is said the oldest forms of these had covers made of birch bark bound with sweet grass. (Pl. 72, b.) Birch bark is combined with coiled sweet grass in the making of a great variety of mats and shallow dishes or trays.

POTTERY

The older members of the tribe agree in stating that in former times their people made pottery and baked it in the fire. One informant said it was "made of clay and sand, mixed with a little glue."

In 1918 the writer visited a locality in the vicinity of Lake Winnipegosis where some old graves had been "washed out." More than 250 fragments of pottery were collected, 110 of which were pieces of the rims or necks of jars. The decorations on these were typical of the pottery found in this region,[76] comprising imprints of roulette, twisted cord, woven fabric, sharp stick, or thumb nail, but

---

[76] Cf. Holmes, W. H.   Ancient Pottery of the Mississippi Valley.   Fourth Ann. Rept. Bur. Ethn., Washington, 1886.

these were combined in such variety that only three or four duplicates were found in the entire collection. Thirty-four fragments of jars were large enough to show the curve of the sides and the size, which varied from a few inches to about a foot in diameter. The color of the pottery fragments also showed a wide variety, including black, orange, and very pale gray, as well as the familiar browns and reddish shades.

Skeletal material was collected and submitted to Dr. Aleš Hrdlička, of the National Museum, who reported that "the bones are those of a male skeleton, in all probability Indian. They are possibly not over a few decades old." The large bones were pierced near one end, the puncture showing the use of a conical instrument and breaking into the marrow cavity. (Pl. 73.)

USE OF DYES

The general process of dyeing consisted in the use of a vegetable substance to secure a color and a mineral substance to "set" it.

Porcupine quills were the easiest material to dye and rushes were the hardest, sometimes requiring numerous "dippings" before the desired shade could be secured. Yarn and ravelings of blankets were among the materials most frequently dyed by the industrious Chippewa women. The colors most used were yellow and brown for large quantities and red for small quantities, as for quills. Black was more difficult to produce than these colors. Purple ("blue") was rarely used and green was never used by the Minnesota Chippewa but was seen as a native dye among the Chippewa in Ontario. The material was boiled in the dye. If a darker shade was desired, the material was either reboiled or allowed to stand in the dye.

The vegetable substances most used were plum, alder, sumac, butternut, oak, dogwood, and bloodroot. The mineral substances were grindstone dust, a reddish substance that rose to the surface of certain springs, and a black earth found near certain springs. These were used in connection with the vegetable products, according to various formulas, in some of which the proportions of the ingredients were designated. (See "Uses of Plants by the Chippewa Indians, Forty-fourth Ann. Rept. Bur. Amer. Ethn., pp. 379–384.)

Wood was given a reddish color by the fumes of a certain "black mud" placed in the fire.

TANNING

(a) *Preparation of hide.*—Otter or other small skins were prepared as follows: The skinning was started at the hind quarters, the hide being drawn forward and the head left on the hide. This was then stretched on a frame. A long frame, as for an otter hide, would have two pegs near the corners at the wide end, these pegs being put through the hide, then the frame, and then the hide again to keep it taut. When dry the hide was removed from the frame, this being the form in which the hides were sold to traders. If the hide were to be used for a medicine bag, it was not turned and put on the frame, but dried right side out stuffed with dry grass. Such a frame is shown in Figure 15.

A deer hide was spread on the ground and sheared with a sharp knife; it was then soaked in clean water for two days, or for a night, after which the rest of the hair was scraped off with an instrument consisting of an iron blade set in a handle. At Mille Lac in

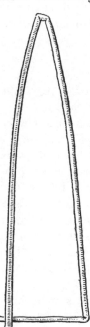

1925 a woman was seen at this work and photographed. (Pl. 74, c.) The hide is spread on a log which is braced against the root of a tree. In tanning a deer hide the flesh next to the hide was removed by laying the hide over the top of a post so it hung down loosely all around. Four cuts were then made in the fleshy tissue, these cuts being where the hide rested on top of the pole. Beginning at these cuts the tissue was worked loose by means of a bone implement, and entirely removed. This implement was made of the leg bone of a moose. It was fastened to the upper arm of the worker by means of a thong, enabling her to use it more easily. The brains of the deer were rubbed on this hide to soften it, as the hide had very little oil in it. A flesher and scraper are shown in Plate 74, a, b.

Another method of softening a small flat hide was to rub the fur side with a bone implement called odjic′iboda′gûn. This implement was the

Fig. 15.—Frame used in drying s m a l l hides

thigh bone of the deer, bear, or other large animal. The bone had an opening in it, through which the hide was pulled back and forth. If there was a little rough place in the hide they " erased " it by rubbing on the inside with a small, smooth bone. Rabbit skins were not tanned but were hung on bushes to let the wind blow away the loose hair, and then used.

(b) *Coloring deer hide.*—The smoking of a hide is shown in Plate 75, a, b, c, the work being done by Zo′zĕd. As she was in recent mourning, her hair hangs loose and is fastened near the ends. If several hides were to be smoked, they were sewed together in such a manner that they formed the same conical shape as the one hide shown in the plate. A hole was dug about 18 inches in diameter and 9 inches deep. Over this a framework was constructed that resembled a small tipi frame. The hide was suspended above this framework and drawn down over it, the circle of cloth around the lower edge of the hide being a little larger than the circumference of the hole, so that it could be spread on the ground and held down by heavy sticks laid flat on the ground. A fire had previously been made in the hole, Zozed using dry corncobs for the purpose. This fire smolders slowly, the smoke giving to the hide a golden yellow color. The hide is almost white before being colored in this manner.

GLUE

An important aid in many forms of handicraft was glue, which was usually made from the sturgeon in the following manner: The cord was pulled out of the backbone of the fish, cut in pieces, and "fried" in a pan. While this was in the pan and warm, the Indian took a little stick and wound the "glue" on the stick. He put this away and, when glue was needed, he warmed the outer surface of the mass and used what was required, allowing the remainder to cool. The Chippewa "glue stick" was probably pointed like that of the Sioux, so it could be stuck upright beside the worker while the glue was moist.

MAKING OF MUSICAL INSTRUMENTS

(*a*) *Drum.*—Two types of drum were in use among the old-time Chippewas, the hand drum, and the Mide drum. (See pp. 95, 96.) In recent years the Chippewa have used a large flat drum, either placed on the ground or suspended from curved stakes. This drum is decorated with beaded velvet and is used for dances or in a ceremonial manner. (Bull. 53, pl. 18–19, pp. 142–180.) A modern bass drum is placed on the ground, and occasionally a washtub is converted into a drum by stretching rawhide over the top and covering the sides with cloth and beadwork.

The simplest form of hand drum consists of a piece of rawhide stretched over one side of a hoop and laced or tied together on the reverse side to form a handhold. A more common form at the present time is a drum having two heads with a loop of rawhide as a handhold. Such a drum is made of a single hide stretched over both sides of a hoop and sewed with rawhide on the outer edge of the hoop. These drums at present are often supplied with cords after the manner of "snare drums." A specimen illustrated in Bulletin 53 (pl. 3) is 18½ inches wide and 2½ inches in thickness, and has three tightly stretched cords inside the drum, each provided with small pegs tied at equal distances. The pegs are tied to the cord before the cover of the drum is put in place, and the cord is twisted to increase the tension, permitting the pegs to vibrate against the deerskin.

Such a drum is commonly called a moccasin game drum, being used during that game. The heads of both styles of hand drum were frequently decorated. A war drum might have either one or two heads. Odijbwe's war drum (Bull. 53, pl. 7) was decorated with a turtle and the lightning, these being his dream symbols. A certain moccasin game drum was painted red with a blue circle about 6 inches in diameter placed in the middle of the drum head. The decorations of Mide drums are separately considered. Little Wolf said that in old times the Chippewa "liked to use several hand drums at once if they could get those that chorded together."

At Grand Portage, Minn., in 1905, the writer witnessed a Chippewa ceremony in which the drum was suspended from the rafters of a log house. The drum was about 20 inches in diameter and had two deerskin heads laced together over a hoop about 6 inches wide. A green star was painted at the top of one side, and below the star a cord was stretched close to the head of the drum. (See pl. 5, b.)

Drumming sticks: The drumming stick used with the last-mentioned drum had a crossbar near one end about 5 inches long. As the drum hung before the leader of the ceremony he struck it with one end of this crossbar. The sticks used with Mide drums were in some instances symbolic and are described on page 96. Frequently the stick used with a hand drum had a small round hoop at the end, the whole drumming stick being wound with cloth. It was the custom, however, to use a stick about 18 inches long with a padded end made by winding cloth around the stick. With the large dance drum a longer stick was used, having a padded end. With the ceremonial drum of the Wisconsin Chippewa there were four drumsticks used by the leading drummers, each covered with soft brown deerskin and decorated with a band of otter fur and long ribbon streamers. There was also a longer stick used only by the owner of the drum in a particular part of the ceremony. This stick was more than 3 feet long. Over the curved end was slipped the skin from the neck of a loon, its glossy black feathers dotted with white.

(b) *Rattle*.—The only use of rattles among the Chippewa was by members of the Midewiwin, and by jugglers who might or might not belong to the Midewiwin. The rattles used in meetings of that society and by individuals when singing the Mide songs consisted of a box pierced by a stick which served as a handle and containing pebbles or small shot. (See p. 97.) Formerly this was made of birch bark or thin wood, but the common form in recent years is a large, round spice box. Another type of rattle resembled a small thin moccasin game drum and was used when treating the sick.

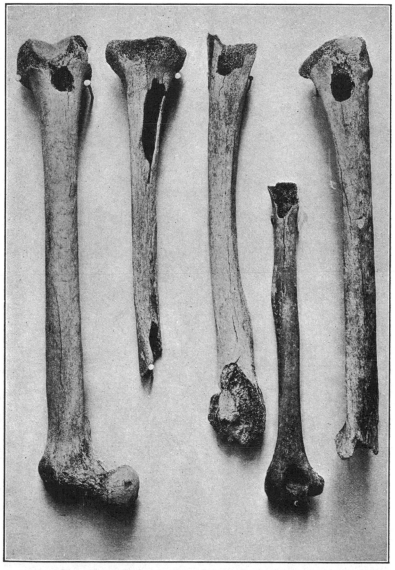

SKELETAL REMAINS

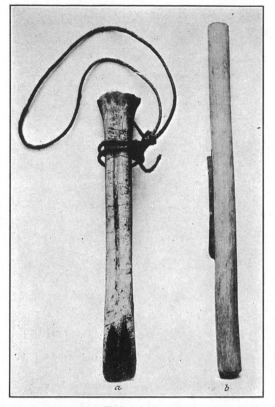

a, Flesher; b, Scraper

c, Woman removing hair from skin

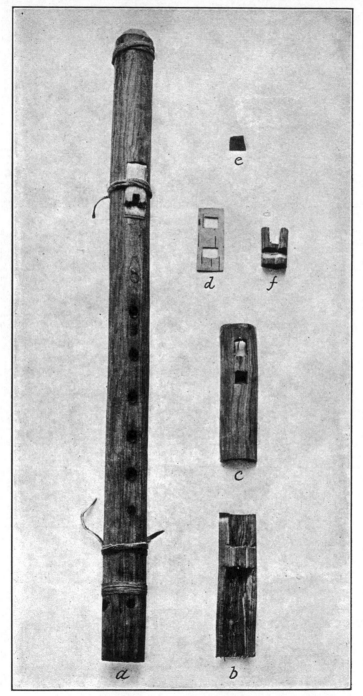

a, Flute; *b*, *c*, *d*, *e*, *f*, Portions of flute

The specimen used in recording songs for the writer was 9½ inches in diameter and one-half inch in thickness. A segment of the drum was painted blue and a smaller segment painted green, a band of the undecorated hide about three-fourths of an inch wide being between the decorated portions. The owner said this decoration indicated that "the weather was fair and we spoke only truth together." (Pl. 39.) It was said that larger rattles of the same type were used in a similar manner.

(c) *Flute.*—The wind instrument of the Chippewa is a flute of the type known to musicians as the flûte à bec, played by blowing into an air chamber at the upper end, the sound being produced by a whistle opening similar to that of an organ pipe. These flutes were either open or closed at the lower end, while the upper end was either blunt, tapered to an opening smaller than that of the tube, or shaped in a manner suggesting a small tube projecting from the instrument and serving as a mouthpiece. The blunt end was preferred by Tom Skinaway, of Mille Lac, who made many flutes in former years, but the second type is commonly seen. The third type is preferred by the Menominee.

All Chippewa flutes had six finger holes, and if the lower end were closed there were five holes in a line around that end. These resemble the holes on Chinese flutes which are used for a silk cord and tassels, but their use on Indian flutes is not apparent. The length of a Chippewa flute was according to the stature of the man who was to use it. Tom Skinaway said the flute should be two "spreads" of the man's hand from the thumb to the end of the second finger, plus one "spread" from the thumb to the end of the first finger. The middle of the whistle opening should be a spread of the man's thumb and first finger from the upper end of the tube. The flute illustrated (pl. 76) is 19¾ inches long. It was obtained on the White Earth Reservation, and the position of the openings is different from the measurements described by Skinaway, who was an expert worker.

The wood used for a flute is cedar, box elder, ash, sumac, or other soft wood with a straight grain. A straight round stick of wood is split lengthwise into two equal parts. Each half-cylinder is then hollowed out, except near one end, where a bridge is left (b), so that when the two pieces are glued together there is formed a cylindrical tube open at both ends and throughout its length except at the point where the two bridges now form a solid stopper, dividing the tube into a short upper portion (the wind chamber) and a long lower portion (the flute tube).

The organ mouthpiece is formed ingeniously as follows: A square opening is cut through the side of the tube just above the bridge, into the wind chamber, and another is cut just below the bridge into the sounding tube (c). A block (f) is so fashioned and slightly cut away on its lower surface that it covers the upper opening and directs the air in a thin sheet downward against the lower, sound-producing edge of the square hole below the bridge. To make this edge of the hole smooth and sharp; that is, to form a suitable "lip" for the pipe, a piece of very thin birch bark (d) is placed between the tube and the block. The junction between the tube and the block is made air-tight in the specimen illustrated by a "gasket" of silk cloth (e); often the joint is closed by resin or other cement. The drilling of the holes is, of course, done before the two halves of the stick are glued together, and is done with a pointed hot iron. The spacing of the finger holes, like the location of the whistle opening, is measured by the hand of the man who is to use the instrument. The measurements are not so minute as to affect all flutes, an average size instrument being made for a man of average stature while a very tall or short man would require the special measurements. According to Tom Skinaway, the position of the first finger hole is determined by measuring half the length of the tube and cutting it a little nearer the mouth end of the flute. He said the instrument would not "sound good" if the first finger hole were half its length. The second finger hole should be distant from the mouth end a spread of thumb and forefinger plus the length of the forefinger, and the third finger hole should be distant the spread of thumb and second finger plus the length of the second finger. The other finger holes were "conveniently spaced" according to the size of the player's hand. The size of the bore should be such as to admit the player's forefinger.

The tone of the instrument is affected by the position of the block over the sound hole. Usually it is held in place by several windings of string or thong so that it may be adjusted by the player, but sometimes it is sealed in a position which is satisfactory to the player.

The Chippewa sometimes used raw deer hide for binding the two parts of the flute. As the hide dried it held the two parts firmly together.

The flute was commonly played by young men to attract or please the maidens. The playing was not a random sounding of tones, as it was said "a young man would never play the flute unless he could play a tune entirely through." The love songs of the Menominee were said to be imitations of the melodies played on this type of flute.

In the old days a flute of the same shape as that used by the young men was kept by one warrior and used by him in giving a signal of danger. If word was received that the enemy was approaching or was hiding near the village he took this flute and went through the village playing it. The intervals were said to be larger than on the young men's flutes and the tune was less lively. The general manner of playing, however, was such as to deceive the enemy while warning the people.

(*d*) *Clapper.*—Among the Chippewa at Grand Portage there was found a clapper consisting of a thin board 14 inches long and 3¼ inches wide. It was used by a member of the Midewiwin and was probably painted to correspond with his degree in that society as it bears three black and two red bands. The sound was produced by four narrow sticks, two of which were painted black and two painted red. It was said these were held between the fingers and vibrated in such a manner that one after another struck the board. An instrument of this sort has not been noted elsewhere among the Chippewa. The clapper is widely used by medicine men on the Northwest coast.

ARTICLES MADE OF STONE

Ax.—A stone was fastened to a wooden handle by splitting the stick and binding the two parts tightly around the stone head with rawhide. (Pl. 53, *f*.)

"*Branch breaker.*"—This implement was smaller than the preceding and had a shorter handle, but was made in a similar manner.

Smooth stones were used in pounding meat and berries.

Pipes.—Both hard and soft stone were used by the Chippewa in making pipes. (See p. 143.)

ARTICLES MADE OF BONE

Awls.—The splint bone of the deer was used as an awl and needed no preparation.

Arrow points.—Any bone that was somewhat pointed was made sharply pointed and used as an arrowhead.

Needles.—The ribs of rather small animals were used in making the needles with which cat-tails were woven into mats. The small needles used in making the netting on showshoes were also made of bone.

Knives.—A Canadian Chippewa said that his people formerly made knives from the "flat ribs" of the moose and deer. He said these knives were sharpened on a stone, and that they cut in a satisfactory manner. (Pl. 53, *d*.) Handles of metal knives were made of horn.

Game implements.—Two sorts of bones were used in making the game implement described on page 117. These were the dewclaws of the deer and a bone taken from the leg.

Hoes.—The shoulder blades of large deer or moose were used as hoes, without being fastened to a handle. (Pl. 53, *e*.)

Ornaments.—The small bones of the hind legs of rabbits were strung and worn as necklaces. (Pl. 13, *a*.)

In treating the sick, small tubular bones were "swallowed" by jugglers. (See p. 46.)   A small horn was also used by a doctor in treating headache.

Pipes.—The small pronged horns of the deer were affixed to handles and used as pipes.

Spurs.—These were made of horn.

ARTICLES MADE OF WOOD

The following data should be understood as representative of-the method of wood making, rather than an enumeration of all the wooden articles used by the Chippewa. The principal tool used in woodwork (aside from the ax) was a curved knife. A man usually had a straight knife also, but the curved knife served the purpose of both a curved and a straight knife if the latter were lacking. Ash was commonly used for lighter articles, while hazel, elder, birch, spruce, cedar, oak, ironwood, and maple had their special uses.

An Indian always whittles toward him, and the handle of his knife is shaped so as to get the greatest leverage. The curved knife, commonly called a "crooked knife," was almost the only tool used by the old Indians. Its blade makes a straight cut when pressed downward, and the end of the blade is bent in a curve.

Bowls.—The Chippewa cut the knots from trees, scooped out the inside when they were green, and hung them up to dry. Later they whittled them into the desired shape with a curved knife and polished them with a piece of leather.

Spoons.—Occasionally a spoon was made with a knot as its bowl; usually, however, the spoon was cut from a piece of wood, the bowl being hollowed with the curved knife.

Clubs and spoons.—In maple and birch trees the grain of the wood turns outward as the trunk of the tree divides into the roots, and a man expert in woodwork utilized this curve of the grain. A "bird's-eye" formation often occurred at this point, and he used this for the bowl of the spoon or the head of the club. It made a strong bowl, not likely to split, and it made a very heavy head for the club.

Mide drums.—A log, usually of basswood, was charred, hollowed out, and made into a drum.   (See pp. 95, 96.)

Frames for snowshoes, sleds, etc.—The wood for frames of this sort was bent by placing it in hot water or holding it near the fire.

Pack frame.—This consisted of a wooden frame laced with either rawhide or basswood cord. (Pl. 77.) It was carried by a pack strap across the top of the head or the chest.

Snow shovel.—The shape of this implement was admirably adapted to its use. The length of the handle gave great leverage, and the narrowness of the blade made it convenient to store or carry. The specimen illustrated (pl. 53, *b*) was 4½ feet long, the blade was 18 inches in length and 4¾ inches in width. Women often used a shallow wooden bowl in removing snow near the door of the wigwam.

Paddles.—These were of many sorts and sizes, ranging from the spatula for powdered medicinal roots, the small paddle for spreading pitch, and the maple paddle used for graining maple sugar, to the spruce canoe paddles for use by men and women. The specimen illustrated is a woman's canoe paddle (pl. 53, *a*) and is 4 feet 10 inches long, with blade 22 inches long and 4¼ inches wide. A man's paddle is usually heavier, longer, and of a somewhat different shape.

Troughs.—These were used chiefly in the sugar camp, one being always needed for graining the sugar, and a large one being often used for storing the sap before it was boiled.

Balls.—A knot of wood was charred, scraped, and made into a lacrosse ball.

The making of bows and arrows is considered on pages 146 and 147.

Wooden implements for cultivating the ground are described in the section on making gardens (p. 124).

ETCHING ON WOOD

The most common implement used in etching on wood was an awl, but any metal point or sharp stone could be used. Some informants said the awl was heated before the work was done, but a particularly reliable Chippewa said the lines were first graven with an awl and then traced with a heated metal point. This produced a brown line. If color was desired, the charred wood was scraped from the groove and the juice of the bloodroot was applied. Several applications were necessary, each being allowed to dry before the next was made. In later times red paint has been used for this purpose. The designs were parallel or diagonal lines and the patterns, generally speaking, resembled the simplest bead patterns and the designs on birch-bark makuks. This form of decoration was applied to bows, pipestems, game implements, and other articles made of wood.

FIRE COLORATION AND ETCHING

This form of decoration was used on pipestems, game implements, and other articles made of wood with a smooth surface. To scorch or "smoke" a piece of wood evenly was a difficult task, and was accomplished by holding the wood over a slow fire of green wood. A reddish color was secured on bows by putting "black mud" in the fire and holding the article in the fumes from the fire. The decoration consisted of (a) a smooth medium brown. This was a color as even as though the article had been painted; (b) a brown color with patterns in the original color of the wood; and (c) a shaded brown. Narrow pieces of green bark were fastened around a pipestem before it was scorched, these stripes showing white and uncolored when the scorching was completed and the bark removed. Marks of identification were sometimes applied in this manner. The frame for beadwork shown in Plate 88 is decorated with shaded scorching.

DECORATIVE USE OF GRASSES AND PORCUPINE QUILLS

We will next consider the use of two materials, one of which was applied to the other for the purpose of decoration. The simplest materials applied in this manner were colored grasses and porcupine quills which were placed upon birch bark and leather. Grasses were the more primitive, as they required less preparation, and it is also said that they were used prior to porcupine quills by the Chippewa. A metal awl was used in making holes through which were inserted the ends of short pieces of grass or porcupine quills, the pattern having first been drawn on the material with a stick or dull knife.

It is said that the earliest use of these materials was in geometric and simple line patterns. Later they were applied in solid patterns representing leaves and flowers. Porcupine quills are dyed red, yellow, and sometimes purple. They are said to be easier to color than any other substance and to retain their color longer. Quills were dyed a brilliant scarlet under the writer's observation, leaving no doubt as to the process. (See p. 163.) The color was similar to that which is often seen on leather tobacco bags, and supposed to be due to the use of analine dye. A bright yellow was also obtained on quills with native dye, the work being done while the present study was in progress.

According to the Handbook of American Indians (p. 341) the quills were flattened "by holding one end firmly between the teeth, pressing the edge of the thumb-nail against the quill held by the forefinger, and drawing it tightly along the length of the quill, the process being repeated until the quill became smooth and ready for use. This flattening process was never done until the quill was ready for immediate use." A small hole having been made in the bark or leather, "the sharp point of the quill was thrust from the back and drawn out on the front side. An end of the flattened quill

a, Pack frame

b, Man carrying pack frame

a, Appliqué work

b, Packets identifiable by knots in string

was left at the back, and this was bent and pressed close to the skin or bark to serve as a fastening, like a knot on a thread. Another hole was made, perpendicular to the first, and through this the quill was passed to the back, thus making the stitch. . . . As quills were always so short . . . the fastening of ends and uniformity of the length of stitches were important points in the technic of the work."

APPLIQUÉ WORK

The materials commonly used in this work were colored ribbons. The work was done by laying ribbon of one color over ribbon of another color and cutting the upper ribbon in a pattern, turning the edges under and sewing them neatly in place. (Pl. 78, a.) The usual pattern was in notches or diamonds. This decoration was used as a border on leggings, also on the cuffs and front piece of moccasins, and on the binding bands of cradle boards. The latter sometimes showed a border 3 or 4 inches wide on each edge, entirely covering the cloth except for a narrow space where the woven braid was tied around the cradle board.

MEMORY DEVICES

A record of time was kept by notches in a stick. This might be a record of time after some important event, or might represent an entire year, a large notch being made for the day of a new moon and smaller notches for the intervening days (p. 119).

It was the custom of Little Wolf, the medicine man, to mark his packets of powdered medicinal roots by means of peculiar knots in the string with which he tied them. (Pl. 78, b.) This marking was known only to himself.

A warrior indicated the number of successful war parties by means of silk threads of various colors wound in narrow bands around the shaft of the feather which he wore in his hair. This was the custom of Little Wolf's father, whose war feather was obtained. This published the number of his victories, as well as kept them in his own mind.

A memory device might be intended also to emphasize a fact. When the Chippewa made a treaty or other important agreement with the Government of the United States they laid a buckskin "hand" upon the pile of articles given them by the Government to seal the agreement. This "hand" was similar to that sent as a war summons (p. 133), except that the latter was smeared with red paint to represent blood. When used in the making of a treaty this "hand" was said to "typify the honor of the Chippewa Tribe." At the conclusion of the negotiation it was kept by the Chippewa, with the articles they had received.

PICTURE WRITING

Pictography is defined as " That form of thought writing which seeks to convey ideas by means of picture signs or marks more or less suggestive or imitative of the object or idea in mind. Significance, therefore, is an essential element of pictographs, which are alike in that they all express thought, register a fact, or convey a message." [77]

The materials used in pictography by the Chippewa were birch bark, cedar, ash, or other wood, and the perpendicular surface of rocks. Drawings were also made in the soft, dry ashes of a fire or on dry earth. The implements were a pointed stick, bone, or metal, charcoal, and paint, according to the material on which the drawings were to be made. The inner surface of birch bark was that most commonly used, but both sides of the birch-bark rolls of the Mide-wiwin (Grand Medicine Society) were inscribed. Cedar and ash were used in flat pieces, either oblong for messages, or long and narrow, as for grave markers. The figures on both birch bark and wood were often filled with red paint. Little is known concerning the pictographs on the cliffs at La Pointe, Wis., and above a lake on the Bois Fort Reservation in Minnesota. The latter are said to be on a perpendicular surface, high above the present level of the water and a considerable distance below the top of the cliff. The drawings in the ashes or in dry earth were usually a map, an illustration of a narrative, or a delineation used in the working of a charm.

The figures included crude delineations of men, animals, birds, and other material objects, and in the Midewiwin symbols representing the sky, earth, lakes, and hills, as well as sounds and "spirit power." A simpler symbolism was used in messages and casual records, including signs to represent days, direction, and duplication of numbers. These delineations and symbols were combined in ideographs, some of which represented progressive action. In a certain Mide diagram this was indicated by a line (fig. 11), and in a certain Mide song it was indicated by the figures of men occurring twice in the same picture. (Bull. 45, p. 27.) If persons inside a wigwam were to be depicted the outlines of the wigwam were drawn and the figures of the persons drawn inside these lines. The subjects represented in picture writing were of two sorts: (1) esoteric, in which the material was understood only by initiates; and (2) nonesoteric, in which the purpose of the writing was to convey information in a public manner. To the first named belong the records, writ-

---

[77] Article " Pictographs," Handbook of American Indians, Bull. 30, Bur. Amer. Ethn., pt. 2, pp. 242–243, Washington, 1910,

ings, and songs of the Midewiwin, the stories of Winabojo, and the drawings used in working charms. To the last named belong "totem marks," the messages left by travelers, the maps carried by travelers, the illustrations for a narrative, records of time, and the names of persons.

To both classes, in a measure, belong the dream symbols which publish the subject of a dream but give no indication of its significance.

(a) *Mĭde'wĭwĭn.*—The purpose of picture writing in the Midewiwin is to assist the memory and to afford a means of record which is intelligible only to initiates in the society. Crude representations of material objects are combined with certain symbols, the significance of the pictograph being largely in these combinations. The principal symbol is the straight or wavy lines which proceed from figures of men or animals, usually indicating "spirit power." If these lines proceed from the mouth they indicate song or speech, if from the ear, they indicate sounds which are heard. An instance is subsequently noted in which they indicated smoke from a pipe. A circle frequently appears in these drawings, and is used to denote the sky, earth, a hill, a lake or a pan of food, the significance being determined by its connection with other objects in the picture.

This writing also shows a representation of the lodge (fig. 12), its contents, and the spirit animals associated with it, and also includes diagrams of various sorts, by means of which the teachings of the Midewiwin are perpetuated within the order. Its use in representing songs was tested by the writer in the following manner:

Typical Mide songs were recorded, and the corresponding pictures secured on one reservation. The phonograph records were played to members of the society on another reservation, and without hesitation they drew the same pictures which had been previously secured. Conversely, the picture was shown, and the corresponding song was sung.[78] An interesting incident concerning an individual song and its picture was related in connection with a Mide bag owned by a woman at Red Lake. (Pl. 49, *b*.) This bag was made of a bear's paw and had been kept many years. Around this bag there was a band of old cloth, dark red in color, edged with small opaque beads. The design outlined in beads on both sides of the band was said by its owner to represent her song. She said that every member of the society had an individual song, and that "anyone seeing this outline on the bag would know it belonged to her because it was a picture of her song." The woman was reluctant to impart the exact words of the song, but said it

---

[78] Cf. Bull. 45, Bur. Amer. Ethn., pp. 27–115, and Hoffman, op. cit., pp. 286–297.

concerned a bird, that the wavy lines issuing from its mouth represented the smoke from a pipe, and the circle above its head represented the pan of food at a Mide feast. The Mide picture writing
could be used to represent the name of a person. (See Bull. 45,
p. 16.)

(b) *Dream symbols.*—The subject of a man's dream might, if he
so desired, be made known by a material representation, or by a
symbol painted on his blanket, or on the hide which covered his
wigwam door. (See section on dreams.)

(c) "*Totem marks.*"—Each gens in the tribe had its mark representing the bird or animal for which the gens was named. Such
marks appear in the messages outlined on birch bark or cedar and
are considered in a subsequent paragraph. For a living person the
outline of the bird or animal was erect, but for one deceased the
mark was inverted.

(d) *Messages.*—The Chippewa had a system of conveying information publicly by means of characters which were familiar to all
the tribe. This was chiefly used in the messages that were outlined on birch bark or cedar and left by travelers for the information of those who might follow them. Such a message, outlined
with charcoal, was placed in the cleft of a stick that was stuck in
the ground pointing in the direction taken by the travelers. A thin,
flat chip of cedar was frequently used as a tablet for these messages,
as it was stiff and easy to write upon, but the ever-ready birch bark
was also used for this purpose. The outlines of these messages
comprised a fairly accurate representation of familiar objects together with a simple system of abbreviation and combination.
Straight lines beside a tipi indicated the number of nights the
preceding party had camped there, and short straight lines in a
canoe indicated the number of children in the party. If the drawing were elaborate these children would be indicated by several
small drawings of animals, this being the same animal used to indicate the father of the family, as the Chippewa children belong to
the same gens as the father. Thus a family in a canoe would be
represented by the father's gens animal at the front of the canoe, the
mother's gens animal in the stern of the canoe, and between them would
appear the proper number of small representations of the father's
gens animal. Such a group would identify a family, the community
being so small that each member was familiar with the history of
each family and the number which constituted it. Thus Figure 16
shows a family in which the father is of the Bear gens and the
mother of the Catfish gens, having three children; also a family
in which the father is of the Eagle gens and the mother the Bear gens,
having two children.

If a camp had been well supplied with food this fact was indicated by numerous small marks around the fire in the tipi, these marks representing bones left from abundant feasts. If no game had been found, the picture would show the tipi as bare and empty.

FIG. 16.—Native drawing. Two families in canoes

Travelers wishing to indicate the direction of their journey put up a stick in the ground, slanted in the direction they had gone. This stick usually had a bunch of hay tied to it, in order to attract attention. After a death the family, if traveling, moved as soon as possible to a new location, leaving a message or " notice " on the grave which told the gens of the deceased and the number of days he had been dead when the family left the camp. Men in health, a sick man, and a deceased person are

FIG. 17.—Native drawing. Men in health, sick man, deceased man

represented in a drawing by a Canadian Chippewa. (Fig. 17.) In this instance there is no reference to the person's identity and the gens animal is not shown.

FIG. 18.—Native drawing. A message

The message shown in Figure 18 was drawn by Nawajibigokwe and would be read as follows: Three canoes started at once. The occupants of two canoes camped here for two days and had plenty of food. The occupants of the other canoe stayed only one day, found no food, and so went away. The identity of the persons in this canoe is not shown. Two canoes are shown in the drawing, the two short lines above one of them indicating that the occupants of these canoes are the ones who stayed two days. In one of these is a man of the Catfish gens whose wife is of the Bear gens. They have four children, who are indicated by the four small catfish. In the other canoe is a man of the Eagle gens whose wife is of the Wolf gens. Short lines indicate that they also have four children. An abundance of food is shown by the marks around the fire in the two tipis.

Perhaps the game was not located on the first day of their stay, and the occupants of the other tipi became discouraged and went away, as there are no marks of food in that tent. The families could be identified by the gentes of the parents and the number of the

FIG. 19.—Native drawing. A message containing a warning

children. Such a sign as this, according to the informant, was often placed at the point where a certain stream flowed into the Mississippi River. A rice field is located a few miles up the stream, and there was a village on the river a few miles below. Thus the message would be placed in a cleft stick pointing in the direction the travelers had taken, and the details of the message would explain why they had tarried so long in the camp.

Another message drawn by the same informant is shown in Figure 19. This message contains a warning and shows after the manner of a map the direction taken by the travelers instead of intrusting the direction to the slanted stick. This drawing shows that three canoes of people camped for two days at a point below the junction of a stream with the river. They saw three Sioux in the direction whence another stream flows into the river. Two of the Sioux had guns. Accordingly, they hastened down the river, as indicated by the line and pointer, though they had found abundant food for their camp. The occupants of the canoes were not families with children. The man at the front of the leading canoe belonged to the Woodpecker gens, the person at the stern belonged to the Snake gens, and those in the middle of the canoe appear to be of a bird gens. The persons at the ends of the second canoe were of the Catfish and Bear gens, and they also seem to have taken a member of a bird gens in their canoe. A member of the Wolf gens was alone in the last canoe.

Nawajibigokwe said that her father's family lived in a village on Sandy Lake (fig. 20, *a*) and her grandparents lived on Rice Lake (*b*), from which a stream known as Rice River flowed to the south. Both

Fig. 20.—Native drawing. A message

families went to the agency at Crow Wing for their annuities, and planned to travel together, meeting at the junction of Rice River and the Mississippi River (*c*). She remembered that once her father found a message on birch bark at this place, stating that her grandparents had already passed on their way to Crow Wing (*d*), traveling with a party in two canoes. The Bear and Catfish in one of the canoes indicated they were with her uncle and his family; the number of children was indicated by short upright marks. It will be noted that this message comprises a sketch of the geography of the country.

(*e*) *Maps.*—Nawajibigokwe stated that maps were sometimes drawn on birch bark for the convenience of persons traveling through a strange country. Such a map was drawn by her, showing the territory traversed by her father and his family in going from Sandy Lake to Crow Wing Agency for their annuities. The downward trip occupied two or three days and the return trip took about six days. This map contained much detail and indicated a general knowledge of the geography of the country. The map conformed to the shape of the piece of paper on which it was drawn, so that relative distances and points of the compass were not strictly maintained.

The principal interests to a man traveling in a canoe would naturally be the intersection of streams and the presence of lakes, through some of which a stream passed, the lake being a widening of the river. The portion of the country occupied by the Pokegama Band of Chippewa and the route to Lake Superior were correctly placed. Rice River, Rice Lake, Crow Wing River, Red Cedar Lake, Rabbit Lake, the Mississippi River, the settlement on the present site of Aitkin, Minn., and the agency at Crow Wing were shown with sufficient accuracy to guide a traveler. Where the Crow Wing River flowed into the Mississippi River there was said to be the first white settlement, which was indicated by a house with windows. This house is shown above d in Figure 20.

(f) *Picture illustrating a narrative.*—Such a picture might be in permanent form, or men seated around a fire might brush the embers aside and draw a picture in the dry ashes, using a pointed stick for the purpose. A picture drawn by Nawajibigokwe (fig. 21) illustrates her narrative concerning the scourge of smallpox that visited the tribe many years ago. This narrative was the personal experience of her father's grandmother, who lived in a village called Wackokagon on the southern shore of Lake Winnipegosis. The smallpox broke out among the Chippewa living at Leech Lake (fig. 21, a). A boy about 12 or 14 years of age left the infected district and wandered around the intervening lakes until he came to a path that led to the village of Wackokagon (b). Following this path, he reached the village, where he had some relatives. He was broken out when he arrived, and some said, "Let us kill him so the disease will not spread among us."

There was a great division among the people, and while this was in progress the boy went into the wigwams of his relatives. Some of the women advised him to go around the village and run into all the wigwams, exposing everyone so that he would not be killed. The Indians who had not been exposed to the disease began to flee from the village and it was decided that those who had been exposed should remain at home. Her great-grandmother was among those who fled, taking with her in the canoe her mother and four brothers and sisters. The great-grandmother was of the Eagle gens (her

father's), while her mother was of the Bear gens. Thus in the canoe
(c) the great-grandmother is indicated by an eagle at the front of
the canoe, and her mother by a bear in the stern, the brothers and
sisters being indicated by short upright lines in the canoe. Many
other canoes started at the same time. The Indians at Sandy Lake
(d) had not heard of the smallpox and were having a good time
when the canoe came in sight. They were dancing, playing the
moccasin game, and enjoying themselves. All at once they heard a
voice that seemed to come from over their heads saying, "The
Indians are dying in great numbers over there." This was so terrible and so unexpected that many fell on the ground in fright.

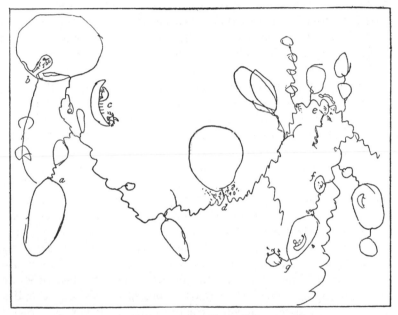

FIG. 21.—Native drawing illustrating a narrative

They all were much alarmed, saying, "This may be the end of us
all." The Sandy Lake Indians all got into their canoes, went
through the outlet and floated down the river. There they overtook
some of those who were fleeing from Lake Winnipegosis and had
developed the disease.

At Pine River (e) a camp was made for those who were sick,
among whom were some from Sandy Lake. Even Nani'bawi (Standing still), a medicine man, was taken sick. Both he and his wife
developed severe cases of the disease, but his wonderful power did
not desert him. The river is wide at that point and has a broad
sweep. Nani'bawi crept down to the river and lay with his body in
the water and his head on the shore, and he called to the people say-

ing, "See, I have turned into a great snake with horns. I extend far into the water." He called to his wife and the children, telling them to come into the water and rub against his body, saying that if they would do this they would recover. They did as he told them and got well. Others saw the benefit and they also went into the water, rubbed against his body and were cured. Children who were unable to help themselves were carried by their parents. Although he was a snake he could talk to them and he told them to wash themselves thoroughly after they had rubbed against him. Those who followed his directions were cured of the disease, but almost all the others died. When the great medicine man crept out of the water he regained his human shape. He lived to be an old man, and his last instruction was that when he died he should be thrown into the river. This was done and in four days he came back. He died again, and they threw his body in a lake and he was never seen again.[79]

The great-grandmother of the narrator did not stop at this camp, but continued down the river toward Crow Wing. She was with a party comprising 10 canoes. They passed through two lakes, the smaller called Noke'zagaïgûn (*f*), and the larger Kĭtcĭbi'kwezagaïgûn, meaning Big Sandy Lake. After this long journey they were taken with the dread disease and all died except the narrator's great-grandmother and a little sister of hers. They were at a point below the large lake (*g*), and the direction of their journey through the lake is indicated on the drawing. These two decided to return to their people, so they selected a small canoe and began their journey (*h*). When they had recrossed the large lake the elder of the two remembered that their mother had cached some maple sugar at that point, so she left her sister in the canoe, went up the bank, and secured the sugar. Then they started on, she paddling the little canoe. After her sister had eaten freely of the sugar she lay down in the canoe. Soon afterwards she died. The elder one went ashore, dug a grave in the sand, and buried her sister. She stayed there until it was almost night, then she went on in the canoe, weeping to think she was the only one that remained of so large a company. As she journeyed day after day she went round a point of land and there she saw a little black dog running down the shore. The dog was whining, and she wondered where he came from, as no one lived near. She talked to herself, wondering where the dog came from, but she did not go near the shore. She decided to paddle all that night. As she went along she heard wonderful music that

---

[79] A similar instance was related concerning a band of Indians fleeing from the smallpox who started toward Lake Superior. They were taken sick and one of their number went into the water and turned into a great turtle. All who rubbed against her were cured of the disease.

seemed to come from a hillside, and she thought she heard laughing and talking in a strange language.

She did not sleep but forgot her grief as she listened to this wonderful music. (Later in her life she heard a violin and the French language, and recognized them as the music and the language she had heard on the water.) The next morning she saw two canoes, one full of women, and the other of men. She heard a voice saying, "Do you see those people in the canoes before you?" She replied, "Yes, I see them." The voice said, "Those are your descendants in the canoes." She returned by the way she had come with her relatives, subsisting on berries and ducklings which she cooked. She also killed some raccoons. Finally she came to some Indians who had recovered from the smallpox. After a time she married a man named No'dĭna'kwûd (Clouds filled with wind). They lived together many years and had a large family, all of whom grew up. She died before her husband. That is the end of the story of Wi'gubĭns (Little Wigub, or wood-fiber).[80]

DECORATIVE ARTS

The materials available to the Chippewa for artistic expression were of a perishable nature and consisted chiefly of birch bark, reeds, and hides. To this, as well as to the custom of burying a man's possessions at the time of his death, is due the limited number of examples of early Chippewa art which remain for our study. One must search for Chippewa art in the minds of those who remember its characteristics and whose fingers retain the ability to execute the old designs. Even this opportunity will soon be lost, as it is scarcely possible at the present time to find persons under 50 years of age who are reliable informants on this subject. The younger Indians are able to distinguish between old and modern designs, but are unable to reproduce the old patterns in an artistic manner or to explain their significance. The perception of art remains, however, as the workers who are commended by other Indians are usually those whose product has artistic merit according to the standards of the white race.

DEVELOPMENT OF DESIGN

(a) *Geometric patterns.*—All informants state that geometric and "line" patterns are older than floral designs. Nawajibigokwe made a "sampler" to show the simple line patterns and their combination in wider and more elaborate designs. (Pl. 79.) The simplest pattern

---

[80] In all the narratives given by Nawajibigokwe the name of the principal character is withheld until the close, the story ending as in the present instance. Cf. legends related by Odinigun, in which the title is withheld until the close (p. 103).

was an interrupted straight line in which the beaded portions and
the open portions were of equal length, three or four beads being
commonly used in such a pattern. This was called the "jumping
pattern," and was varied by making the beaded portion longer or
shorter than the open space (*a*). Thus a double row of interrupted
lines with equal spacing might be connected by lines of equal length
in such a manner as to form triangles or a " block pattern " (*b* and *c*),
and a double row of diagonal or zigzag lines placed with points
together formed a succession of diamonds (*d*). Extending the space
between the crossing of the lines produced a new outline (*e*), and
a combination of these produced the "ottertail pattern" (*f*). One

FIG. 22.—Birch-bark transparency

section of this is prob-
ably the most frequent
pattern in Chippewa
beadwork, unless it
be the simple zigzag.
The ottertail pattern
is said to have been
received by the Missis-
sippi Band of Chip-
pewa from the Otter-
tail Band, but this
seems conjectural, as
the pattern is so
clearly developed from
simpler forms. It is
used as a narrow bor-
der and also in various
widths and combina-
tions (*f* and *g*). In
a typical "ottertail

border " there are two, three, or four diamonds between the straight
lines and the pattern has a straight line of beads on each side. (Cf.
pls. 80, *c;* 81, *b;*.88.)

   (*b*) *Birch-bark transparencies.*—A different type of geometric pattern is seen in the transparencies made of birch mark, which were
copied in woven bead bands. These patterns were adapted for bands
from 1 to 4 or 5 inches wide, and probably suggested the patterns for
the woven pieces 10 or 12 inches wide that formed the pockets of the
old "bead sacks." The principal geometric units in these patterns
were a star and a cruciform combined with various lines and angles.
The patterns, in great variety, were formed by folding and refolding
the thin birch bark and indenting with the teeth. The unfolding of

the bark revealed the pattern. Many of these patterns contained units with curved outlines combined with strictly geometric figures. Among such units were a conventional rose, a star, a heart, and a butterfly. Such a transparency, with a diagram of its foldings and a detail of the indentation, is shown in Figures 22, 23, and 24. (See Forty-fourth Ann. Rept. Bur. Amer. Ethn., pls. 59–63.)

Mention should here be made of the "edging" of beads which in early times was used on leggings and moccasins and which borders the "sampler." This was always made of small white opaque beads and chiefly used in connection with simple line patterns. (See pl. 33.)

(c) *Patterns with angular outlines.*—The patterns considered in this paragraph are different from the patterns already described, and some may be said to resemble the "drawing in planes" by artists of the white race. The geometric patterns, with their intersections of lines, were

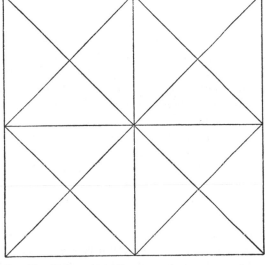

FIG. 23.—Manner of folding the transparency in Figure 22 for indentation

especially adapted to woven beadwork, but the patterns with angular outlines were best adapted for use in applied design. The simplest are the moccasin patterns cut by Nawajibigokwe, which show serrated edges. In one or two instances these edges, either inner or outer, are on a sweeping double-curve pattern. Other angular patterns represent leaves. A combination of angles and curves appears in conventional patterns by Zozed and in a representation of a bird by Mrs. Razer, the latter being intended for use as a dream symbol.

FIG. 24.—Detail of indentation in Figure 22

The star was a favorite pattern, both as a dream symbol and for decorating. (Pl. 80, *a*, *b*, *e*. Cf. also pl. 11 and fig. 5.)

(d) *Patterns with double-curve motive.*—This is described as " consisting of two opposed incurves as a foundation element, with embellishments more or less elaborate modifying the inclosed space, and with variations in the shape and proportions of the whole. This

simple double-curve appears as a sort of unit, capable of being sub-
jected to   *   *   *   a variety of augments." [81]   (Pl. 85.)

After reviewing the occurrence of the double curve among the
Algonquian tribes north and south of the St. Lawrence River, Doctor
Speck says, " The Ojibwa, contrary to what might be expected, show
even less of the double curve than their neighbors, their art being
so overwhelmingly floral." [82] Three informants at White Eearth
included among their cut-paper patterns double-curve motives for
the fronts of moccasins, these patterns (pl. 85) bearing a close
resemblance to the double-curve patterns etched on birch bark by
Montagnais Indians living on Lake St. John. [83]

(e) *Floral patterns, conventional and modern.*—In early designs a
conventional rose frequently occurred in combination with the lines
and angles of geometric patterns. The wild rose may be considered
a representative flower of the Chippewa, as it grows in profusion
throughout their country. This flower appears in the simplest of
the conventional patterns used in their beadwork. (Pls. 80, *d;* 86, *a.*)

In some instances it is shown with its leaves as a pattern for
the frontpiece of moccasins and in other instances it appears as a
grouping of dots. It was said that the "round-bead pattern" was
one of the oldest, and the grouping of four dots with or without a
smaller dot in the center is a natural development of design. [84] Two
forms of "round bead pattern" are shown in Plate 80, *a.*

It appears that in the development of Chippewa design an interpretation of nature through conventional flower and leaf forms preceded an imitation of nature. It appears further that the spirit of
real art decreased as the imitation of nature increased until the
floral patterns in use among the Chippewa of to-day have no artistic
value. The Chippewa women distinguish clearly between the old
patterns of flowers and leaves and those which have prevailed since
1860–1870. These dates are approximate and differ among various
bands of the tribe, but they represent the period when the Chippewa
came extensively under the influence of the white man.

At that time the whole culture of the tribe changed, the old standards were discredited, and there arose a tolerance of poor workman-

---

[81] Speck, Frank G., The Double-curve Motive in Northeastern Algonkian art.   Memoir 42,
Geol. Surv. Canada, Department of Mines, Ottawa, 1914, p. 1.

[82] Ibid., p. 13.

[83] Ibid., fig. 15.

[84] In this connection the following statement by John Ruskin is of interest : " The first
order of arrangement, in substance, is that of coherence into a globe ; as in a drop of
water, in rain and dew—or hollow, in a bubble ;   *   *   *   then the second orders of
arrangement are those in which several beads or globes are associated in groups under
definite laws, of which, of course, the simplest is that they should set themselves together
as close as possible ;   *   *   *   these are the first general types of all crystalline or
inorganic grouping."   Ruskin, John, " The Laws of Fésole," London, 1904, pp. 384–385.

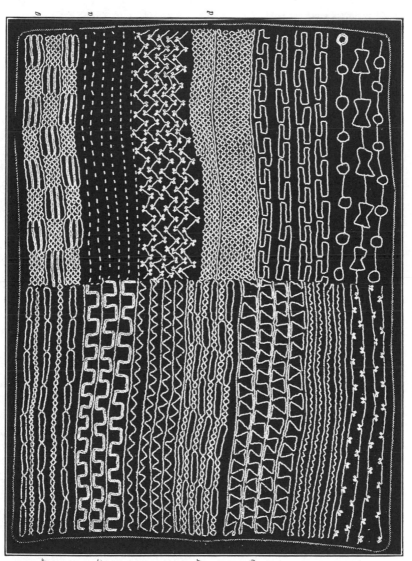

OLD DESIGNS USED IN BEADWORK

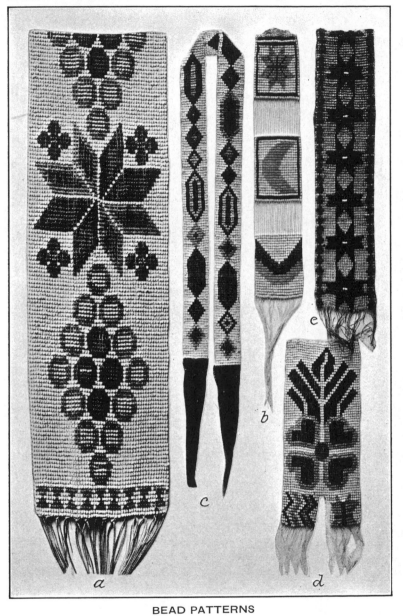

BEAD PATTERNS

a. "Star" and "round bead"; *b,* Dream symbols; *c,* Otter tail; *d,* Conventional flower and leaf; *e,* Star

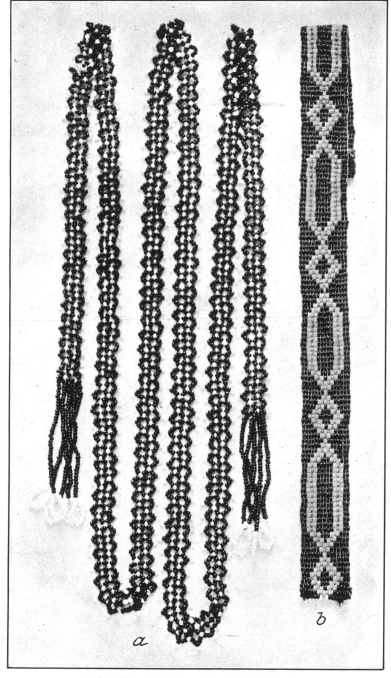

a, Bead chain in imitation of lace; *b*, Otter-tail pattern

CANADIAN BEAD PATTERNS

MODERN DESIGN USED IN BEADWORK

PATTERNS CUT FROM BIRCH BARK

DOUBLE CURVE PATTERNS

a, Beaded bag, old design; *b, c,* Partially completed beadwork on black velvet

ship in design and technic which remains to the present day. An important element in this change was the great amount of material which became available. Instead of a limited supply of beads, the Indians were able to secure large quantities of bright-colored glass beads. At about the same time the traders brought flowered chintz and calico. To what extent the art of the Chippewa was influenced by the trader's chintz must remain a matter of speculation. In this connection, however, it is interesting to note the cleverness of Chippewa women in imitating what is strange to them by using familiar material. Thus, a certain type of bead chain made in black and white (pl. 81, a) was said to imitate lace and to have been made at about the time that lace making was introduced among the Chippewa by missionaries of the Episcopal church.

Patterns of beadwork used in southern Manitoba, Canada, are shown in Plate 82.

All informants stated that the old floral designs were conventional. Such flower and leaf patterns are best exemplified in wide belts and on the pockets of bandoleers. (Fig. 26.)

One of the chief characteristics of early floral patterns was their truthfulness. The chief characteristic of modern Chippewa art is its lack of truth and its freedom of expression. Roses are placed on the same stems with oak leaves, and we are shown bluebells growing on grapevines. A typical design of the present period, drawn in pencil, is shown in Plate 83. Doctor Speck states that three-petal flowers or leaflike patterns are found north and south of the St. Lawrence River.[85] A triple pattern appears in the small beaded bag in Plate 65, a, which resembles those illustrated by him more than the bead patterns of the western Chippewa. According to Ruskin, "groups of three, though often very lovely, do not clearly express radiation but simply cohesion.[86] The old conventional patterns of the Chippewa frequently indicate "not merely order of construction but process or sequence of animation." [87]

The floral designs originated by certain women are found to have the same characteristics as the women themselves. Thus the patterns created by Mrs. Roy and her sister (pl. 12) are upspringing in their lightness, and even the conventional patterns show a certain freedom. These women are cheerful in disposition, with a ready pleasantness of manner. Mrs. Frank Razer is a different temperament; serious, steady, and always industrious. Her original patterns are more constrained, a larger proportion are strictly conven-

---

[85] Speck, op. cit., p. 10.
[86] Ruskin, op. cit., p. 396.
[87] Ibid.

tional, and there is evidence of painstaking care throughout her
work.

PATTERNS CUT FROM BIRCH BARK

Every Chippewa bead worker has a box of patterns cut from
birch bark or paper. These are the units which she combines in
forming her designs and are chiefly used in applied beadwork, but
could be used in etching on birch bark or any other decorative work.

a

b   *c*

Fig. 25.—Three patterns for beadwork, representing three generations of workers. *a*,
Native drawing of pattern (first generation); *b, c,* patterns cut with scissors (second
and third generations)

They comprise every sort of pattern which can be outlined, such as
flowers, leaves, angular patterns, and double-curve motives. If
lines are to be placed inside the pattern, as veins in a leaf, they are
indicated by pencil marks. The earliest patterns of this sort were
cut without scissors in the following manner: The outline of the

pattern was pricked in birch bark with a sharp fishbone, the pricks being placed close together, after which the bark was cut along these lines with a knife. The Chippewa first secured shears from English traders, and it was said these shears were better than the shears brought by early American traders.

Scissors were given the Chippewa with their annuities at an early date, and were carefully treasured by the women. Nawajibigokwe, who gave much of the information in this section, said that her grandmother had a pair of scissors that she kept hidden under all her belongings lest some one should use and dull them. It was with considerable difficulty that Nawajibigokwe, then a young girl, obtained the scissors and began her art work by cutting patterns from birch bark. The writer's best informants on this subject could not

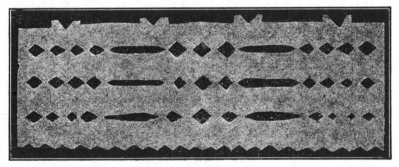

FIG. 26.—Stencil pattern for beadwork

use a pencil easily, but could cut patterns with entire freedom. Cut patterns are of two sorts—those in the nature of stencils and those having no open space within the boundary lines. Among the angular moccasin patterns cut by Nawajibigokwe are several stencils, the opening in the pattern appearing as an inner row of beads, or as an area of beads in the finished work. (Fig. 26.) A few of the stencil patterns cut by Mrs. Roy's sister show a square opening in the center of a conventional rose, while in others the outline extends a short distance within the pattern itself. This necessitates the folding back of part of the pattern when the design is traced. Mrs. Roy and her sister outlined their patterns with a pencil before cutting them, but their mother cut her patterns in the old way without previous tracing. (Cf. pl. 84, lower right corner.)

The women seldom exchange patterns, but a good designer is often asked to trace patterns for less gifted workers. Frequent additions to the supply of patterns is made by bead workers, a few leaves of particularly pretty outline often being placed with the cut patterns. The writer has seen a woman pressing leaves for patterns when she was visiting on a reservation, saying that such leaves did not grow near her home and that she wished to copy them in her beadwork. While this perception of natural beauty indicates an artistic sense the results have not the atmosphere of the old art forms. (See p. 186.)

A portion of the conventional flower and leaf patterns in Plate 84 was cut from birch bark by Mrs. Louisa Martin, whose Chippewa name is Ajawac. (See pp. 80, 81.) Others in the group were cut by Zozed of Red Lake, including four conventional designs of a rose berry.

It is interesting to note the inheritance of artistic ability in five generations of Chippewa women at Red Lake. The oldest living members of this series are Magi'dins and her sister Zozed, the former of whom said that she learned weaving and other handiwork from her grandmother, while the latter cut a scroll or whorl which she said that her mother originated and used in her beadwork. Zozed stated that she did not know what this represented. A whorl of the same proportion forms part of the design on the cover of a Montagnais birch-bark box illustrated by Speck.[88] Zozed cut many interesting designs which she herself originated. Her daughters are expert bead workers, and her granddaughter did needlework that showed a good perception of color, as well as neatness and dexterity.

Magidins and Zozed could not speak English, their daughters could speak English but were not educated, and the granddaughter was a student at a Government school. Like other Indian women of the present generation, she knew nothing of native craftsmanship, and her standards were those of the "school system." Mention has been made of the whorl originated by the grandmother of Zozed. An adaptation of this was seen in a pattern that Zozed used on moccasin fronts when she was a young woman, and a suggestion of it appears in the conventional clover-leaf pattern outlined in pencil by Zozed's daughter, Mrs. Roy. A comparison of the first and last patterns in this group shows one of the differences between old and new Chippewa art. The whorl originated and admired by Mrs. Roy's grandmother was a purely conventional pattern, while the pattern drawn by Mrs. Roy, though conventional, was said to represent a natural form. (Fig. 25.)

BEADWORK

The first beads used by the Chippewa were obtained in small quantities from English traders. Later they were brought by American traders and were issued by the Government with annuities.

---

[88] Speck, op. cit., Pl. IX.

The first beads secured were small, opaque white beads, then larger opaque white beads, and in comparatively recent years the Chippewa obtained large quantities of clear and opaque beads of all colors. The native word for bead is *manido'mĭnĕs* (*manido*, spirit or wonderful; *mĭn*, berry or bead; *ĕs*, diminutive ending).

(*a*) *Applied design.*—This method of using beads is simpler and undoubtedly older than the woven work described in a subsequent paragraph. It consists in sewing beads on cloth or leather. In early times the bead embroidery was placed on the broadcloth of which a garment was made, but in more recent times the embroidery is placed on black velvet, which in turn is applied to the garment to be decorated. Fine strands of deer sinew were originally used for this purpose, and are still used if the work is to be very strong. Thus a little case often hung on a child's cradle board was beaded with sinew. The simplest patterns, and those probably used first, were the "jumping pattern," the zigzag, and the "ottertail pattern." These were embroidered with small opaque white beads on the " front piece " of a woman's dress, and on the cuffs and " front pieces " of moccasins. They were also used as borders on the leggings of both men and women.

The cutting of patterns for use in applied beadwork has already been described. These patterns were laid on the material to be decorated. In the old times it was customary to outline the pattern with long stitches of white thread, this being especially adapted to the serrated patterns described on pages 34 and 35. At the present time the bead worker lays the patterns on the material to be decorated and traces a line around them with flour paste.

In a set of tracing materials obtained, the container for the paste was made of birch bark, and the stick for tracing was very soft so that the marking paste was wiped along the desired lines. The woman who provided this set said that she kept a stiff feather in her box to brush off any of the flour and water that was accidentally put on the velvet outside the pattern. The writer watched the drawing of a design by Mrs. Razer. Much thought was bestowed upon the selection and arrangement of the cut patterns. (Pl. 86, c.) The design began at the left, after which the right end was decided upon and the cut patterns arranged in the intervening space. These were connected by scrolls drawn with the paste. In preparation for this work the velvet was basted on calico to give it firmness. Each color of beads was strung separately and wound on a roll of cloth. A string of beads was laid along the traced pattern and fastened in place by stitches at intervals of two or more beads according to the fineness of the pattern.

The original form of applied design consisted of an outline of the pattern as described. This decoration was used chiefly on the "front piece" of a woman's dress. As beads became more abundant, a second line was introduced, making a double line of beads, and it is said this double line was used for a long period. Two unfinished pieces of such embroidery are shown in Plate 86, *b, c.* With the abundance of colored beads and the use of elaborate floral patterns, the Chippewa began to fill in their beadwork solidly by sewing one row of beads inside another, a style of beadwork in use at the present time. In admiration for masses of color the women lost much of their appreciation of graceful lines, and the art value of their work is further impaired, if not entirely destroyed, by the use of a background consisting of solid rows of beads sewed on cotton cloth. White beads, either opaque or opalescent, are commonly used for this background.

(*b*) *Woven beadwork.*—It has been said that this is a survival of an early form of porcupine-quill work. In this form of beadwork a number of cotton threads representing the warp are stretched taut and a string of beads corresponding to the woof is fastened in place by means of a needle and thread. The strung beads are held horizontally beneath the warp threads and pressed upward so that one bead is between each thread. A threaded needle is then passed through the beads above the warp and then back again through the beads below the warp, holding them securely in place. For many years this work has been done on a wooden frame, but before the invention of this frame the threads were kept in position by passing them through a double piece of birch bark. (Pl. 87.) Holes were made for each thread by passing a needle through the birch bark, and the threads were tied in a knot at each end. These warp threads were kept taut by fastening one knotted end to a post or other stationary object and fastening the other end to a stick placed beneath the woman's knee or to a cord tied around her waist, as in the braid weaving described on page 159. It is said that the first bead frames were made of ash tied with sinew at the corners, and were almost square.

The bead frame shown in Plate 88 is decorated by smoking the wood. The threads that form the warp were wound over the length or the width of this frame according to the length of the band to be woven. The specimen illustrated is about 11 by 15 inches. With a more lavish use of materials, the frames were made longer, those in use during the last generation being about 27 inches long, permitting sufficient warp for a woven band of twice that length. This could be made continuous by slipping the finished portion of the work over the end of the frame, or the band could be cut and a tassel put at each end. The frame is tilted when in use. (Pl. 89.)

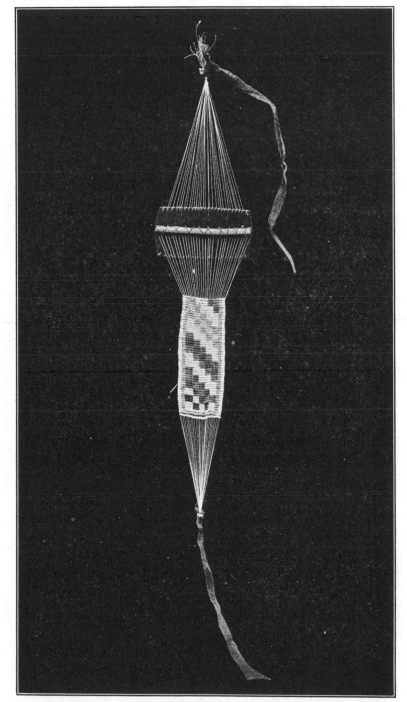

BIRCH-BARK WARP HOLDER, WITH UNFINISHED BEADWORK

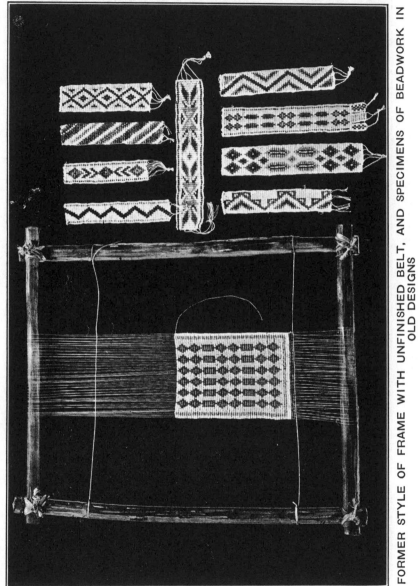

FORMER STYLE OF FRAME WITH UNFINISHED BELT, AND SPECIMENS OF BEADWORK IN OLD DESIGNS

WOMAN MAKING BEAD CHAIN

BEAD PENDANTS, COMPLETED AND PARTIALLY COMPLETED

If the work is done in a house, the lower edge of the bead frame rests on a table and the upper end is suspended from the ceiling by a cord. The worker has her box of beads beside her, the beads being in bunches as purchased from the trader. She places a few beads of each desired color in a saucer or shallow dish, from which she

FIG. 27.—*a*, Conventional design for shoulder bag; *b*, design for shoulder strap of bag

picks up one bead after another with her needle. The colors are not separated in the dish, but the worker rapidly selects the number of each color in sequence corresponding to the design she wishes to weave. As already indicated, the number of warp threads is according to the width of the band to be woven. A neck chain is usually about five to seven beads in width and requires one more than that number of warp threads. A headband is about an inch wide, an arm or knee band is 3 to 5 inches wide, the shoulder band of a bead sack is about 6 inches wide, and a bead piece for the pocket of a bead sack is about 12 inches wide.

The maker of woven beadwork never has a pattern before her as she works, and rarely repeats a pattern. Some workers use the birch-bark transparencies as a suggestion for these patterns and others "have the pattern in their heads." An expert maker of woven work at Red Lake said that she never used a pattern, but had the entire design clearly in her mind before she began a piece of work. The difficulty of this can be imagined when we consider that she made woven work about 12 inches square for the pocket portion of bead sacks, the pattern being a unit with corners and a border. She said that she seldom made two alike. The designs illustrated (fig. 27) were said to be a conventional leaf with roses in the corners intended for the pocket of a bandoleer similar to that shown in Plate 15 and a smaller pattern of rose and a leaf for the shoulder band of the same article. One of the oldest patterns in woven beadwork is the "round dot" shown in Plate 80. A majority of the patterns in woven work are superior to those used in the applied beadwork. Dream symbols are also more frequent in woven work.

(c) *Bead pendants.*—Two methods of construction for these ornaments are shown in Plate 90. The foundation of the simpler is a ball of some soft material covered with white cloth, over which strings of beads are sewn in rows, round and round. The more interesting is made by weaving beads in the manner illustrated, forming diamonds of any desired proportion with strands of thread in triangular form between them. By drawing the threads together there is formed a little bead bag, which is stuffed with cotton and sewed along the edges where necessary, forming a pendant which can be attached to various forms of bead bands.

AUTHORITIES CITED

BARAGA, FREDERIC. A Grammar and Dictionary of the Otchipwe Language. Montreal, 1882.

BUSHNELL, D. I., Jr. Native Villages and Village Sites East of the Mississippi. Bull. 69, Bur. Amer. Ethn., Washington, 1919.

CULIN, STEWART. Games of the North American Indians. Twenty-fourth Ann. Rept. Bur. Amer. Ethn., Washington, 1907.

CUOQ, J. A. Lexique de la Langue Algonquine. Montreal, 1886.

CURTIN, JEREMIAH, and HEWITT, J. N. B. Seneca Fiction, Legends and Myths. Thirty-second Ann. Rept. Bur. Amer. Ethn., Washington, 1918.

HEWITT, J. N. B. See Curtin, Jeremiah, and Hewitt.

DENSMORE, FRANCES. An Ojibway Prayer Ceremony. Amer. Anthrop., n. s. IX, pp. 443–444, Lancaster, Pa., 1907.

—— Chippewa Music. Bull. 45, Bur. Amer. Ethn., Washington, 1910.

—— Chippewa Music II. Bull. 53, Bur. Amer. Ethn., Washington, 1913.

—— Teton Sioux Music. Bull. 61, Bur. Amer. Ethn., Washington, 1918.

—— Northern Ute Music. Bull. 75, Bur. Amer. Ethn., Washington, 1922.

—— Uses of Plants by the Chippewa Indians. Forty-fourth Ann. Rept. Bur. Amer. Ethn., pp. 275–397, Washington, 1928.

GILFILLAN, JOSEPH A. The Ojibway. New York and Washington, 1904.

HANDBOOK OF AMERICAN INDIAN LANGUAGES. Bull. 40, Pt. 1, Bur. Amer. Ethn., Washington, 1911.

HANDBOOK OF AMERICAN INDIANS NORTH OF MEXICO. Bull. 30, Pts. 1–2, Bur. Amer. Ethn., Washington, 1907–1910.

HOFFMAN, W. J. The Mide'wiwin or "Grand Medicine Society" of the Ojibwa. Seventh Ann. Rept. Bur. Ethn., pp. 143–300, Washington, 1891.

HOLMES, W. H. Ancient Pottery of the Mississippi Valley. Fourth Ann. Rept. Bur. Ethn., Washington, 1886.

JENKS, ALBERT E. Wild-Rice Gatherers of the Upper Lakes. Nineteenth Ann. Rept. Bur. Amer. Ethn., pt. 2, pp. 1013–1137, Washington, 1902.

JONES, WILLIAM. Ojibwa Texts. Edited by Truman Michelson. Publs. Amer. Ethn. Soc., vol. VII, pt. 2, New York, 1919.

ORR, R. B. Snowshoes. Thirty-second Ann. Archaeol. Rept., App. Rept. Min. Ed. Ont., pp. 19–37, Toronto, Canada, 1920.

KAPPLER, CHARLES J. Indian Affairs. Laws and Treaties. Vol. II (Treaties). Washington, 1904.

MALLERY, GARRICK. Recently discovered Algonkian Pictographs. [Paper read before the American Association for the Advancement of Science, at Cleveland, 1888.]

MICHELSON, TRUMAN. Preliminary Report of the Linguistic Classification of Algonquian Tribes. Twenty-eighth Ann. Rept. Bur. Amer. Ethn., pp. 221–290b, Washington, 1912.

—— The So-Called Stems of Algonquian Verbal Complexes. Proc. 19th Int. Cong. Amer., 1915, pp. 541–544, Washington, 1917.

OFFICE OF INDIAN AFFAIRS (WAR DEPARTMENT). Reports, 1833, 1834, 1837, 1838, 1839. Report of the Commissioner (Department of the Interior), 1850.

RADIN, PAUL. Some Aspects of Puberty Fasting among the Ojibwa. Geol. Surv. Can., Dept. Mines, Mus. Bull. 2, Anthrop. Ser. 2, Ottawa, 1914.

RUSKIN, JOHN. The Laws of Fesole. A familiar treatise on the elementary principles and practice of drawing and painting. Vol. I. Sunnyside, Orpington, Kent, 1879. (In The Works of John Ruskin, edited by E. T. Cook and Alexander Wedderburn, vol. xv, London, 1904, pp. 333–501.)

SKINNER, ALANSON. Material Culture of the Menomini. Mus. Amer. Ind., Heye Foundation, Ind. Notes and Mono. [Misc., no. 20], New York, 1921.

SPECK, FRANK G. The Double-curve Motive in Northeastern Algonkian Art. Geol. Surv. Can., Dept. Mines, Memoir 42, Ottawa, 1914.

VERWYST, F. CHRYSOSTOM. Chippewa exercises, being a practical introduction into the study of the Chippewa Language. Harbor Springs, Mich., 1901.

WARREN, WILLIAM W. History of the Ojibways. Colls. Minn. Hist. Soc., vol. v, St. Paul, 1885.

WILSON, EDWARD F. The Ojebway Language. Toronto, 1874.

INDEX

INDEX

○